An Amazing Life

TO GEORGE AND TANYA MOGYOROS WITH MUCH OF LOVE AND AFFECTION. Thin August 21, 1990. George Cronin

AN AMAZING LIFE
Escape from Rumania

George Crisan

VANTAGE PRESS
New York / Los Angeles

FIRST EDITION

Copyright © 1990 by George Crisan

Published by Vantage Press, Inc.
516 West 34th Street, New York, New York 10001

Manufactured in the United States of America
ISBN: 0-533-08581-0

Library of Congress Catalog Card No.: 89-90202

To my beloved wife, Eunice,
and our wonderful sons and daughter,
George Stewart, Patricia Ann
and John Titus

Contents

ACKNOWLEDGMENTS

To you dear friends, in America or Europe, for your love shown to me and your constant encouragement that I should write my Memoirs, my life story, ever since you first heard me talking of my escape, my new start and my new life; my flight from behind the Iron Curtain to my new and blessed home country, America.

There is a quip which here and there I express: "I lost everything behind the Iron Curtain except my faith and my accent, and I mean to keep them both for life!"

My thanks to my very dear wife who made me feel and become an accomplished husband, father, and lawyer. Our children, indeed, are like jewels in our parental crown.

Thanks to Rhea Williams, my editor, who so dutifully, and wonderfully, edited and reedited my manuscript, and greatly encouraged me, ever since 1977, to continue and finish it.

All the blessings on you dear friends, old and new, wherever you are and on all the readers who take time to read this amazing life of George Crisan, born in the Transylvanian Alps and becoming an attorney with the greatest government in the world, the government of the United States of America. A note from my readers will be greatly appreciated.

INTRODUCTION

By the age of ten George Crisan had seen his tiny village of the Transylvania Alps occupied twice—first by the Bolsheviks and then by the Romanian army. Later, as the first student to leave his village of Tisa for schooling, George found himself ridiculed by students and teachers alike because his father had become a "repenter" who had "sold his soul to the Devil" by leaving the Romanian Orthodox Church to become a Baptist.

Despite these obstacles, George excelled in college, placing first in the baccalaureate exam. His extensive knowledge of the Bible and classical literature served his studies well. He received a full scholarship to the University of Cluj, the finest school of medicine in Rumania, but quickly discovered that the "chopped corpses" used for study were repugnant and debasing of man, who was created in the image of God.

George abandoned medicine for law and was admitted to the district bar during the depths of the depression. As a result he often worked without pay and, as the only Baptist lawyer in Rumania, was frequently called upon to defend his "brothers in faith," leading the struggle to have the community of Baptists recognized as a denomination.

With the approach of World War II, George was forced to abandon his legal career in order to defend his country against Hitler's impending invasion. The dreaded invasion never came, however, as Hitler's compact with the Soviet Union resulted in great parts of Rumania being divided between Hungary and the Soviet Union. Despite the heroic efforts of its Light Horse Artillery, Rumania was eventually occupied by the Russians.

In 1945, George found himself jailed as a "political" prisoner because he had dared to divulge publicly that President Truman had told the Russians at the Potsdam Conference they would have to withdraw within their borders as they existed before the war. George continued to speak out against the human rights abuses of the Russian occupiers of his homeland and soon found himself a marked man. In 1947, he was taken away again, this time in the middle of the night. Through the entreaties of a Communist friend he was eventually released, but was forced to live underground, unable to appear in public.

During September 1948, seeking freedom in the West, George managed to escape from behind the Iron Curtain, crossing seven hostile borders in the process. After three long and harrowing months, he made his way to Paris, where he met the former American Baptist missionary in Rumania, with whom George had become friends ten years earlier. The missionary made George the missionary's assistant in managing the Baptist Relief Program for refugees. Because of his activity and interest in relief and church work, he was granted a scholarship to study theology at Colgate-Rochester Divinity School, Rochester, New York.

At forty-two years of age, with no friends or relatives to meet him, he came to the United States to embark on a course of study in theology. After graduation, while living and working in New York City, he was offered a job in the Law Library of the Library of Congress in Washington, D.C., where he wrote numerous articles for Congress and co-authored a reference book, *The Church and State Behind the Iron Curtain*. He also broadcasted for many years for the Voice of America.

At the age of forty-eight, the author met his future wife, a nursing instructor, in West Virginia. He married and enrolled in law school for the second time in his life at the George Washington University Law School. After graduating, he was admitted to the bar in Maryland and the District of Columbia and worked at various positions in the United States government, including the Foreign Claims Commission, where he served as an expert on foreign law in General Services Administration, and the Department of the Navy, where he served as attorney adviser general and trial lawyer.

Over the years, the author counseled many Rumanian-American Baptists and wrote many articles for and served as editor of a Rumanian-Baptist monthly. He is affiliated with the First Baptist Church of Washington, D.C., and taught Sunday school class there, the same one former President Carter subseqeuently attended when he became president. The author was invited to the White House for a reception for the president of Rumania.

The author's belief is that this whole Odyssey was possible only because God had not lost him from his sight in War or Peace, Jail or Freedom. *Faith is the reality of things unseen.*

AN AMAZING LIFE

I

CHILDHOOD

MY PARENTS

MY earliest recollection of my mother and father goes back to the age of three or four when my grandmother, Mother's mother, took me by the hand and walked to the mill with me to see Mom and Dad. Though I enjoyed walking, the mile from my grandmom's home in Big Run Valley to the mill on the other side of the Cris River seemed a long way.

Later when I was able to understand, my grandmother told me my parents had married young, my mother was about sixteen and my father eighteen. When they were seventeen and nineteen respectively, I was born, the first child of these young parents, themselves still teenagers. So when I was about ten months old, I was weaned, and Gramdmom took me to her home. There I stayed with Grandmom and Grandpop until I was six and ready to go to school, which was about three miles away in the county seat of Halmagiu.

From my grandmother I learned how my father married my mother. My father's father, George Crisan of Ann, had been mayor of the town for many years, having been elected and reelected every five years. Though illiterate, he won great respect from his village because of his ability to make quick and clear decisions while acting as a justice of the peace for his village.

Grandfather wanted Father to get married at sixteen. He said to him, "I found a girl for you, George. She is from a good and honorable family. I have talked already with her father, and he has agreed to it."

My father replied to Grandfather, "I do not want to marry that girl. I would rather leave the mill and even your household and go on my own. I do not want you to choose a girl for me."

Grandfather was taken by surprise that his oldest son, the manager of the mill—who was also to inherit the mill and lands—had rejected his decision. He did not believe it. It did not dawn on him that his son was in earnest. He thought my father was a serious boy and, more so, he wanted only Father's good.

1

Weeks later, Grandfather said, "Son, we have arranged for the wedding to be in two weeks. The preparations are well started."

Father then told him, "You may have a wedding but without me. I told you I would not marry the girl you chose, and I will now go on my way."

Grandfather realized this was a serious matter. He asked Father whether he wanted to marry at all and whether he wanted to stay at the mill and manage it.

"Yes," said Father, "I want to marry, but I want to marry another girl, Elizabeth of Mary from the Big Run Valley."

"But she is the only child of her parents, and they will not give her away to come live with us at the mill," said Grandfather.

"I don't care about that," said Dad. "I will either marry Elizabeth or no one."

Grandfather cautioned Dad that there were several boys in the village who wanted to marry Elizabeth and, as son-in-law, take over the responsibility for managing their father-in-law's household. Such boys, he said, might plot against Father and even kill him.

Dad was not moved. Either he would marry Elizabeth or no one, he insisted.

My mother at that time, close to sixteen, had long, blond hair and black eyes. Later, Father told us that he thought Mother was the prettiest girl in the world. Her parents, while not rich, were well-to-do, having a pair of oxen, two cows, pigs and sheep, and quite a few parcels of land, including a summer pasture, summer stables, and a cottage for summer grazing the cattle in the hills. What a delightful place it was! It had air and spring water like no other place in any other village in the area. When my father saw my mother she was grazing the milk cows on the pasture up on the Big Run Valley pastureland.

Grandfather, who was very quick in his movements and decisions, immediately went to see Elizabeth's father and mother. When George, the mayor, came, Mother's father, Theodor Roman, was in the yard.

The mayor called Theodor over to the fence. "Good day," he said.

"Good day to you, Mayor."

The mayor then said, "I came to talk to you on an important matter!"

"Would you please come inside," invited Theodor.

2

Inside, without further ado, the mayor said, "I am here to asks you for the hand of your daughter for my son, Giutzu." (Giutzu was my father's nickname.)

Mom's father was certainly taken by surprise. He called in his wife, Mary, and told her, "Look, the mayor is here, and he's asked that we give Elizabeth to marry Giutzu!"

My mother's mother, Mary, was more talkative than my grandfather, Theodor. So she answered, "First, we do not have a daughter ready to marry. Elizabeth is only a child herself and not ready for marriage. So far, we have not given a single thought to such an event since she is still too young."

"Why don't you talk to her tonight when she comes home with the cattle?" replied the mayor.

"We will!" said my grandmother.

"I would like to have your word by Saturday when you go to the market and pass by the mill," he called as he left, walking along the street as fast as usual.

Before Saturday came, the mayor went again by the Romans'. He said to Theodor, "I happened to pass by your place, and I thought I had better stop and talk with you on the matter we were talking about last time. Have you talked to Elizabeth?"

"Yes," said Mom's mother. "She said she would marry Giutzu, but we are entirely unprepared, and we believe we should not hurry this matter; we want to do it in a fashionable way, as our position in society calls for!"

"What sort of preparations are you talking about, folks?" George demanded. "I have not asked you for anything but your daughter's hand for my son!"

Mother's mother replied, "Well, George, we are not the type of people to marry off our only child without having made all the expected preparations for the event!"

"Look," said the mayor, "I asked you one question, and you want to beat around the bush, although you have your daughter's consent. Let's be reasonable. The children want one another; let them get married and all other things will straighten out. I did not ask you for any dowry in land or cattle; all we want is a daughter."

Mom's parents were staggered at the mayor's quick decisiveness. They had known the mayor as a quicksilver type of man, but they were dumbfounded by his fast propositions. Grandfather was breaking all the traditions established over centuries in the village

3

of Tisa. It was 1905, the beginning of a new century, and changes were coming fast. Who on earth had ever heard of marrying a girl from a well-to-do family without a dowry? It was unbelievable!

They were married in the old oak-log church, which had been built in 1760 by five families in the village, among whom were the Crisans and the Romans.

My father became very attached to his in-laws—so much so that once when Dad had a disagreement with his father, the mayor, he packed his locker and left to live with the Romans. Mother stayed at the mill and eventually persuaded Father that the mill was where they should live.

When I was born, our village belonged to the Austrian Empire, and the official language of the country was Hungarian; few villagers would have anything to do with the Hungarian-speaking clerks at the town seat or with the county court. In such a case they had to spend a lot of money to hire a lawyer who knew both languages, Rumanian and Hungarian.

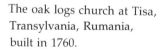

The oak logs church at Tisa,
Transylvania, Rumania,
built in 1760.

4

FAMILY AND VILLAGE LIFE

The house where I was born was a rather large structure of stucco, with oak beams and a front porch all along the house; a pantry was next to the entrance. The floors were of hardened clay and the fireplace was sheltered by a huge canopy, covered with layers of clay inside and outside so as prevent the fire from getting to the wood. The smoke accumulated from there and went up to the attic and through the straw roof. The smoke gradually smoked the pork hanging on wooden rods in the attic. I remember how excited I was when Grandmom let me climb into the attic and cut a piece of smoked sausage for myself to eat with green onions or green peppers from the vegetable beds in the clearing on the slope right next to the backyard fence.

The straw roof with the slowly oozing smoke reminded me of the steam rising from a perspiring horse early in the fall. This was the big, rather dark and mysterious house in which I was born. The house faced the courtyard, and the gate led to the street, which followed the big run where my grandmom was laundering the white clothes. Along this very stony and muddy—or dusty, when it was

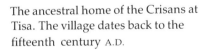

The ancestral home of the Crisans at Tisa. The village dates back to the fifteenth century A.D.

5

dry—street my grandmom was taking me by the hand to my mom at the mill, where she was living.

My grandmom had nine children. All had died in infancy but the last one, my mom. Mom married George, the mayor's son, and settled at the mill to manage it. This was the only business in the village. My grandfather had bought the mill almost forcibly, because no one else wanted it. Nobody had the money or the skill to run such a noisy and constantly moving thing—a water mill.

When I was born, my mother was barely seventeen years old and my father was nineteen years old and was managing the mill. I remember now my mother said that she married so young she did not know how to even make cornmush for the table. My father taught her many things, including how to make thin pancakes and how to flip them in the air above the stove to turn them on the other side. I always liked the thin pancakes and marveled how Mom was able to flip them up in the air and get them crisp and brown on both sides. Really, I thought those crepes were the best I could expect for eating.

Because my mother was so young and my grandmother had no other children, when I was ten months old and weaned, my mother took me to her parents' home in the Big Run Valley for them to take care of me. I understood much later that my grandmom took me almost daily to my mother and father at the mill, or my father took off and ran for about two miles to see his firstborn at the home of his mother-in-law, or "Sweet-mom" as I called her.

My first remembrance of the quaint, strawroofed old house must be from when I was four or even younger. The place was so mysterious with its dark corners and immense attic where all the best things were stored: smoked sausages, pork ribs and, of course, several halves of pork bacon hanging from the beam. The bacon, which we ate only cured and with onions or peppers and in the off season with pickled cucumbers or sauerkraut, was the chosen food, more so when the bacon had a lot of red, tender strips of flesh along the cutting. Sometimes I thought that the thick salt, black pepper, red-hot pepper, and garlic were too strong, but Sweet-mom told me that the seasonings made the bacon good and in the summer it would never get rancid when it was well seasoned with all these things.

6

The house had one very large room and next to that, a pantry. But the large room was divided into two by the fireplace with its huge canopy over it and, next to it, the little cooking stove. The canopy was necessary so that the smoke would not go straight to the attic and ignite the straw roof. The smoke would gradually go to the attic and there spread all over so as to smoke the hanging chunks of pork. Of course, it was pitch dark in the attic, and I was thrilled that I was allowed to hold the hand lamp for Sweet-mom to see what she was looking for, or to cut a slice of pork for the cabbage.

At the end opposite to the stove there were two small windows screened with chicken wire. Above the window frame there were two icons; one of our Lord, the Christ, and the other of the Lord's mother. They were painted on glass, and Sweet-mom had one of the prettiest colored woven towels above them as a crown. There was another, smaller window toward the courtyard on the long side of the room—on the long porch side. This had no screen, and often a wooden jug with fresh water and one of the baked clay jugs for drinking were set in the window. It was handy. Grandfather would fill the jugs with water and set them in the window from the outside. Sweet-mom would take them from inside and use the water for drinking or cooking. I was not able to handle the big jugs because they were too heavy for me. I had my little baked earth enameled jug for drinking water. The handle had a little nipple, and I drank water from it. I could get the water from the little jug belly either by tilting it or by sucking from the nipple.

In the back of the room next to the big canopy, opposite the entrance, there was a little window. In fact, it was a little hole covered with a piece of glass. You could not open it because it was built in. It was strange to me because it was so small, and yet one could see almost to the top of the hill when it was light outside. I asked why was it so small and set in the wall. Sweet-mom told me that it was there so that Grandpop might watch that nothing frightful might come—like the so-called "doghead men." These creatures, heads like dogs (*capcauni*) and bodies like men, barked. They would watch some women when their husbands were away at work in the forest or even faraway to work in the mountains at their summer cabins on their mountain pasture meadows. If a woman came out of her house, the creatures would capture her and take her away forever. Nobody knew where they lived but they were thought to have their abode in the darkest forest, and no man would have dared to go deep into the forest to look for the victims. They had carried away girls or even little children. They were never known to try to capture men or even wrestle with them. Once in a while, listening to the older women talking to my grandmom in the evenings when they came to spin hemp fiber for making cloth, I heard stories that the doghead men were even devouring small children because they were savage creatures.

What really helped us all against such creatures were the sign of the cross, and the house itself was sanctified every Saint John's Day, when the winter is at its depth. Inside, we had holy basil bunches under each of the icons, and on the long beams there were beeswax candles pressed into a cross form, which were lighted on the day when the priest and cantor came to sanctify the house and the stables against evil and bad luck. Holy water was sprinkled toward the four corners of the house with a bunch of basil, which itself became holy and was kept until the next year or even longer.

Basil was picked from our own vegetable rows, when in full bloom, and hung out on a wooden pin on the porch column until it dried. Then it was put in the big and small wooden chest among the homespun cloth. It smelled so good! So fresh! Above all, it was the best thing to chase away many evil things. I well remember how it helped me. Granny said that I was probably charmed by an evil eye and got sick. She called Baba Johanna (Grandmom Johanna) who knew how to chase away the evil spirits by her own words. She dropped red coals into the "unstarted" water, sprinkled it over me, and made me sip a bit. I got well amost in no time. She dropped several little bits of basil in the water. Baba Johanna was saying her chant, "Evil eye, evil eye, you go to places where the bird does not sing, where the owl does not hoo-hoo, where there are no men or animals, no plant or living spirit, in the desert, and there do your evil look and evil charm." She had to repeat the chant sometimes three times and again sometimes three times a day. Grandmom was repaying such a service with a slice of wheat bread or even with a slice of bacon. Such services, I understood, should never be unpaid: do not expect anything for nothing. It was Baba Johanna's living. She was also the self-made midwife for most of the villagers, and to all the hamlet of the Big Run Valley.

8

Once I remember when I must have been very sick. I don't know what I had. But after some weeks in bed and with Grandmom watching over me day and night, I felt better one day. She asked me to sit on the bedside and she put my shoes on. Then she lifted me down on to the floor. I was not able to take a step—I did not know how to walk. But Sweet-mom, holding my hand, encouraged me, "Try hard, dear, try again!" I did and I was able to lift my foot and make the first step and then the second and then I was able to walk again. How happy I felt! It was not the sickness that made me feel bad but the fact I was not able to go out, to play in the Big Run or just try to climb a bent down apple tree in the garden which was behind the house and the stable. The apples were so big and so cider-tasting. Granny told me it was a wild, ungrafted, apple tree which had grown there way back before the stable was raised on the place. But there were no better apples for cider and early apple pies than the wild apple tree apples.

When my father came to Big Run Valley he would lift me up and hold me in his arms. He had a very thick mustache. Then there came a time when Father did not come to see me. I did not see him at the mill, either. He was drafted into the army, and went far away to a city called Gyula in the plain of Theis. At that time Franz Joseph was our king and emperor of Austria. Our village was in the district of Arad, which is part of Transylvania province, and that province of the great empire of Austro-Hungary came more and more under the Hungarian administration and language.

I do not know how long Father was in service, but when he came back I did not want him to touch me or hold me. He had shaved his mustache off and he looked strange and unbecoming. Even Grandmom asked him, "Why did you do that? It is unheard of and uncustomary in the village, and you really look strange!" I do not remember what Father said. Eventually, I accepted him, though for a long while he looked very odd to me and to Granny.

Of course, my mother's father had long hair. Once a year or more often it required clipping. I remember how it fell down on his shirt and how he had his sheepskin vest over it or over the heavy black woolen winter and bad weather overcoat. Grandmom clipped his hair with scissors that were very clumsy since they were made by the village gypsy blacksmith. They were the same shears with which granny used to shear the sheep and cut the hemp cloth. Well, my grandmother was dismayed when Grandpop let himself be in-

9

duced by my father to shorten his hair. It was such a revolutionary thing in the village and was the talk of the hamlet that Giutzu, my father, had gotten strange and foreign ideas in the service. He even had learned to speak Hungarian, which was alike to abomination to any Rumanian folk.

I am not sure whether it was at this time that my father decided I should have a hair cut. According to century-old tradition the children, either male or female, did not have their hair cut until, as adults, the hair was trimmed a little longer than the collar of the shirt. Of course, it was kept in shape or close to the scalp by anointing it from time to time with melted butter, which was kept in a little baked earth mug. This was put on the hair when, say, going to church or to the market. It was a must at Christmas and Easter. My granny said it smelled rancid, but how else would it smell, being kept so long? But butter was a rare product because the milk was needed for cornmush or homemade wheatflour cereal in the morning and sometimes in the evening. When the milk cow was heavy with calf, there was no milk at all. That period lasted about nine months of a year. Then the needed milk was obtained from neighbors.

My hair was long and heavy and white. Granny told me Father decided to cut it short to be like the boys he had seen in the city of Gyula or even Arad, the district seat where he went twice a year for some iron parts so much needed for the mill. My granny saved some of my white curls and stuck them against the long beam with beeswax from the little candles she made every year before Easter. I thought it was white wool, but Granny assured me that it was my own hair, which was so much darker now since my father cut it short.

"We have lived so peacefully and contently so far," Granny said. "Now your father has started all these things—I am uneasy! I do not know what he wants to do. All our forerunners were born, lived, and died as respectable people in the hamlet; they have been happy and kept the customs of their forefathers; now Giutzu wants to change it. I don't believe God wants us to change the things that way! Be like Giutzu: he is good, kind, and loving to us and your mother, but what is this change all about? Why should we do things when we have been quite content with the way of life we have kept like that of our parents and other people in the hamlet?"

10

Of course, I agree with Granny. I loved Granny and Grandpop dearly. I also loved my father and mother. My father brought me presents when he came to see me—like an iron spoon and a little cup, white inside and blue outside, which would not rust. Granny fed me with a wooden spoon and from wooden bowls—God-given material from which to eat. These things were made by the carvers from fine poplar wood, which was light and would never crack. To put in your mouth an iron spoon was not only against the natural way of living, but would damage your teeth and mouth, Granny said, and who could tell, it might even affect your health and life. "We are God-fearing folk and he wanted us to live with the things he gave us: our food, our implements are all made of the things that grow—trees, fruit trees, wheat, barley, corn, potatoes. No matter where you look, these things God gave us to use and enjoy. Now, we try to change these things and that does not sound good! It may be sinful. It may bring upon us evil things or even pestilence," Sweet-Mom said. She related this to the other women who came in the evening to spin. They all agreed. But some said, and Granny agreed, that "What can one do? Giutzu, the mayor's son, was in service and saw new and unheard-of things. He has traveled by train, which in itself is an awesome thing; it may be that the whole world is about to take another course. It may be that God will bring it to an end because of too much inequity among men. Look, fewer and fewer go to church, the priest comes only once a month or even more rarely, especially when the roads are flooded or he is sick. He has to come by horseback from his hamlet, Magulicea, about five hours to Tisa." They discussed the fact that the priest was assigned his parish by the bishop. And that was the end of the matter—no matter how things may change, man cannot avoid his fate. "What is written in the book for him that is also written on his forehead." Nobody may switch from his fate!

Sometimes, Granny talked about the "foreigners," those folk in the city, where neither she nor Grandpop had ever been, but had heard about, who were living all crowded into houses close together, having no courts or gardens. There were only crowded houses on streets. They worked inside, not as the Rumanians in the fields and meadows and in the forest or orchard. I took in all these stories and my fantasy ran along with the repeated tales. How could these people live like that? What do they eat? They have no orchards, no chickens, no cow for milk, no sheep for wool. How can these people live in such crowded houses—like ants or bees? My fancy ran riot. I decided I would never like that kind of life. I felt happy to go into the garden, in back of the stable, climb up into the plum tree and find the best ones, or to climb up into the big cherry tree and eat all the cherries I wanted.

Grandpop was not very talkative, but he smiled a lot. He would lift me up onto his shoulders once in a while, allowing me to go into the stable attic to look for eggs in the hay. Several of the laying hens hid there and were laying their eggs there. I was ever ready to crawl in the hay and look for the nest. Once I found a dozen eggs in one nest. My grandmother examined them by the light of a little beeswax candle to see whether they would hatch. If they were, we left them back in the hay until the chicks were ready to hatch.

When the hens hid themselves so and then suddenly came out from the hay in the attic with chicks, it was early in the spring and too cold for them outside, so Granny brought them all in the house and tied the mother hen to a footstool next to the stove. I loved to hold the chicks in my hand, no one was like the other, golden silk, hair-like down, sprinkled with dark brown and even black. There were completely black chicks and I recognized and named them one by one. There was the balky, the sprinkled, the brownwings, the black legs, et cetera. I was always ready and glad to feed them with moist corn flour, which we kept in a small wooden trough under the big bench along the wall toward the entrance of the house.

When the chickens grew big enough to be butchered, Granny took two at a time and, after cleaning them, would take one wrapped in a baked earth bowl and a kitchen towel in a hand hemp bag to Mom at the mill. Sometimes, Granny even put in some peeled potatoes with the chicken.

Granny cooked for me alone the livers, gullet, and hearts together with potatoes fried in a chicken fat. It was delicious! She would often say to me, "You must eat good to grow. We have to feed the chicks well so they will grow. So it is with people and children. They must eat good things to grow and be healthy and strong to take over the plow and fork when Grandpop grows older." She would usually wind up with saying, "I don't think you would like to live at that mill, where the dust from the flour falls all over you and where you cannot sleep for all that noise of the water wheels and the deafening shake of the entire structure of the mill and the room where your father and mother are staying." When we went to the mill to see Mom and Father I was always ready to return with Granny to her home in the Big Run Valley. That was my home and there I felt happy and knew every bit of the place: the trees, the big cabbage plants that were saved for seeding and the purple onions for seeds at the end of the rows in our vegetable and hemp plot on the slope.

In Big Run Valley the sun seemed to rise later because of the steep hill on the right and seemed to set earlier under the peak of Gorgona. What a high mountain it looked to be, all wooded far away on the West Horizon. Oh, how I would have liked to climb that mountain. It was far away. Older boys said the mountain was covered with wild ivy that was green all winter long, and they gathered it in amounts to decorate the wooden jugs for weddings and other occasions. Later on I thought Gorgona was the right name for the mountain because it was remote from us. When the sun reached the peak in its course and disappeared, darkness was upon the village and Big Run Valley.

The steep hill facing the house was covered with tall grasses. Here there were plentiful strawberry vines and scattered hazelnut bushes. Only the goats and, once in a while, small children would climb it, "with care," as Grandmother said. Children's feet were more secure since they were smaller. I would climb the steep slope and pick strawberries and stick them on fern branches to make it look like the branches were full of berries. I even stuck them on a long haystem. I remember how fragrant they were. Whenever I took some of the berries to Granny she was very happy and, after tasting one or two, gave me the rest, saying she had had many in the past and that I should eat them all. I also brought fresh hazelnuts from the bushes above the rock for her, but she remarked that her teeth were not good to chew them. I thought the hazelnuts tasted delightful. I thought they were better than the freshly peeled walnut meats.

Once Grandpop found a rabbit nest in the alfalfa field when he was cutting the growth. He found a little rabbit and brought it to me. It was the climax of happiness for me. I had even dreamed of holding a little rabbit, and now the dream was in my lap. Grandmom helped me feed it milk. We put a little milk in the wooden saucer and dipped his nose in the milk. He would lick his funny lips. Then we dipped his nose into the milk again. He would not do it by

13

himself. He started shivering, and I covered him with a cloth and put him in a basket. I glanced in every five minutes to see if he was sleeping. His eyes were open, and Grandpop said rabbits slept with their eyes open.

The little rabbit grew fast, and in several weeks I could not catch it. In an empty pigsty it was hard to catch him unless he was cornered, and then he scratched your hands with his sharp paw nails. Granny cautioned me about giving him plenty of water so that his fur would look much shinier. He would not drink milk or a handful of fresh clover.

One day I opened the door so that he could run in the courtyard in the sun to stretch his legs, but he would not come out. I went in to chase him out, and he suddenly jumped out with a high hop and ran straight across the yard and stopped in a corner. I went after him, but he would not let me pet him. He started running and stopping and in less than a quarter of an hour was gone. He jumped over the footgate to the backyard and was gone forever.

I did not know what to make of it all. I was concerned that Granny would scold me for letting the rabbit out. But she looked at me and saw that I was very sad. She asked me what was the matter and I burst out crying. She asked me to sit on her lap and tell her what was the matter. Through my sobbing I told her the rabbit was gone. "Oh," she said, "Grandpop will bring another one next summer." I thought she relieved all my worries. Several days after that, Grandmom told me she saw the rabbit in the hayfield next to our backyard, but it would not come into the yard. I was concerned that some dogs might catch it and kill it, but Grandmom assured me that the dogs could not run fast enough to catch the rabbit no matter what and that he eventually would find his way back to the hills and bushes where his kin lived.

My greatest wish was to go to the Big Run Valley pastures, just outside the hamlet toward the run's springs. One morning Granny came to my little bed and asked me whether I would like to go with the children to watch the pigs in the rugged pasture up the Big Run Valley and on the slopes where they were rooting in the sod and finding sweet roots and, after a little while, going back to the warm ponds along the stream and having a mudbath. The pigs liked that in the summertime and sometimes they even fell asleep and snored.

The day was hot. The pigs took to the ponds and the children took off shirts and pants and took a swim in the large, dammed stream. I remember in some places the water was up to my neck. Almost as soon as we were in the pond an incredibly dark, almost black, cloud appeared to rise from behind the Craven Stone Range. It was shaped like a dragon, and one of the boys said there was going to be a fight between two dragons and no one could predict the outcome. The dragons were getting closer and closer as they rose from behind the Craven Stone Range and we realized they were coming toward us.

On the other side, the sky was clear and the sun was burning hot. Then hail started falling: ice in all shapes and sizes, some as big as a goose egg. The pigs started squealing and running around looking for shelter. Some of them were bleeding from ear and back cuts. We, the children, took shelter under a big rock, where there were several foxholes. We were told by other boys long afterward that in the nighttime stray ghosts stayed there. The valley and slope were covered with ice in no time. We were crossing ourselves and asking St. George to chase away the dragons. It was dark as night though it was the middle of the day.

While the hail was coming down in various shapes, mostly round, we heard a noise from upvalley and one of the boys said he saw a wave of water as big as a house coming rapidly, carrying stones and trees and logs. We were almost sure that the end of the earth was near, as we could sense it then and there.

The waters were now from slope to slope. The pigs were gone and everything was covered in water. The flood was almost nearing our foxholes under the rock on the slope, yet, it did not rise to the rock. We were spared from being carried away. The plum and pear trees in the valley were entirely submerged. They, too, might be carried away with the rolling waters—the woods, hemp, pigs, uprooted trees and everything in its wake. I was sure some of us, like me, were closing our eyes and saying some prayers in our heart, that the almighty St. George might overcome the dragons or even God Almighty would get involved and bring us to safety.

How long did the storm last? No one can say. Was it minutes or hours? But as it started from nothing the dark clouds started to vanish and the sun appeared again. The waters started to recede almost as fast as they fell. The ice covered the ground almost knee deep as the water receded. But we would not dare to get out of the hole!

After a while, when there were almost no clouds, I was sure I heard a voice. It was the voice of my granny, calling, "My child! My child! Where are you? Are you alive?" I was not exactly sure that it was the voice of my granny or some other voice, which in such fearful times would call children only to catch them and take them away or even suck their blood. We knew that for sure those demons existed. But it was still daylight, and certainly evil ghosts did not come out from their holes before the sun set.

I whispered to the boy next to me that I heard my granny's voice. He did not answer. We were sitting squat under the rock, petrified and completely mute. But now I was sure the voice was Granny's. "George, my dear child, are you alive, are you saved?"

The voice was close, and I burst from our hole and there was my granny coming along the slope almost straight toward our shelter. When she saw me she started to cry, "Oh, my dear, oh, my dear, God Almighty saved you from the flood. God guided your feet to the rock to find shelter."

She grabbed me and fell on her knees, thanking God for the miraculous saving of her grandson, who she thought might have been carried away with the waters of the deluge, which in minutes had carried away people and animals and houses along the riverside.

I remember quite well that Granny said it all happened because of the sin of the people. God wanted them to know that he was still almighty, he still could destroy everything, but in his kindness had only an outburst of anger to show to people that they should be good to one another, there should be no swearing, no stealing, no encroachment on lands of others, they should remember the poor. Granny told me that God was often mad but restrained in his dealings with people. She said too many people were blasphemous and unloving, really possessed by the evil spirits.

That coming fall Father wanted me to go to school. Granny tried to reason with him that I was too young—I was barely six years old and no one of my age was going to school and the school was too far away for a child of six. It was at least one hour of hard walking to Halmagiu, the county seat where the schools were. But Father

16

had to prevail. Granny knew Dad was right in his thinking but wrong with regard to the welfare of his child, who was too young to be sent away to school and taken away from his grandfather and grandmother, who would then be really alone. I was hoping and praying that Dad would reconsider his decision, but he did not.

One Saturday morning he came to the Big Run Valley place and asked me to go with him to the market. I was not pleased or happy, as I did not know what he wanted. People went to the market to buy or sell such things as salt or kerosene, and sometimes Dad would bring me some hard candies or a white roll shaped like a crescent, which was good with warm milk. We went in our horse-drawn wagon and Dad put several bags of corn in the wagon to sell. I wondered why he would sell corn, since I thought everyone who came to the mill brought his own corn and oats for milling.

It seemed a long way to the market. There were other people going too. It must be a fair. Maybe the Saint Mary's Fair in August. The road was packed with people going in the same direction, bringing along by ropes cows, goats, and sheep. There were many women with baskets on their heads carrying eggs, chickens, or even butter. I thought it was bad to sell eggs and butter or sheep as they were good for eating and the sheep were giving milk for the lambs and wool for spinning. I had never seen Granny sell anything! She gave to the poorer neighbors such things as milk and occasionally eggs. Of course, they helped Granny to clean and spin the wool. I did not ask why these things were so; I only thought in my mind that they were not so wise as my granny or my grandpop or even my pop. But my dad was selling corn by the measure from his bags. That was another matter, I thought, since he had plenty as grain token for the grinding of the corn.

There was a lot of dust along the road, and it was a warm day. The people chasing their pigs or cattle talked to them—"Hei, Hei, Joanna, this way, dear." Some even cursed the cattle, which tried to get away from the crowded road. Eventually we arrived at the middle of the town, where three roads met. There was a long building, which Dad told me was the courthouse. In the backyard was the jail. What is jail? I wanted to know. He explained there was a room with iron bars in the windows and the gendarmes placed people who had broken the law, like killing somebody, there. It was incredible to me—who would kill someone and what for?

We got down from the wagon and Dad took my hand and led me to a canvas-covered table on which were only hats. The man behind the table greeted Dad by name, and Dad said, "Look, this is my son. I want a hat for him—he is going to school this fall." I thought the heavens would fall in on me—I wished it would! I did not want another hat. I had one on my head. Dad picked out a hat and put it on his head. He then took off my hat and put a big, new hat on my head. I was very unhappy and wished that I could be far away from this place, somewhere like my granny's backyard or even in the Big Run valley with the pigs. I did not want this ugly hat on my head.

The man behind the table handed a frame to my father. It was a mirror. I knew each house had a mirror like that on the wall for Dad to see in to shave, but to have a mirror on a handle was just nonsense! Dad showed me the mirror to look in and asked me how I felt. I shrugged my shoulders, saying nothing, and felt near to tears. I was pleased, however, when the man behind the table, who was wearing a hat with a wide brim like the one on my head, said to my father, "George, you have a nice boy! He is a little bit shy, but that is the way young boys are!"

Dad shook hands with the man and he stretched his hand to me and I shook hands with him. I remembered he had a strong hand and was friendly in manner.

There was another tent nearby that one had to go in by a little opening like behind a curtain or canvas. Dad almost dragged me in. In the middle of the canvas enclosure there was a wooden box set on top of a wooden tripod. The man sitting on an upside down box got up and came to Dad saying, "I guess you want a picture of this handsome boy!"

"Yes," said Father. "He is my son and he is going to school this fall. I want to have a picture of him!"

What was he talking about? I had seen pictures in the papers. But I could not understand why Dad was having a picture of me made here in this tent. The man instructed us to stay very close to the canvas wall. I was unhappy having this picture made of my dad and me, especially in this new hat, which I hated. But how could I tell Dad how I felt? I felt I had only to obey and shed tears later.

Soon the man removed a cap from the end of the box and told us to stand still. After that we got a piece of paper on which, lo and behold, there I was with Dad next to me, he with a stern face and me not far from sobbing.

Dad moved along through the groups of people, chatting or stopping to look at the things people were selling, such as eggs, early apples, or pears. Here and there were chickens with their legs tied together, struggling to get away. *What cruelty*, I thought. These people did not love their fowls at all!

We went farther along by the tables with fabrics and kerchiefs for women. What a crowd. They were looking at everything, asking the prices and feeling the cloth. I did not understand how all this merchandise could arrive here. How did these people come to the market, where were they from, and how could they leave their homes and come to this dusty place? I even thought, *Why are they not at home, in their fields as my grandpop is, taking care of the cattle or cutting the tall hay and piling it in stacks?* But Dad took me even further. I did not like the market, but I was fascinated watching people to see how many different costumes they were wearing, quite different to the men and women I saw at our church at Easter.

Then we went on to the next tent. The tables were stacked with black vests covered in shiny buttons. Dad wanted me to try one on, but I refused to budge. My father explained that he only wanted me to look well, and by this time the tears were rolling down my cheeks. My father further said he wanted to make me a gentleman. *What a curse on me*, I thought! I even thought he wanted me to look like a chimney sweep or other town dark-clothed people. *May God save me from such*, I thought. *How cruel of Dad!* I felt that Granny would not like this sort of thing, but she was not here. But she always said that Dad only wanted what was best for me.

Dad put one of the vests on me and asked whether I would try a pair of the pants. That was it! I sobbed, "No, no." Father said something to the man, handed him several coins, put the vest on his arm, and off we went.

Several people greeted my father, saying, "Miller, is this your son? How much he has grown. How handsome he looks."

I only thought they should mind their own business and not be concerned with my appearance! Did not my granny tell me I was a good boy and did as she told me—such as minding the onion and hemp seedlings from the sparrows and other birds. We went back to the wagon and found that the big bags of corn were emptied. Adam, our good old servant, had sold all of it. The horses were enjoying their hay from the end of the wagon, occasionally raising their heads and shaking their manes against the flies.

I was ready to get into the wagon and go home to my granny, but Dad said that the school was not far away and he would like to show it to me. I had never said no to my father, and now I waited. Soon we walked by the low house next to the only two-storied building in town, the Big Inn—also called the Sodamaker, because this was the only place they made carbonated water used in lemonade. Some people even used it in wine. We passed a house that Dad explained was the doctor's house. He said he would take me there for "a scratch with medicine."

I had heard that at the age of seven children were taken to the doctor's office. I resolved that it would not be me. I did not understand the reason for this initial visit. Then we came to a very large building with many windows. It was the school. It was all white with a red tile roof. There was a very large yard at the end of the building, which had a very unusual enclosure, half wall and half wire mesh fence. There was a small gate, which was open, and a large one, which was closed. Not far away was the church—a real, solid-walled church. I stared in amazement. How could they build such a high building covered with some sort of metal sheet? Our church was made of oak logs and covered with oak shingles, and I thought all churches were alike.

"Well," said Dad, "this coming fall you will come here every day except Saturday. You will come with your aunts, Betty and Mary, who know the way. And when there is very deep snow or flooded roads, Adam will come with the wagon and bring you here together with your aunts."

I listened but with no enjoyment. I thought that since my dad so wanted it, I had no choice but to obey.

From here we went back toward the center of the town and the marketplace. We stopped at a little house all by itself next to the creek. We went in and Dad asked for two hard rolls, crescent shaped. The big lady behind the table asked Dad whether I was his son. My dad said yes and that I was going to school in the fall. She asked how old I was, and, when Dad said that I was six, she answered that I was very young to start to school. She added that her children had started school at seven. Dad assured her that I would be all right, as I would be going with his two young sisters. I was still hoping that he would change his decision. That was the summer of 1913. That September, after Saint Mary's Day, school started.

PRIMARY SCHOOL

It was a sad day for me to leave Granny's home and go to stay with my father and mother in the house at the mill. I looked forward to Saturday and Sunday when I would go to the home of my grand-mother and grandfather in the Big Run Valley. I felt that was my real home, and I hoped the "school business" would end somehow. Grandmom and Grandpop never went to school, and I wanted to be like them. My mother never went to school, and everyone talked about how beautiful and good and thoughtful she was.

We left very early in the morning for school. I had a little leather-backed book and case with a strap for the shoulder. Most of the time, Mother made a bowl of mashed potatoes with fried onions mixed with pumpkin seed oil for my lunch. It was good. With this I had a slice of good bread. I discovered some of the children had corn bread with mashed potatoes. Their bread was dark brown. My bread was fluffy and raised.

I soon realized I did not like to play with other children. They played games I had never heard of, and many of them cursed and used all kinds of words I had never heard. I was told that only wicked people cursed and used foul language. I was told to pray to God, even in my thoughts, to help me to cross over bad things unsoiled and unharmed. Some of the boys told me and even said behind my back that I was mild like a girl. I did not swear—I resented this talk. I did not want to be like a girl, although my best playmates at home were my aunts and Lena Fisherman's daughter, who did not go to school. Her father and mother decided she need not go to school, since they did not expect her to be a priestess. How right they were, I thought!

About this time, I met a boy to whom I was told we were related. My father called his father and mother our cousins. So, I too called him cousin. That is to say, we were related through my father's father's mother, who of course died long ago. However, I knew that my father's grandmother had been from Lestiora and that Miron's mother had too. She had been married in the village of Bodesti. Miron was taller than I, but he would not play outside much, I noticed. Then I discovered that he had a minor limp on one foot. He preferred to watch other children at play, and often I would stay near him rather than participating in the games.

Another boy I liked was Pompil. He and Miron were dressed differently from me. I was sent to school dressed "as a child should" in *vigan*, which was a one-piece dress and then my lambskin jacket. When it was colder I wore my woolen short overcoat, which had warm side pockets for my hands. Miron and Pompil wore britches which ran from the waist to down below the knee. They wore dark cloth jackets just like the gypsies wore, except their were much neater. I wondered why we were not all dressed alike. Perhaps they did not have fields of hemp and herds of sheep to have the home-spun cloth and wool cloth. Pompil's father was a priest and his mother was a teacher. We wondered if they were just like town folks or like the tinsmith who came to the village occasionally ready to repair the tin pans.

The most amazing things I experienced during my elementary school years were the several trips we made, instructed by our teacher to go two by two and hand in hand. It was a sunny day when we went to see the tunnels made in the dark period of history in which the people hid from an enemy, like the Turks or anyone else who was trying to invade our country—mistreating the people and carrying off the sheep and goats and cattle and sometimes killing people who resisted and even burning their villages. We had studied about all these things in school. It was incredible to me that these things had happened. And now the teacher told us we would go into the tunnels by ourselves.

We walked along the margin of the road until we came to the bridge over the Halmagiu Run and then crossed over and climbed up a steep hill along a rather narrow pathway often broken by trenches and ravines of reddish clay-like soil.

Next we approached a small area of forested ground, and shortly after we went around it we came to a big hole in the side of the hill. The teacher lighted two kerosene hand lamps and asked

22

the children to follow in. I was curious to see the tunnel, my first one. I knew foxes had their burrows and holes and some of the boys I knew had tried to capture foxes from their holes or dens. These tunnels were not in rock, and the thing that amazed me was that the clay stayed as it was dug out for a long, long time. The bottom of the tunnel was muddy. As we went further we could look back and see the light of day through the opening we entered. One of the teachers told us that some tunnels were very long and had several openings but some of the openings might break in because of rain and snow. We also were told that some daring people had explored some of the tunnels, searching for gold treasures that possibly had been hidden in the tunnels. Awesome! It might have been that those treasures had burned with flame at midnight of the New Year. I had heard some of the boys saying that if you only knew the area and stayed there during the New Year night under a forsaken harrow, which had no iron nails in it, you would certainly see the flame of the golden treasure. You could then run there and stake it out, and go there the next morning to dig for the treasure. One thing for sure, the older boys said, never tell anybody these things, because if the gendarmes heard it they would take away the spoils found. I wondered why the gendarmes could take away treasures found by someone else and finally decided it was because they were Hungarians and we the people, peasants, were Rumanians.

I began to hear that the people in dark clothes were almost, if not all, Hungarians. They were intruders and despoilers of many things in our land. Why were these dark-clothed people coming among us? They were exacting tolls, I understood, and even from people going to the market. I did not understand why. Was not the land God-given to the Rumanians? Surely the land belonged to the Rumanians because they were born there and so were all their forebears back from the time of creation of the earth. I was beginning to understand that there were other peoples speaking other languages, even Hungarians. Why was this? The Rumanian language was spoken by everybody. Where was the need for another language? How could a cow or sheep be called by some other name?

When the term of school was over, I was so happy! The summer vacation was on! My grandmother allowed me to take the milk cow by a rope and go to the grazing fields together with my aunt Betty, who took two other cows by a rope. For one week we went to one grazing patch and then the next week we moved our location. The cows were gentle but became quite excited when the boring bugs came buzzing about, and they ran into the bushes or into deep water to escape the painful bugs. Betty and I sang the songs we had learned at school and talked about what a sweet language was our mother language. We even sang songs, which, we understood, would not be sung within hearing of the gendarmes! Why was this? Because the subject of the songs was about the Rumanian three color flag; red, yellow and blue, and the Hungarian flag was red, white and green!

One evening when I came home with Joanna, the cow, I could see at once that Grandmother had something of importance to tell me. She did. She told me that Father would have to go into service because of a bad happening. A foolish young man had killed the emperor's nephew and his wife while in Sarajevo, Bosnia. The matter could not be settled except by going against Serbia, from which country the student had come to Bosnia. Then I heard the word Sarajevo.* What did it mean? Father came and told us because he was on active duty he would have to go, but that the conflict would probably last only a few weeks and he would be back home, because the Austria-Hungarian Empire is so big and powerful that Serbia would be defeated in no time. From Grandmother I learned not only Father, but five others from our village were going to fight. Dad came in the evening and kissed me on the forehead, and I kissed his hand and he said they would take a train very early in the morning to go to Gyula. It was August 1914.

Granny told me I might be needed at the mill, that my mother might need me to watch over the crib of my brother, John, who was about a year old. While I did not like the idea of staying at the mill, I would not refuse Granny. I never said no to her. How could I? She knew what was best for me. I remember how she had cared for me when I was sick, when my arm was broken. I remember when she had let me go out into the Big Run Valley to play with other boys and even allowed me to swim in the pond. Now, when she asked me to stay by my little brother's crib, I could not possibly say no!

*Sarajevo was the capital of Bosnia. In 1914 Francis Ferdinand, heir presumptive to the Austrian throne, was shot to death by a nationalist Serb. A month later the First World War started when the Austria-Hungary Empire declared war on Serbia.

It seemed everybody came to the mill with his bag of grain to have it milled; there was corn, wheat, barley, and oats. Some of the women commented about how much I had grown; that I had been to school, though only six years old; that I would soon be seven.

Grandfather, Father's father, was now the mayor and the miller in the village. He was often at the mill, since Father was away. Quite often he went to Halmagiu, where the town clerk had his office. From time to time when Grandfather came to the mill he brought along some printed papers to be posted in a box that had a wire cover. The entire frame of the box was painted green, except that at the very top of it there was something like a little crown and a sort of shield, which was painted in three colors; red, white and green. I thought the little box would make a very fine bird cage, but it was really too narrow. The printed paper was put in the frame and locked in with a tiny key. I could not read the words, although I had been taught at school to count to ten in Hungarian and to say good morning and good day.

I wondered how a war would be carried on against the Serbians. People who came to the mill talked amongst themselves that the fighting would be done with sabers, which I had seen hanging down from the sides of the gendarmes. Some people talked about the soldiers from our village who had been away in service as long as seven years, and one for fifteen years. Some even thought the soldiers were just lured into joining the army and leaving their families behind. One man, almost an old man, who was called John the Soldier (Catana Onica), had been away so long that he no longer knew the pathway to his home, nor did he recognize his wife. He had been gone at least fifteen years and it was said he battled on the Austrian side against the Germans at the Curly Dog, which they said was the name of the place and which sounded funny, Königgretz. I thought this was comical—to call a place by a dog's name.

I began to think that it was interesting to stay at the mill, to see many people coming and going and to hear stories of faraway places and of people who were different from us—like those Serbians who killed the emperor's heir and his wife. I thought of the story of Sophia, the fool, who set fire to the house where she was not received. Maybe this was the reason in some way that the Serbian felt; he must have been unhappy and as the fool he took revenge on the prince and his wife. Then I thought what my grandmother had said must be so, that no one could escape his fate—if God so willed, so it would come to pass. Again that off-repeated phrase came up: "What is written in the book for you that is also written on your forehead!"

Mom had no time at all to chat on all these things because the bell on the millstone dropped, which meant the big chest was emptying. After she filled it up again with grain she came in and took up her wool spinning. Other women would watch and pick up a rod and ask her whether the thread was for weaving or for knitting. I thought it was an amazing process—the thread had to be held with the teeth to make it even and strong.

People would inquire about Father, and Mother told them that he must be all right, as she had heard nothing from the town clerk. Mother said that in reality no one could say what the end would be. But it seemed like God's punishment, because people were quarreling among themselves and constantly going to the town court with their grievances instead of settling things before the justice of the peace as they used to do. Now some even went to the district court as far away as the big city of Arad, to the district chief supervisor. My mother, I was sure, had never been there and had no wish to go that far away by train. But why would she have reason to? We had everything we needed. Grandpop was the mayor and had more lands than anybody else. He had a mill and even sold salt and kerosene. Many women came for salt and kerosene and paid with eggs because they did not have *kritzars* (pennies).

Then came Saint Mary's Day, but school did not start and how glad I was! We did go into school, though, to work for the soldiers. I heard from other boys and girls that their fathers, too, had been "called in" to go fight the war. The teacher explained that Russia's emperor, whom the Russians called tzar, jumped in to help Serbia, and that Russia was a big country, though weaker than Austria-Hungary, and had many men, like ants swarming all over the place. The teacher went on to say that now our country needed more men in this battle against Russia.

It was fall, October. The children, two by two, were led to the nearest hills covered with bramble bushes and a lot of black raspberry bushes, which were thorny with sharp needles. We picked leaf by leaf from the black raspberry bushes and put them in our

26

book bags. At school we emptied these on a large table, which had been covered with a hemp tablecloth. We were told that the dried leaves would be sent to the front for our fathers and other soldiers to use as tea leaves.

I thought this was strange. I thought only the leaves of the linden flower were good for tea, when someone had a sore throat or a cough. Perhaps, there were no more linden flowers, as it was fall, and so tea would have to be made from black raspberry leaves. But these leaves did not smell like the linden flowers!

Our contact with the war raging somewhere in foreign lands or at the edge of our empire were the songs taught by Mihai Vidu, our teacher. For example, the "Sweet language that we speak, there is no other sweeter language in the entire world like the one we speak; the heart listens to it with pleasure and it brings honey to the lips when spoken." Another song was the "Three colors I know in this world; that I behold like a holy flag; it is the red like that which pierces my heart with the yearning for freedom and for my country's love; it is the yellow, like the proud golden sun is our future; forever in flourish time and with unperishable shine; blue is our faith for our nation like the sky above; serene and immaculate and with the eternal hope for the clear future of our nation."

We had heard my dad singing and my mother humming a song that if the gendarmes heard the singer would be taken away! Why? It was explained that it was a long song talking about the Rumanians to awake from their deadly sleep and carve another fate for themselves; they have glorious forefathers, the Romans, and their fate is to move forward in the glorious path of history already drawn by their ancestors. Some of the words I did not understand, for example, "secular enemies." Who were they and why were they our enemies? We were doing nothing wrong. We were Rumanians since the beginning of the world, as Granny so often told me, and why should we have enemies? Why should the gendarmes take one away who was singing such a nice song?

About this time I discovered that my mother had a beautiful belt that she had never worn. It was of silk and knitted in three colors lengthwise, red, yellow, and blue. It was hidden in her chest, and I asked her why she did not wear it. She explained that the gendarmes would destroy it if she wore it. But she did not explain why these three colors were kept in secret. But I knew the Hungarian colors were red, white, and green under a big, bejeweled, cap-like thing. I did not hate them. I thought they were nice. But why the Rumanian colors were not liked by the gendarmes was a mystery to me.

I heard my grandpop, and once in a while my mother, say that in Serbia even the women were shooting guns from their house attics. *Shooting at what?* I wondered! I thought it must be awful that the Serbian women had to take guns in their hands and shoot at my father and others. I soon heard my grandfather telling people who came to the mill with their grain that Giutzu, he was sure, was no longer on the Serbian front but in Galicia. Where was that? Well, they said, that was a very mountainous place with a lot of marshy valleys and wooded areas; the Russians were coming that way and Father was transferred there in the fight against the Russians. I knew the Serbians as well as the Russians had the same church as the Rumanians. It was amazing to me that people speaking different languages had the same church.

It was in the spring of 1916 I believe my mother told the other women at the mill that she had had a dreadful dream. There were several soldiers including my father in a fight in which there was clashing of sabers and she saw my father with blood on his arms and suddenly she awoke. She said she prayed that God's will be done, but at that time something must have happened to Father. Sure enough, several days later the town clerk sent word to my grandfather to go to the office, and he told my grandfather, as the mayor of the village, that my father had been wounded on the Galician line—a shell had hurt his left hand and his left thumb was gone. When Grandpop gave this news to my mother, she said she was sure that it had happened in the night of that dreadful dream and that it may have been God's will that for Father it was the end of the war. Granny of the Big Run Valley sobbed as she heard the news of father's wounds. "Oh, my dear Giutzu, what a fate has been given to you."

But my mother said to her that it might have been for the best for herself and for her family that now he might be able to come home. "It's better than being killed," Mom said. "After all," she said, "our fate is written by God; we really cannot shift that assigned way."

My grandfather wanted to go to see my father in the hospital, but he did not speak the language used there, Hungarian. The town clerk, Mr. Steger, who was always friendly to Grandpop and had been wined and dined at Grandfather's house, offered to go with him to the hospital. The whole trip took three days, going and coming and seeing Dad in the hospital in Gyula. I thought Mr. Steger was very kind and thoughtful to go with Grandpop. I had seen him but could not speak with him because he was such a high ranking gentleman, dressed in fine dark clothes, and had been everywhere. Grandpop called him a very good and kind man. The position of town clerk was the highest next to the county's chief officer, whom my grandpop had seldom seen and then only in conjunction with and upon the town clerk's advice or direction.

The county chief officer was Hungarian and spoke only Hungarian. His son was a friend of my uncle Alexander, who said they had been good friends when they were students at the state school, where the spoken language was Hungarian. I was amazed when my uncle said he could speak Hungarian and that at the school he spoke only in Hungarian. My uncle Alexander said he wanted to continue in school with his friend, the county chief officer's son, but Grandpop explained that he did not have the money to send him on to higher education.

In essence, my grandfather seemed to be saying that although it is nice to know dignitaries, it is better not to follow what they say. He repeated the saying that the laundry should be washed at home, not at Halmagiu, that is, at the town and county seats with the help of the Town Clerk Steger or the county chief officer. He was saying that it is all right to listen to what the gentry has to say, but, he added, "Whoever plows with the gentry may end by harrowing with his own bottom!"

Uncle Alexander taught me how to count to ten in Hungarian and even in German. I felt very proud of this accomplishment. I was able to count in Rumanian up into many hundreds. I was now ready for the third grade. My mother asked me to read from my books, even from the *Dream of Our Lady*, a little book that related that a small stone fell from the heavens. It was small but incredibly heavy and, lo and behold, there was an epistle in it—a letter was my way of saying it. That epistle told the people that God's angels were walking on the earth with Saint Peter or Saint Paul and they performed miracles and even at times punished wrongdoers. That was long ago, the story said, but people talked about these things. They said people are the same today. When the saints walk among men they are looking for shelter for the night and so on. Those who are generous to the travelers, giving them food and shelter, will be rewarded for their good deeds.

I was never very excited over these stories. I thought it was a matter of course that such people of God had walked on this earth since God made it. But I especially remembered that Grandmother and Mom had never left anyone wanting in our house without offering him a slice of bread and some bacon. That is right, they were saying—anyone in their house was a guest. It never occurred to me that it should be different!

Just as many people who came to the mill with their grain to be made into flour brought to Mom some forest mushrooms or earliest cherries or plums, or pears, apples, or grapes, so Mom never turned anyone away empty, but put flour in their bags in extra amounts. I remember Mother prepared the mushrooms with onions and sour cream and she remarked that it was better than any chicken!

That summer in 1916, Father came home. His hand was in a sling attached round his neck. I cried seeing my father. I kissed his right hand and he kissed my forehead. I was wondering whether he would be able to handle the Flober gun and teach me how to aim at the wild geese or ducks along the river Cris and the ponds in the winter. Or how would he be able to lift those big bags of grain? It had seemed easy for him before to carry the bags from the wagon to the mill. And could he go to the forest for firewood? All these thoughts flew through my mind when I saw him. I was thinking of a miracle to cause father to be able to use his hand and arm.

Father had to return to the hospital at Gyula many times to have his hand checked and to learn whether he would be able to return to the army. It was a long time until I understood that he was rated a 25 percent disabled veteran of the war and that it was temporary. This rating gave him some benefit. He received a 25 percent discount on travel by train—about four times a year. So he was able to go to Arad for some of the things he needed for the mill, like the steel heart of the millstone or the steel axle of the waterwheel.

Father had more leisure time in the evening, and once in a while he taught me some Hungarian words and listened to my work on the multiplication tables. I felt I was quite good on that. It was simple. You only took what was already in your mind and added a couple numbers more and there you were. In reading I was good, I thought, and when Father put a big map in the mill hall I was amazed at the colors of the mountains and the valleys. We had a map at school, but there was only Austria-Hungary. This was the map of the whole world.

Suddenly it was spring, then summer of 1917. Father told us we were going to have war prisoners, Russians, who were captured by our armies. There were about twenty in all. They had to stay at our place because nobody in the village had as large a barn and house as ours. I was puzzled about why the prisoners should come to us. What can we do for them? Were they like other people? How did they look? Since they were Russians, were they our enemies? Must we keep enemies in our barns? Then I heard Dad talking at the mill to others about all this. The prisoners were assigned by the executive of the county to help work in the fields, since so many of the able bodied men had gone to the battlefields. But would they know how to work in our fields since they were Russians? I was anxious to see the Russians but somehow concerned that they might be strange creatures. I heard some of the people saying among themselves that the Russians were almost like us, that they were a God-fearing people and had churches like ours and that they were not pagans!

One day, early in the morning, I heard that the prisoners were there at the barn. Father had to distribute them to people who needed help for the fields, but quite a few of them were to stay with us at the mill. I heard that two of them were Rumanians. They were Bessarabians—Rumanians from Bessarabia. How could Rumanians be Russian prisoners? Dad explained to me that as he was a Rumanian in the Hungarian army, so these prisoners were Rumanians in the Russian army. They were really from a country called Bessarabia, which was full of Rumanians, and they went to Rumanian churches, but the Russians had drafted them to fight the war against Austria and Hungary.

They wore an awkward fashion, I thought. There were large pants of an ugly color, almost like grass, and their shirts were without buttons, with a sort of string to close it up at the neck.

What impressed me no end was the fact that they got together to sing. Their voices were strong. They sang all kinds of songs—songs I had never heard before, but which were nice. The two Bessarabians sang beautifully even though none of the words were like ours. I remember one of them, Adam, had taught me the words of the song and it was similar to our "Christ is Risen Today" but different, too, e.g., *Christos Vaskress a varabezi odaravast*! Adam told me that it was like our words in Rumanian, but theirs were in Russian and they sang that song at Easter in the church and through the Ascension Day. They greeted one another during these six weeks just like the Rumanians: "Christ is risen!" and the reply, "He is risen indeed!" They celebrated the days between the Ascension and Pentecost just like the Rumanians did.

Adam, whose name was just like my godfather, Adam Crisan of "Crisani" (Crisans's hamlet of Tisa), taught me to count in Russian. It was not difficult to learn but sounded so funny to me. Now I could count in four languages: Rumanian, Hungarian, German, and Russian. I thought it was all easy and wondered why my mother did not know other languages, since my father could count in other languages. She did not see any reason to learn to count in any language but her own.

Mother went on to relate how busy she was all the time in the many areas taking all her time: cooking, laundering the clothing, sewing, embroidering, spinning, and, of course, teaching other women the art of weaving the hemp thread into cloth, and how to mix the cotton and wool thread to weave into cloth for towels or for bed and table spreads. Mother went on to comment that there are many kinds of personalities—some who learned fast and others who had slower learning capacity, and then there were those who were lazy and did not do as well as they could. She thought being lazy would be the most boring way to be.

At school I learned that a country by the name of Rumania had attacked our country, Hungary.* They were making advances into Transylvania. The teacher made no comments one way or the other on these things. But at the mill people talked about Rumanians advancing into Transylvania, and soon we were told that the big roads and the country roads were jammed with oxen carts and

*The author was born in Transylvania, which was part of Hungary in 1918. Only after 1918 did Transylvania become a province of Rumania. The new spelling of Rumania is *Romania*.

carriages loaded with household goods all fleeing from the advance. Why were the people fleeing? People said it was really the order of the Imperial Office that the Rumanians may not capture our goods and oxen and horses. God forbid! Why should these things happen? That was the order and nobody knew anything additional. Only we saw people with their oxen and horse-pulled wagons. It seemed their wagons were bigger than ours and the oxen heavier. We were told these people came from villages where the land was excellent for tilling and for pasture, not like ours along the river valley or here and there on the slopes.

This chain of events did not last long. The flow of people ceased. The people at the mill said the Hungarians, with the Germans' help (because the Keiser's army was very strong and the Germans better fighters), were able to overcome the Rumanians. The Germans, I heard, were a well-planned, very hard-working people. Some of the villagers said they had been servants to the German farmers on the plain and they had had to work very hard for their pay. The Germans themselves worked very hard—not only the servants or the hired hands in the fields. These people talked about the big horses of the Germans pulling the plows and used in the harvesting. Their milk cows were something of a wonder, too, as to the amount of milk they furnished. But, they said, the cows were fed with grain and cow beets—not like our little cows only grazing in the pastures and once in a while having a little grain. There were places, I thought, in our country where there were no hills where they had milk and butter in great abundance and where the farmers slaughtered several pigs at Christmas. But here in my village only a few beside my father and grandfathers slaughtered any pigs. Why didn't they? Because, Mother said, there was not enough grain for themselves, much less the pigs. But the pigs could not get fat without grain!

At harvest time, my mother and my grandmother from across the Cris cooked for the harvesters. They cooked cabbage with chunks of bacon and pork ribs. It had such an appetizing aroma! My grandmother said it was well to put an extra amount of pork in the cabbage because the workers must be well fed to do their work. She added the bit of wisdom that just as the axle of the wheelbarrow or the axle of the ox cart needs oiling so it is with man, who needs the "belly greased" in order that he may do his best work, whether it is plowing, cutting hay, cutting wheat, lifting the sheaves onto the stacks, or piling them into the wagon to take the sheaves to the threshing pad.

Grandmother from across the Cris gave us more of her philosophy. She said that really people were not lazy. They were hungry. When there is a poor diet such as onions with cornbread, day after day, and year after year, you cannot expect people to be eager and quick, just as the cow who only has a poor diet cannot give rich, creamy milk. And the manure from poorly fed cows cannot produce an enrichment for the land. I figured out that people were poor because they had no lands on which to build and raise good crops.

My father sang in *strana* as a cantor ever since I remember going to church. He would stand in the right-hand *strana*, which was just a sort of high enclosure that had one shelf with a stack of books on it. Father and Old Mihai (Michael Darau), our neighbor from the mill house, chanted when the priest, Old Ilie Sirca, was not saying something behind the iconned wall. Father took me with him in the *strana*, but I felt I did not belong there and wanted to be back with my grandmother. At my age, boys and girls were standing by themselves in the church. I thought I would stand with them in the front row, just before the little elevation on which the *strana* were set at each side. There were two big wooden candlestands there, and in front of each was a little desk with old icons, which many of the old women and even the men kissed. Of course, before entering the church, people crossed themselves, as do all Christians. Then, when in the church, you put your hat under one of the side seats that were not taken, as there was plenty of room—except at Christmas and Easter. My father's father, George, the old mayor, recited the creed at the conclusion of the liturgy, the Lord's Prayer. No other man had accomplished this part of the service. I heard from other people that my grandfather knew it all from heart and was able to recite in a strong, clear voice.

Now, my father, back home from the war, read even more books than before. He ordered many expensive books from Sibiu, from the Metropolitan Printing House, all bound in red leather with golden clasps. Father went to the church even when the priest was not there. Ilie Sirca, the priest, lived in Magulicea, a village in the mountains, about a half a day away by horse or one day by foot. Many times he was not able to come because of illness or because the footbridge had been carried away by a flood, or just because he had to care for his household and his lands. On his visits he usually arrived by Saturday market time in Halmagiu and from there he would come straight to my grandfather's house, where he always found his boarded-floor room waiting for him. It was the best room in my grandfather's house.

My father told the priest that the liturgy had been mostly babbling words without meaning. He went on to say he had read that only pagans do that—praying and repeating words to no end and without meaning. Father said he considered it better to have fewer words that made sense than to have many words without meaning. Father had an interesting book, which he called *The Writings* and from which he often read. Father also brought home several new songs. He succeeded in teaching me and Mother one of them, "Home Sweet Home." The song said there was no place like home where sweet words are heard, and the humblest home would not be exchanged for even a palace. I agreed with all this and thought of the home of my grandmother where I had been raised in the Big Run Valley. How sweet everything there was! Even the cold cornbread tasted better than any other food elsewhere.

My granny told me that she had a cousin who went to America, and when he returned became a "Repenter." I did not understand what she meant by the word *repenter*. Granny explained that it was because he did not go to church anymore, the church of our Christian people, among whom we had been brought up. He read from a black book that said it was not necessary to go to listen to the liturgy but to read the black book, which was the true "writing." He told people not to pray like a pagan—repeating words after words without meaning—and he stopped smoking and drinking and using foul language, greeting his fellow men with such words as, "May the Lord Bless You" and urging others to repent from their way of life and come to the Lord.

Granny said she was very distressed about her cousin. She did not see him for many years. He was from Ciuciu (Varfurile) and was the son of Granny's cousin who married in Ciuciu, Joachim Crainic's father. Now it seemed that Dad was trying to be like Cousin Joachim (or Keemu, as he was called). I heard Granny talking to Elizabeth across the fence and relating our family standing in the community and how the strange ways of my father would bring shame upon our family, whose forebears were founders of the church and were

35

upstanding in every way. It was bewildering that father was not satisfied and happy with the belief followed by the Rumanians since the dawn of their existence—probably ever since Saint Peter and Saint Paul lived on earth!

Father brought home books I had never seen before. They were different from the books on the shelves at the church *strana*, where the books were kept for singing the liturgy responses. Father had often sung the church chants; now he sang some other songs! I wondered where he had learned them. But some of the words and the music appealed to me and to Mother—especially the song about home. It was appealing and sweet. One song I remembered well. The gist of it was, "Young friend, listen, the sin may ruin you. Get away from that type of life, Jesus calls you now!" Once in a while I heard the name "Jesus." *It must be like "Christ" spoken in church,* I thought. That seemed reasonable to me. It seemed that the first name was Jesus and the family name was Christos. Just like we all have two names. So all people of the world must have two names in order to tell to which family they belong.

As far back as I can remember, Dad and Mom were called to be godfather and godmother to many weddings and to the newly born babies. They would hold them in their arms while the priest sprayed holy water on the baby with a bunch of dried lavender—which smelled so fresh! It was blessed water because it came from the little trough where only holy water was kept. This water was taken from the run at the January 6 holiday, the baptism of Christ, when the priest, together with young and old, took the holy cross in procession to the river and, after the liturgy was said, poured the old water into the ice opening or in the barrel. He made the sign of the cross over it with the lavender bunch and so it was that the water and the river were sanctified. The holy water, taken in wooden jugs or liter bottles, was used for many unfortunate happenings such as illness among the cattle wherein several drops of holy water on the grain made the cow well again. These rituals also stopped coughing or a runny nose. Father and Mother were given a beautifully woven towel. These were treasured and kept in the big chest, or some of them were put on the wall around a colorfully painted saucer. I always enjoyed the decoration it all made—the pretty towels around the saucers or around the icons above the windows.

I did not like the idea that Father considered declining going to weddings or baptisms. He felt there was too much drinking and foul language and bad stories rather than seriously praying and thanking God for all His goodness to man, for our health and all the things we had. He even said that all such affairs were pagan and should be abandoned. He felt that God did not like them, and that ceremony was not ordered by God or Christ, but was of pagan tradition. He turned more to *The Writings*, which showed the true way God wanted His people to follow.

All these things were strange to Granny and to me. I enjoyed listening when Dad talked about these things. Of course, I never heard him speaking any foul language, nor did my mother or grandparents speak it. But I had heard other boys and even other adults cursing and using words I had never used or heard my parents using. I thought people who talked that way did not know any better. It did not seem obnoxious to me because I did not use such words, and for this reason I was all right. I could recall boys at schools who used bad language, and there were others like me who never used such bad words.

One day one of the boys with whom I was walking to school remarked, "George, you are like a girl—shy and do not curse. You are like those born in faraway places, where people know how to speak and how to show good eating manners; you are not rough at all!"

In such moments I secretly wished I could prove to be as rough-and-tumble as any of them. I disliked being considered too delicate or so different from my older friends. Yet each one of them was ready to take my defense if the occasion arose. Such remarks, however, made me stop and think for a few moments about whether I was like I was because my mother and father would disapprove of any sort of foul language or rough behavior.

Granny told me that there were people better in speech and work than others, because that was the way God made the world. There are the good and the bad and they all live together like grain and weeds—they all grow together. You plant many seeds in your vegetable garden, but there are the weeds also growing with the good seed. You must watch constantly and pull up the weeds so they will not choke the vegetables. And in the wheat field it is necessary to destroy the darnel, or the bread would be bitter. So it is with people, she said. Some are born into families who know no better. Unfortunately they are like a black sheep—different from the rest of the family. Granny said children from such families were just like their parents and grandparents. I thought this was an interesting thought—that a child may behave like his parents or his grandparents!

Granny had a brother, Demetrius (Crisan) from the hamlet of Crisani who was notable for his cursing. His house was much smaller than Granny's. Granny remarked that my uncle's wife did not know very much. She was good, of course, but did not raise her eyes too high!

My father's mother had a brother, Gilgore, from the hills, the same place from which she came to marry my grandfather, the mayor. Gilgore was a good man. When he came to visit us he would sit at the corner of the table in the kitchen to have a snack. He brought in the earliest cherries or pears or grapes from his yard on the slopes. He was a quiet man who moved about slowly and had very little to say. My granny told us he was a poor man who had to raise a family of several children alone, as his wife died many years ago.

There was a remarkable difference between the two grandfathers, Theodore Roman, Mom's father, and George of Anne's, my father's father, the old mayor. I thought there was a bigger difference between these two families than any other families in the village! It was just like Granny said, there are many living things created by God, but all are so different, one from the other. She concluded, "One does not expect to make a silk sieve of pig hair." She had two sieves in her kitchen, one was of horse hair she sifted corn flour with, the other was of silk, which she used to sift wheat flour for preparing flour cakes at the holidays. The silk was so thin you could almost see through it and the sifter part was sewn to some white cloth, which was fastened along the wooden round margin.

I thought she was so wise. She illustrated what she was talking about as she constantly pulled weeds from the vegetable beds or in the hemp field or the corn rows or the wheat fields. She showed me the difference between vegetable seedlings and the weed seedlings. It seemed that the weeds were vigorous and ready to choke out all the vegetables. In her illustrations she explained to me that some people get their reward right here on earth and some will receive an award after death. Because, she explained, all will receive

38

a reward of some degree. I remember old aunt Johanna, who said, "What is written for you is there on your forehead! No one can change it!"

However, Father's words and actions were different. Of course, he had gone to school five years at Halmagiu and then he was in the war and discharged as an "invalid" of the war. He told people who came to the mill that God really wanted each of us to be His children, if one would repent of his evil ways of life. He mentioned such things as smoking, drinking, cursing, attending drinking or dancing parties, even memorial dinners or wedding parties where, usually, there turned out to be eating, drinking, and foul talk. All these things, he explained, were pagan in origin. Well, Grandmom from the Big Run Valley thought that George was working in a big way to lead people to a different way of life, yet it seemed futile. But the world would not change. "God will punish those who get out of bounds and he blesses those who follow the good way. So, that's the way it is and forever will be," she said!

I thought about this and I thought my granny was right and my dad was right too, each in his own way! I thought it was the same way with my schoolmates along the roadside going home from school or going to school. Some of them acted wild and others walked along in a quiet, orderly way. I remember some jumped into the mud puddles, splashing those who were near and then laughing at their sport. Others avoided mud puddles. I wore boots, and I certainly avoided any muddy places. Once when I was trying to show just how close I could walk on the edge of the ice I had an accident. The ice broke, and I got wet up to my waist. When we got near to school, one of the women—one of those artisans (I believed they were sheepskin tailors)—called me in to get dry. I was embarrassed. I had to stay there until noon, thereby missing a half day of school. My aunts insisted that I stay and get dry. I wondered who told that lady that I had fallen in the water. I never found out. But whenever I passed that house I looked at it with interest, and whenever I saw the lady or the man there in the yard I called a greeting to them and they answered. The man usually said, "To your health, my boy!" How funny! I thought this was the way grown-ups talked. He might have said something like "Long live the young man!"

Regardless of my granny's belief that the way we were living was the right way and should not be changed, Father knew another way. He became acquainted with all kinds of people from other villages as Ciuciu, Aciuta, and far down the Cris Valley to Buteni and other places farther on.

Sometimes, on a Friday evening, some people came to the mill dressed in white clothes. The vest was bluish in color and had many silver buttons. The overcoat was of white, homespun wool. They certainly looked different. I heard that they were vine growers in their villages. We had only a few grape vines on the upper slopes where my uncle Gilgore lived. Several times father brought grapes home from the Saturday market, and they seemed sweeter and jucier. Father read from *The Writings* with these people and heard someone say that a repenter is saved when he is baptized. This seemed incredible to me. We had all been baptized when we were about eight days old, either at home or at the church with the holy water, so that we had been Christians all our life. I thought all this discussion was strange.

I heard Grandmom say that her brother had been put in jail for six months because he, along with others, had been stirred up by the "other priest" who lived in our village and had assaulted several people in the home of John Banciu, the American. "Those people had come to make trouble or to find themselves in trouble," said Grandmom, and they knew no better than to come to John Banciu's home, on the Grui, where they sang and prayed. I thought all this strange. We went to church to worship. John Banciu came from America and we considered his ways strange. He was quiet, did not smoke or drink, and did not come to our church. One Sunday a group of people came to his home to sing and talk and pray. Several men, including Grandmom's brother, Dimitrie Crisan, broke into the meeting and started beating the people there with poles pulled from the fence. The gendarmes came to stop the disturbance. Several of the offenders were taken to Arad, and the judge sentenced them to six months in jail. My granny remarked that her brother had been wrong to listen to others stirring up trouble. She also blamed John Banciu, who came from America to try to change people's way of thinking. She blamed both sides of the question. She ended the discussion with her own philosophy, "Whatever you are looking for, you will find it!" I was very distressed about my uncle's trouble. After that incident, John Banciu returned to America, and we never heard anything about him afterward.

40

The old priest, Ilie Sirca, discussed the incident with my father and grandfather. The priest was concerned that the bishop might hear about Dad's bringing to his house those people who had forsaken the church of their forefathers. He even said he might be in trouble by just talking to Dad and Grandfather. He talked about the true Rumanian tradition and belief and the church liturgy that had been passed from generation to generation and that we would be betraying our ancestors and even their souls if we changed our way of life and belief. "Do we not pray for those who have passed on every Sunday when the liturgy is served?" He said it would be a betrayal to our own orthodox way and only true belief to forsake the way of our ancestors.

I remember one time Ilie Sirca, the priest, said to Dad, "Giutzu, if I changed the liturgy and followed readings from *The Writings*, which I surely believe are correct and good, I would lose my job as priest and even my retirement, if the bishop heard about it."

The Easter holidays were the most exciting times of all that I can remember. Grannies and mothers and children were busy decorating Easter eggs. The girls were making haste to finish embroidering their new blouses to have them finished by Easter Day. We school children in Halmagiu had a two-week vacation. At Easter the lambs were taken out to the side slopes, like the one next to the church, to graze and enjoy the balmy weather. We could hear them bleating after their mothers, already taken to the hills early in the morning.

The story of decorating eggs at Easter, we were told, was that of a woman who went to see Christ on the cross. She was on the way to market with a basket full of eggs. She was sorrowful and put the basket down on the ground near the cross in order to wipe her tears away. When she picked up the basket she saw that the eggs were splotched with blood, making the most marvelous designs imaginable. She turned and went back to her house, and the women in her neighborhood came and looked at the wondrous designs on the eggs. This was the origin of the decorated Easter egg. All the women started the new custom and vied with one another to see who could make the most beautiful decorations. Other details were added to the story; that even Satan could not resist the beauty of the decorated eggs and would fall asleep while staring at them. In this way, souls tormented by him in the Realm of Darkness would have a respite. Of course, I knew this was only a story, but thought

41

it was interesting that even Satan could be lured by something beautifully done.

Dad reminded us that although the story of the Easter eggs was indeed beautiful and the embroidered blouses and the white shirts and the white trousers were all attractive, the whole thing was a pagan tradition. He said people would be better off to read the word of *The Writings*, which was unadulterated by old women's superstitions. I believed Dad. But I also noted that my grandmom said that Dad was right—he could read and write—but at the same time one must pay attention to the way of life we inherited from our forefathers and established for all Rumanians. All these things Dad read from books were new but they had to come from somewhere—perhaps from foreign people—not Rumanians. It was all peculiar to her. She said she was an old woman but had never heard anything like these things. Maybe some of it came out of the war. Granny never told her son-in-law to his face that he was wrong; she seemed only concerned that our family might be placed in a shamed or scorned position before the villagers, as our family was of notable reputation not only in our valley but in all the many villages in our mountains, back from the dawn of remembrance.

I don't remember Mother expressing views similar to those of Granny. She may have occasionally said that Dad should not insist too much about expressing his views, that some might listen while others were just plain dull—what went in one ear went out the other. I thought about this and came to the conclusion that Mother was right. It was the same with the teacher at school. She said some students retain what they listen to and others allow the information to come in one ear and out the other. I thought perhaps grownups were like this, too. I remember Grandpop, the mayor as well as justice of the peace, saying that some people are so stubborn in their thinking that they are hard as stone.He said that even sometimes horses and oxen are the same way. He went on to explain that the burden animals were trained to follow direction either by voice or stick to follow the right path or furrow. So it is with people, he said. Some had flexible minds easily trained while others had stony minds and it proved difficult to teach them new things.

My grandpop of the Big Run Valley was not a talkative man, except when he was spoken to. He merely expressed himself by saying that when a neighbor asked for a shovel or a fork, let him have it. But it is not his business to instruct the neighbor how to use it or what to do in his yard or field. This would be resented, because every man knows how he wants to conduct his business or how he wants to cultivate his fields. If he were asked for advice, then that's another matter. He would relate to the neighbor his own plan of the cultivation and whether the neighbor agreed to this plan was up to him.

Mom's father, Theodor, occasionally smoked a pipe. But my father's father, the old mayor, never smoked. Grandmom told the story that he had a pipe when he was young, but when he smoked it for the first time it made him sick. Next day he broke the pipe and threw it out in the trash along with the pipe tobacco and never had a pipe again. He never drank. Once he was asked whether he smoked or drank. His reply was typical of him: "Why should I burn up my savings? If God had intended me to smoke, he would have put a chimney on top of my head to release the smoke." As to drinking, he said one should not drink because if he did he was drinking his mind along with the brandy.

At school some of the boys were talking about the new young teachers who had come to teach fifth and sixth grades. I remember they said that the teachers were really ordained priests, though trained as teachers. It was said they were not to be drafted to go to war. They were Vichentut Catana and Alexandru Sirca. I was never assigned to their classes. Sirca's sister Lucretia was a good friend of my aunt Betty and, of course, of myself. In fact, they had the mill above my father's and managed the same millwater canal.

In the fall of 1915, I was assigned to a woman teacher, Mrs. Teaha. Her husband was a priest in Leasa. She was tall and walked with a limp. She was of a mild temperament, and I liked her. We called her "Miss Teacher." I remember that I had never especially liked another teacher, Mr. Mihai Vidu. In Mrs. Teaha's class I met her son, Pompil. He was about my age. Also my cousin, Miron of Bodesti, was in my class again.

This teacher taught us many interesting things, like the meaning of the maps of Europe. We learned that between one continent and another there were great bodies of water called oceans. If the body of water was smaller it was called a sea; for example, the Mediterranean Sea and the Black Sea. We learned that the Americans were on the other side of the Atlantic and that it was only a matter of time until they would enter the war—on one side or the other. We were told that this was war like no other war in the past and that almost all the countries were fighting on one side or the other!

Pompil dressed like the town folks, as a priest's son usually does, in dark clothes. But so did Miron, who was not the son of any mister or artisan. I thought that it probably would not do me any harm to dress like that too, and it would even please Father.

I enjoyed reading my books even ahead of the lesson assignments. It was interesting to learn all sorts of things about people in other countries and their way of life. Some of these stories related the great daring of the seafaring people, who had traveled across oceans and found new lands. It was learned that America was discovered by mistake by an Italian by the name of Christopher Columbus of Genoa. I felt that such pursuits must be the most exciting life of all. How exciting it must be to see other lands and see other races of people other than my own! Even reading about the islands of the Pacific was fascinating indeed. Imagine a place where the woods were always green and there was no snow! Was it possible that there was a place without winter? But the teacher and the books were showing us that this was so.

The years went faster and faster, and all of a sudden I finished my fourth grade. My father said he planned to take me to Brad, at the Gymnasium (High School); that he had talked to Miss Teacher about it. She would teach me and her son Pompil additional grammar and arithmetic during the summer so that we (being very young) would be able to keep up with those boys who were ahead of us, being fifth and sixth graders. I enjoyed going places with my dad, but I was not happy about going to summer school. I would miss Granny, Aunt Bethy, and hiking after the cows and sheep on *Magura* and *Plesa*—the meadow and range. My father assured that the summer plan was to my advantage. He said the time would come that I would be able to see some of the places I was reading about and studying about. He reminded me of the people from our village who went to America and made good and were able to send money back to their families.

For several weeks that summer of 1917 I went to Halmagiu, to the teacher's home. I took either milk in an earthen jug or eggs or cottage cheese for my lunch. The teacher asked me about my homework, whether I could repeat the multiplication tables. Yes, I knew the tables by heart and had no trouble with the four arithmetic rules: addition, subtraction, multiplication, and division. I was better than Pompil, so I thought. After some writing, either copying from the book or answering some questions, and doing some arithmetic problems, Pompil and I were free to go in the yard and garden where we usually played with dolls, such as burying them with a church funeral service. In such case, we played the priest and cantor: singing "Remember, O Lord, your servant" and the answer—"His memory be forever remembered." The teacher had to call me to leave for home. Then I walked back the 3 or 4 kilometers back.

AWAY TO HIGH SCHOOL

September, 1917, was a most wonderful fall. My pet rabbits had multiplied their family and the young ones were spotted white, yellow, and black. They were kept in Granny's hemp pantry. She told me not to worry about them, that they would get hay and cabbage leaves. But my heart was not so much with the rabbits as with my Granny and Grandpop in the Big Run Valley home. When Dad came after me to take me to the mill, he told her he was taking me to Brad the next day. She cautioned him, "George is so young, you should not estrange him from you and Elizabeth. You have only two children and there is plenty to share; Theodor is getting old, becoming tired. Who is going to help him?"

"Granny," said Dad, "George will be all right! I want something good for him; I want him to be able to see the world as it is now, a new world. He will have a better and easier way of life if he goes to higher school! God willing, we were able to get along so far regardless of my wound received in the war. We will be able to carry on!"

That day Dad gave me his military locker. I liked it. It had a covering tray that was divided and the space below was for articles of clothing. Mom helped me to place my things in it. There was a space for apples, nuts, and hazelnuts. Dad gave me the book *Transylvanian Tales*, which I had read several times. In the covering tray he put two pencils, a pen, an eraser, and a notebook of about twelve pages, on the back of which were the multiplication tables.

Next day it was time to leave for Brad by train. Mother packed my shoulder bag with smaller bags of food such as beans, potatoes, nuts, flour, and a jug of pork lard. These "goods" were the first installment for room and board to the landlord and landlady. Dad told Mom and Granny that the landlady was a very good woman. Her husband, Professor Mihail Stoia, was the teacher of physical education and music. He was a violinist and gave private lessons to the children at school.

Brad is about one hour by train from Halmagiu. It was a long trip to me, yet when we arrived, it seemed like the trip had just started. The station was bigger than anything I had ever seen. It had two stories and there was fancy woodwork on the front and large porches. It was the end of the line, and all the people got off the train. Dad found a cab with a platform on two wheels. We put our bags and packages on it and started moving. I had never seen such a funny cart—one with two wheels. We pushed through an alley and came out on a graveled road, passing a tall building of three or more stories. I later understood it was all fenced in by a wall fence, but we could easily see that there was a well-organized garden. After we passed this school building it seemed we were in the countryside. There were only a few houses and there were long strips of cultivated land with wheat or corn. Some of the corn fields had been harvested, leaving the corn stalks' stumps.

Afar off to the left we could see a big, red building four stories high. When we came nearer we could see it was not finished. There were piles of brick and sand and other building materials piled about the unfinished structure. My father explained that it was the new building of the Lyceum being erected by the Rumanian Orthodox Church. Across the street from it there was an "L"-shaped house in which Professor and Mrs. Stoia lived. I was told that they had boarding students, about seven in all, from the first class of Gymnasium.

Professor Stoia was a well-proportioned man, a little taller than my father, with a little beard and mustache. His wife was a plump, youngish-looking lady with a pleasant voice and a motherly approach to us. At this point the only boys whom I knew were Miron and Pompil. Later I met the others. There were John Popian, nephew of Professor and Mrs. Stoia, Luciu (John) of Cristesti, Tripon of Bucium, and Pompil Sirban from Halmagiu. There we were, seven children boarding at the Stoias. Miron, John Popian, and I were assigned to sleep in the big bed behind the oven in the kitchen. I put my locker under the bed and stored my books in my assigned corner of the big shelf.

At the school we were aligned in one long row according to height. I did not like that. I was not the last one, but there were five or six smaller than I. We were numbered "one, two, one, two"; then we stepped forward to the right and marched a couple of times in the yard before being disbanded, after which we ran to our classrooms. There were about forty boys in our class. We understood it was the largest class ever had by the school. In the fourth class there were about ten pupils. In our first class, I was among the youngest ones (about five were my age, ten), and the other students were at least twelve and some were fourteen years of age.

I became closely acquainted with another boy, about my height and age, Niculita Obadau, who was from Brad and whose father kept a grocery store and bakery. Their house was one of the biggest in town—it had two stories and faced the marketplace.

The marketplace there was different from the one in Halmagiu. It was paved with stones of all shapes and sizes. Every Thursday, people from all the villages as far away as 15 kilometers would come to display their goods and to buy and sell. There was a row of tents in which fabrics were displayed and other tents with tables piled with all sorts of marvelous things like penknives, little mirrors, little whistles, and so on. All these things were expensive, I remember. I did not ask my father to buy anything for me. But I would have liked a penknife or a small mirror. I knew it was all too expensive and really not appropriate for small children. I further consoled myself with the thought that I had a good penknife, and even though it had only one blade it served me well in sharpening my pencil and cutting my paper as well as some sticks with which we played the game "popic" when we had time for play.

The books from which we studied were on religion, the Rumanian language, Latin, Hungarian, arithmetic, civics instruction, botany, music (no book was available) and, of course, physical education. Equally important was conduct, which included our responsiveness toward others, toward our studies, our books, our desks, and our greetings to our teachers and our fellow students from the upper grades. I never heard that any student had an unexcused absence. There was no need for it. We were all there together and well established and watched over by the boarding lady who was cook, master, and a real supervisor of the students.

The boarding lady proved to be a mother to us with all the authority to admonish and even spank us when necessary! Of course, the teachers had authority to swat the palm of the hand with a bamboo stick or with the ruler, but this was rare.

Did I study seriously and well? I thought I did what I could. It was not hard for me, but I considered it was time consuming to go over and over the Latin words to memorize them or to memorize poems in Rumanian. I liked to memorize the poems but did not dare to raise my hand to recite. I was perhaps too shy and lacked the poise others showed in reciting a poem with real talent. I watched and admired them. My favorite subject and study was botany, which was natural because of my background. I came from the fields and valleys full of wildflowers, from the forest where there were berries, shrubs, and mushrooms of all kinds and sizes. Then, watching the cows and sheep along the lanes, I was able to learn what plants they liked and what they avoided. It seemed easy to me, and all I had to do was to learn the Latin names for each thing and give the description and genus. What a herbarium I compiled! I received a grade of 10, which was the highest grade a teacher gave. I enjoyed searching for a rare flower, pressing it between soft paper for several weeks, and then placing it on white paper for display, labeling it with its Rumanian and Latin names, place where found, season, and of course my signature, which I tried to do like my father—writing in my regular hand my name, George Crisan, and then a sort of elongated loop under my name which meant "manum propium" (your own handwriting). This expression now had a meaning for me.

I remember how much I enjoyed reading *Transylvanian Stories*. I learned there were more volumes of these works. There was also a collection of short stories, funny ones, by Anton Pan. I never got tired of reading these stories.

Soon after school started I learned that my father wanted me to begin violin lessons, with Professor Stoia as my teacher. I did not oppose the idea and agreed with father's plans for me. I had to practice the scales every day and had a two-hour lesson each week with the professor. He was stern; I don't remember that he ever smiled, but he did not seem angry. I thought he was just a plain professor whom I tried to please by doing my homework.

One of my bedmates wetted the bed several times, but we did not dare tell Mrs. Stoia. Eventually, she realized the difficulty and removed this boy. Then she placed Pompil (Teaha) in with us.

An interesting event was going to take place, we were told. The entire school body was to take a trip by the narrow-gauge freight train to the gold mines located at Gurabarza (Storkbeal). There were no school classes that day. We left early in the morning, each carrying his own lunch, a bacon sandwich, wrapped in a towel or paper. We traveled by train in open platform cars in which mineral stones containing gold were carried from the mines to the mill. We saw the big stonemill grinding the mineral rock, then allowing it to fall into the water in the long and narrow troughs. The water came down and ran into the river, looking as white as milk. Now an old mystery was solved for me. Our river, the White Crisus, sometimes looked just like milk as it ran by our village. Cows did not drink it, but were taken to the big runs or Yugarun for watering.

Some of the boys were quite excited about trying to catch some gold stones. Many made all kinds of jokes, and some even swore. I thought of my grandmom and grandfather as well as my mom and pop, and how unhappy they would be to hear me talk in such a fashion. However, sometimes I had an almost admiring feeling about some of these boys and thought they were smart and outgoing and knew so many tricks and jokes I had never heard about. I felt somehow lonely when someone said to me, "George, why don't you play this or that game with the other boys? You look so shy—like a girl." I did not agree with this obersvation, but I said nothing. I knew the games well and felt I even knew more than those "smart" ones. But I tried to carry on my daily tasks at my homework and tried to help John or Pompil or others with the arithmetic, botany, and the Latin words I knew.

Late in the fall of 1917 and my first year away from home, I remember one evening we saw the entire sky was flashing with lightning without thunder. We were scared and began to hide behind our beds. Soon we heard crackling sound. We thought the world was coming to an end. Mrs. Stoia came and explained to us that it was the noise of war. The enemy was the Rumanian army, which was trying to divert the front in the west and weaken the Austro-Hungarian armed forces on the facing two fronts, on the west against France, Italy, Great Britain, and now on the east, Rumania, which herself was aligned with the Allied powers.

The greatest joys I had this school year were the vacations: Christmas, two weeks, Easter, two weeks, and then the summer vacation. My grades were good without being anything exceptional. At the end of the first semester, I had almost all "Good," with one "Sufficient" on the Hungarian language. There were several "Very Good" grades. So I came to the end of the first school year.

During the summer my special thrill was grazing the cows with my aunt Vetuta—Elizabeth. We led the cows by a rope across the Cris and to the pastureland, between the Crises. This was a large plot of land that was good for grazing only because it was covered with small bushes of red willows, which we cut for the basket maker in the village, the Georgita of Josana. Several times we had to take one or the other of the cows to the village of Ociu, about five miles away, for breeding purposes. I enjoyed the walking and looking at the houses or trees or the long strips of cultivated land along the way. Most of the houses had straw roofs and appeared well kept with whitewash. We had no occasion to see inside any of the houses. The man in Ociu was the only man in the area who knew how to correctly castrate the calves. On these trips we had the opportunity to take a quick swim in the Cris where it formed a bend. There the water was above my head, but I had learned to swim a long time before.

During the summer I enjoyed going to the summer grazing meadows at the Littlewells. It was fun. We had to climb up the hills by foot about an hour's time to reach the Littlewells. There was the cottage in between the two stables. There were the cherry trees that I enjoyed climbing. I could see the big, almost black, juicy cherries. I remembered the white mushrooms found in the beechwoods and fried on the open embers, flavored with a little salt. When we found the orange-colored mushrooms it was real excitement. These were especially delicious.

The summer flew by so quickly! It seemed I barely got to pick up the hazelnuts above my granny's house when I heard my father say it would soon be time to return to Brad. I thought, *What dreadful news! I hate the thought of going away from these loved places and from Grandmom and Grandpop.* But they all encouraged me, saying that it would be no time until the Christmas holidays. They assured me my pet rabbits would be well cared for in my absence. Dad reminded me that all would be well with me in trusting God to watch over me and asking him to direct my path in all things. I remembered Grandmom mentioning that Dad wanted me to be a gentleman.

Some asked, "Why is that Giutzu sending his boy away to Brad? Does he want him to be a priest or a teacher or what?" Some women spoke in my hearing that whoever is not dressed in white clothes is not a Rumanian, but folks who dressed in dark clothes were city folks, and city folks had nothing but the clothes on their backs. Some wondered why Giutzu wanted to make his son one of these people.

My father did not let me wonder about all these things. He said to me, "Son, I don't want you to be with your feet in mud as I am. I want you to have an easier life."

The fall of 1918 came far too quickly for me. I learned that I would have another boarding house with another landlady. It was the Steels' house, where Aunt Mariuta was boarding five boys. Now I would have only one bunkmate, Miron.

I remember how beautiful October was. The weather was ideal. And I was homesick. The river nearby reminded me of home when I used to walk barefoot on the grass and the sandy beach by the river there. I pulled off my shoes and walked on the sand. But the beach here was not as nice as the beach back home. There were bones and even horns of animals scattered along the beach. I understood that a tanner had his business up the river aways and this accounted for the occasional stench.

My professor of Latin, Dr. Pavel Oprisa, who was once director of the gymnasium, suffered a nervous breakdown and was taken away to the hospital. I could not understand why such a highly educated man would have a nervous breakdown. But I learned that education had nothing to do with mental illness. It could happen to anyone. So it was with Dr. Oprisa, who attained his doctorate in Budapest. I had to accept the fact that anyone could become mentally ill. Then I remembered the old saying that one's destiny was written on the forehead.

I remember that at about the time I had a terrible dream one night. I dreamed that while I was walking barefoot, a man hit me with a stick on my left leg. It was so painful I awoke and started crying in pain. The next morning Aunt Mariuta comforted me by saying I might have taken cold in my leg while walking along the river barefoot. She sent word to my father, who came and took me to the doctor, Dr. Tisu. He told Father I had got cold and asked that a hot cloth be put on my leg and gave Father some sort of white powder for me to take by mouth. The pain was becoming worse. Father carried me in his arms to the train. Mother met us at the station with the carriage and wrapped me in a big down blanket. I wanted to be taken to my grandmom in the Big Run Valley home.

I was put in bed and the pain increased day and night in my leg. The priest from our church said a special mass for me. Grandmom wanted to call another priest who was located at some distance and who had the reputation that his masses had greatly helped in cases of illness, but my father was reluctant to do this. In any case it was not done probably because I could not be moved and could not stand without great pain.

Later, I understood that there was no doctor to see me because the doctor who had an office in Halmagiu, about four kilometers away, and other officials of the county seat had left since the war was over, but the Rumanian army was advancing and occupying Transylvania. On the other side, the capital city of our country, Hungary, had been held by Bella Kuhn and his Bolshevik army. My grandmother was trying all kinds of leaves on my leg, the part above the ankle was so painful and red. Eventually, she put a skin of a rat, just caught and skinned. The pain receded and the suppuration erupted. There seemed to be chips of bone coming with the ugly, black suppuration.

The pain in my leg became less, but I could not move it.

I learned that the war was over. The time was November 11, 1918. There were many men returning home from the war. We heard about the ones who were captured by Russians would be allowed to return home too. We also heard a revolution was going on in Russia. What was a revolution? My grandmother told me about a revolution more than a hundred years ago, when the peasants were going to set fire to the landlord manors. This was unbelievable to anyone who believed in God and His justice.

At Christmas I was taken by carriage to my other grandmom to meet with my aunts and other children. By now, I could take a step or two. No one knew what kind of illness I had. It was unheard of that a young boy could have such a serious infection. After the

Christmas holidays the weather was like spring, and I was able to go out for a few steps with the aid of a cane.

Then the effects of the revolution began to realistically affect us all. The officialdom of the county—the county executive, his deputy, the county clerk, and the judge and the doctor, all left, fearing the approach of the war, the advance of the Rumanian army. We were "a village without dogs," as the saying goes. When the peasantry learned that officialdom had fled, they began breaking into homes and offices and took whatever they laid their hands on.

A few years later I heard the following story from my village teacher: In a tuckaway in the upper valley village the priest was invited to baptize a new baby boy and was then asked to stay to dinner. The lady of the house brought in a fancy porcelain pot, white with a handle, filled with golden chicken soup with fine, homemade noodles. The priest seemed reluctant to serve soup from the fancy bowl. But he asked where the soup bowl had been purchased. The lady of the house answered, "My husband, Peter, got it from the executive house. We only use it on special occasions." The priest then understood that the bowl was a plain nightvessel of the county executive.

It seemed at this time that everything was in tormoil. There were many oxen carts in the yard. There were too many people everyplace in the mill hall. Many people had taken refuge from the neighboring village of Leasa in our mill house—the only house in the area having a stone foundation. A baby was delivered in our kitchen in the basement.

Eventually the armored train of Bella Kuhn crossed the river at Leasa and stopped at the Halmagiu station, which is only a half kilometer from our mill.

My father was the mayor of the village at that time. One evening a group of soldiers in Hungarian uniform but without the rank on their shoulders appeared at the mill. They saw all the people there. They took my father and grandfather and made them march in front of them to the station. Next day another group came and told mother and the people that my father and grandfather had been tried and found guilty of resisting the advance of the Bolshevik army and that they had gathered all these people in the mill to oppose the advance of the Bolshevik army. Their treason was punishable by shooting on the spot—which they deserved. But if they would deliver one cow or young ox to be butchered every week and thirty or fifty kilograms of wheat flour, they would be released.

I remember many women were weeping and people were saddened because of the sentence laid on my father and grandfather. My mother said we must pray that God might change the minds of the soldiers, that they may see the truth. She went on to say they might be killed, but their souls would live on. Father and Grandfather came home and began to arrange for delivery of supplies to the army.

After about three months the army of Bella Kuhn withdrew almost overnight. The Rumanian advance guard occupied positions in our area, awaiting the main bulk of the army. These guards were organized by the former officers in the Hungarian army, of Rumanian background, to keep order and law until the Rumanians came.

Several young Rumanian soldiers led by an officer came to the mill and took my father and grandfather and made them march to the guards' headquarters in Halmagiu. They were indicated as traitors—because they had fed the Bolshevik army of Bella Kuhn and they had instigated the plunder of the house of the priest, not far from our mill.

Before carrying out any sentence of execution, the general commanding the army had to approve the sentence. General Mosoiu said that the sentence was vindictive, that there was no evidence of treason on the part of my father or grandfather, that any army occupying a village may ask the civilian officials to feed them and give them supplies as long as they are in the area. That was the saving word for my father and grandfather.

I was impressed with my mother's attitude, that no individual may escape his fate or the lamentation accompanying, it but an earnest prayer to God can alone change the thoughts of men.

The next fall, 1919, my father took me back to high school in Brad. Arrangements had been made for me to board in a room right near the school. The school was now next to the railroad station, which building used to be the civil school in Hungarian language. The janitor of the school had two large rooms. One of the rooms was used as the kitchen and the other room was for the seven boys boarding there. There were the two Gligor brothers, Aurel and Peter, the sons of the priest from Halmagel, there was John Sortoc, son of the station master, Gyuri was my bed mate, and there was Luciu John. Later, another young man joined us, Jonita Giurgiu, who had finished his accounting school and was an apprentice with the Crisana Bank of Brad.

In addition to the subjects we had in the first year of high school, we now studied french instead of Hungarian.

My mom sent me twice a week ready-to-cook chicken, potatoes, or pork. Of course, I always had on hand cured bacon, which could be used when needed. Mrs. Mary Halmagean, rotund lady and wife of the janitor, was very kind to me. She taught me how to cook my chicken, making it last for several meals. She went through the recipe with me. For example, she showed me how to proceed with the onions in the pork recipe, adding the paprika, et cetera. The bread Mother sent was dark but tasty. It was baked from the wheat flour ground in our own mill. One round loaf of bread would last me about two weeks.

The boys I boarded with shared the kitchen, each doing his own cooking. I was teased about my shyness and rosy cheeks, which I hated. I made no comment. They asked me about my girl friends and so on. I knew they were joking, but it made me unhappy. I was thankful to God, however, for saving me from my serious illness, and I began to think of the times when I would be able to be outside again, enjoying the trees, the plants, and going for a swim in the summer. I felt sure that God would see me through any unpleasantness here among these strangers.

Jonita Giurgiu had a different attitude toward me. Once he taught me how to read the clock by minutes and quarters. I never forgot his kindness. He had not made fun of me. He commented that I was better in the Latin and Rumanian languages than the older boys there. I was in the second year and they were in the third and fourth years. Gyuri Farcas was first year, but he was much older than I. He was quite tall and thin. I remember he was quick-tempered and would strike his opponents.

The professor of Rumanian language, Mr. Stefan Albu, once asked me why I was in the second class when my previous classmates were in the third classs. I told him I had been ill and had missed one year.

I rarely went to town. My chief interest was in the bookstore and in new storybooks. The ladies in the bookstore soon knew who I was and directed my attention to some new books, which were smaller and of reasonable price. I discovered that a certain story-teller, John Creanga, had many short stories about himself. They were quite funny and I read them with interest and curiosity, because the things he wrote about could happen to me too.

I read by myself when I had time from memorizing Latin or French words. I was even called a bookworm by some of the other boys. I stayed with my nose in a book and never looked at a girl. At times they talked about such and such a boy who was in love with a certain girl. I thought what they were missing by not reading good books or by not having heard a real story as told by our neighbor, Aunt Magdalena, or stories about the saints who had walked on earth or were walking on earth doing all kinds of amazing things.

I did not especially like any of the subjects taught, but I thought zoology was an interesting study. I had to prepare an insect box, and I paid close attention to the type of insect to catch and how to place it in the box and let it die under the naphtha powder. I received VG (very good) on my collection and I was quite happy with my grade. Other grades were G (good), and probably in French and Latin I got S (sufficient).

In my third year at the now-named Avram Lancu Lyceum, I stayed at the same rooming place. The studies were neither harder nor easier. It seemed they were sort of keeping one busy with memorizing poems in Rumanian and French. Another study was added: German. It was a little difficult, but there were rules of grammar that were easy to keep in mind.

In January 1921 I had not heard from home for some days, and I decided to go there for the weekend. I left Saturday at noon by train. On my arrival, I received the greatest shock. My grandfather, Theodor Roman, my mother's father, had died of influenza and had been buried over a week ago. One week later my beloved grandmom died, and the funeral services were to be held the same day I arrived home. I was deeply grieved. I could not understand why my father and mother had not notified me. I later learned that my father and mother were trying to spare me this great shock and were waiting until it was all over before notifying me.

I deeply felt the loneliness and loss. I remembered my grandmother had told me that in heaven children and their grandparents would be reunited and would never be separated again. Of course, I didn't want to die but was comforted in the thought that we would meet again. Now I had a clearer understanding of all these things.

Along about this time I noted that my father became more interested in reading the Bible. He gave me suggestions as to reading assignments that would be of interest to me. He also explained the meaning of some of the hymns to me.

When I went home on Easter vacation, I saw that my father and mother did not attend the church services. Instead, people from another town came to our home and held services, singing and praying and reading from the Bible. I could understand what they were saying. I remembered the services at the church at home. I never understood what the priest was mumbling and why the *strana* singer repeated over and over, "God have mercy" and what the constant crossing of the chest was all about. Of course, my grandfather recited the Creed and, very clearly, the Lord's Prayer. I had never understood why the altar was a forbidden place and people never walked beyond the altar platform.

Then there were so many icons in the church. Some of them were taken out in procession. I thought the procession was fun and enjoyed walking along. But now repenters came and said they would not bow down to icons or kiss them or kneel before them because that was idolatry and God did not like it.

I was mixed up. I was having doubts either way. My grandparents, now gone, had never accepted such a thing: to hold a service in a private home, without a priest, without cantors and icons. On the other hand, this type of so-called service at a meeting or gathering in a home appealed to me. The appealing songs were full of enthusiasm and yet warning to repent and come to Jesus. For the first time, I understood that Jesus taught people a new law, a new order not to smoke, not to drink, not to swear or curse, not to cheat, and that one should pray for himself and for his family and friends, never for the dead ones.

Aunt Elizabeth was very good in singing, and I listened to her and learned to sing stanza after stanza. She had a good memory. She could hear a song one time and could repeat the tune and words she heard. The words were beautiful, telling us that no matter how lonely one is, he can find a friend in Jesus. I thought I probably needed a friend since my grandparents were gone.

That summer of 1921 my father wanted me to go to Arad, the capital city of our district. I was not especially enthusiastic about going but still somewhat curious about how a city like Arad might be. It took us six hours by train. We went by the large marketplace, and I have never seen anything like it. It was located in the middle of the city and was paved with square rock blocks. It seemed that there were hundreds of women there displaying all kinds of produce on white cloths—fruit, vegetables, pottery. Then there were long tables on which were cheeses of all kinds and also dressed chickens. We made our way through this marketplace and arrived at the street with all kinds of clothing. My father stopped at one of the tables and explained that I was his son who attended school in Brad and that we were looking for a suit for me. The man found a corduroy, greenish-looking, two-piece suit. He asked me to try on the coat for size. It was too large, as were the pants. The man went on to say that the suit was a very good one and in just a couple of years it would be too small for me. Anyway, my father bought the suit and put it in his shoulder bag. From the clothing vendor we walked to a big building. The steps leading from the street to the gate were large, and the gates to the building were enormous. On the top of the building was a large statuary like a woman dressed in a bedsheet and holding an oval shaped board in her hand. Much later, I learned that the statue was the Goddess Minerva holding the shield of wisdom that protects the student from stumbling in his learning.

We looked at the lyceum, as Father called it and now Father said, "Do you think you'd like to come to this school in the fall?" I shrugged my shoulders in indifference. I had lost interest in the old home in Big Run Valley. It made little difference to me where I attended school. "It might cost more," I remarked to my father. He agreed that it might, but he had several Jewish friends who would help him to find a good and less expensive boarding room for me.

There was little discussion about it. But within, I thought it would be a good thing if Father would take me to Arad. I was becoming tired of Gyuri anyway. I was tired of the jokes he played on me. I remembered he always left the basket of food for me to carry, although he was bigger, and he never said "thank you." But I was not unmindful of the fact that my mother was able to send food to me twice a week because of the help of Gyuri's father, who was a flagman on the train, and this privilege was duly appreciated. These packages came to me via the freight car of the passenger train.

II

LIFE IN A BIG CITY

I remember so well the city of Arad. It's a large city, spreading out in all directions. Street after street was paved with some sort of black material. Workers continuously repaired worn places in the pavement with steaming black tar from a huge caldron over a fire. From the railroad yards to the downtown area a little train plied back and forth, and here and there a train pulled onto a sidetrack waiting for an oncoming train. I remember the line of carriages, each drawn by one horse with the driver seated on a high seat above. And I remember the shout, "Wagon, wagon," calling for a conveyance. My father soon had transportation for us.

In less than half an hour we arrived at a wide plaza. In the center were statues of a group of people, who, I later learned, were thirteen martyrs who had fought for freedom and independence. But I did not learn at the time the meaning of the freedom and independence for which they fought because the statues were soon covered and removed. I heard later that they were of Hungarian origin and in the new Greater Rumania they had no meaning.

The landlady of the house where I was to stay was away when I arrived, and her godfather and mother placed me in their dining room, where I was to sleep on a couch. Soon I noticed that every Friday evening two candles were set on a brass holder on the table, which was covered. When the table was uncovered and set for dinner, there were dishes and silver for each of us—two of them and me, the boy of fourteen.

The lyceum was not more than ten minutes' walking distance from Mr. Sam's home. My boarding family lived in a three-room apartment; living/dining room, one bedroom, and the kitchen. To reach the apartment I had to go under a long and dark tunnel-like gate in the big building that faced the plaza. At night the heavy wooden gate was locked.

When the landlady returned home I moved there. It was a very narrow street and an even more narrow hallway led to a little apartment in the courtyard. Several nights later, I discovered there was something burning my skin all over. I did not know what to do. I dreaded to see evening come and have the same experience over again. It was discovered that the sofa was infested with bedbugs. I wrote to my father, who came at once and placed me in the school dormitory. It was expensive, I thought, and I did not really want to live in the dormitory. It was within walking distance from the school. There were about two hundred boys living in the building, comprising all ages and grades. In my study room there were nine of us and a supervisor boy of eighteen by the name of Nicholas Maghiar. (About fifty years later, in the United States, I met one of his cousins, a Baptist fellow in Detroit.)

The sleeping room was on the third floor. We numbered thirty in one room. Once a week we had a shower. I remember I was quite prudish about taking a shower with the other boys. *But one has to bear it*, I thought.

In my class of forty boys, I sat behind a tall boy who called me and my deskmate "just plain peasants" who had come to the city from one of those remote villages in the mountains. Later, this boy Emil Rosvan became a good friend of mine. I learned that his father had been an engineer and had surveyed the forests of Tisa and had lived in my grandfather's house for several months during his survey.

I felt that I was a stranger among strangers. Because of my previous illness of myelitis, I was excused from strenuous sports. For this reason, I took no part in soccer, which most of the boys were playing at the time. In the physical education classes I did some exercises the professor asked me to try. I did well road climbing and even rope climbing and some of the other exercises. But I was poor at the parallels or horse jumping.

I remember the only boy of Jewish faith in our class was Felix Landes. He was an excellent scholar in mathematics, French, and German. I learned he came from the old kingdom of Rumania. His father, a physician, had been killed in the war. He came to Arad to live with his uncle, mother, grandmother, and sister. His uncle was the director of the power plant of the city, which also generated an electric train connecting many villages from the foothills of the Metalic Carpathians. I thought that all trains were driven by a smoky locomotive like the train that brought me to Arad.

George Ionescu was our counselor-professor. I considered him a very pleasant teacher and the nicest man I ever met. He was friendly, patient with the students, and was even known to say to a boy who had made a bad grade that next time he would get an A if he came up with better answers.

Professor Ionescu came to Arad from the old kingdom. His language was beautiful Rumanian. He taught geography, which was a physical or geophysical study of Rumania as well as an economic and political study of the country. He was the first teacher I ever had to tell me in front of the class that my answers to questions were good and my maps were excellent. This was a great boost for me. It attracted the attention of other boys to me. Boys who had not spoken to the student coming from the "countryside" became interested to know me and to learn of my success in making good maps on Rumanian geography or economic resources.

My paramount work for this teacher, Professor Ionescu, was a map of Rumania with mountains and rivers and political districts. He was very enthusiastic about my work on my maps. My father encouraged me further by having my map put on canvas and taking special interest in my school work that first year at the Moise Nicoara Lyceum in Arad.

By the end of May 1922, I had completed the secondary work, called the Gymnasium level of a Lyceum. I was not awarded any prize for scholarship, but I ranked probably among the top ten of the class. My father never went into detail about my school work, only asking me if I had passed all my tests. But he was mindful that his son was the first and only boy in the family to go to Arad to attend secondary school.

In the Rumanian language classes we studied syntax and grammar, which I enjoyed. Some of the boys had a difficult time distinguishing such parts as gender and tenses and analyzing a sentence or a paragraph. When the school term was over I was eager to go back to the mountains and the Big Run Valley and to walk and run through the fields and woods and to renew acquaintance with all my friends and neighbors there. I especially enjoyed driving the milking cows out to the grassy pastures between the rivers with Aunt Vetuta and joined her in singing all the old songs we loved so well. We remembered the songs we had learned in elementary school at Halmagiu, and these were added to our joyous outdoor concerts! We also remembered the Rumanian flag colors, red, yellow, and blue, and knew we'd never forget its meaning in our lives. But the Hungarians did not like any mention of anything Rumanian.

Everyone, old and young, who came to the mill stopped and talked to me. Some asked, "George, is it not hard to attend the city school and study all the time?" Others asked if I became homesick with only walls around me and pavements to walk on with no fields of wheat and corn to see. Still others were sorry for me that cherries or pears or apples had to be bought in the market in the city. I then began to realize that most of these people had never been out of their neighborhood, had never been on a train, and the extent of their travel from home was the Halmagiu market, where they traded in sheep or goats or cows or oxen, to match the animal they had at home. There was even a comment or two as to my difficulty resting and sleeping among hundreds of boys, all dressed in dark clothes—so different from our peasant Rumanian garb in snow-white linen or our winter coats and britches of white wool, products of the land and sheep.

I remember I was even asked what I intended to do with my education—what I wanted to be, a priest, a teacher, or a clerk in the county clerk's office. I hated such interrogation, and I just shrugged my shoulders and answered that I did not know what I wanted to be. In fact, at that time I had not thought of any profession or a definite place in the world.

In the fall of 1922 my father located a boarding room for me at 31 John Calvin Street, about a twenty-minute walk from the lyceum. It was really a small apartment—a little kitchen and a large room in the basement of the house. Two other boys lived there with me. Our landlady, Aunt Mary, spoke both German and Hungarian. I liked my roommates, Ponta and Funata, and we got along well together. We were not interested in serious study, but I concluded that I must study because I could not put my mom and dad to shame. So I tackled the French, German, Latin, and algebra problems assigned. I was soon asked by other classmatess if I was able to solve the problems given us and they wanted me to explain how to go about getting the right answers. I tried to do this and I got the idea that they did not know where to start or even how to start. I explained that solving a problem was like building something—you have to put big stones at the corners and then lay big beams onto them. Then you proceed erecting anything—even a corncrib.

Our Latin professor was an elderly Catholic priest. He was an amazing teacher—mild in temperament, fatherly to us, friendly, and yet wise. How could I ever forget his saying, "Boys, in your life when you think that you have great burdens and you are in deep despair, only look around you and see those who are blind or crippled! Then you will realize how fortunate you are."

The mathematics teacher took note of my explanation of certain problems at the blackboard and he added his sage advice, "Mathematics is a subject you do not learn by memorizing. That will not help at all. It must have a logic of its own. When you find the logic, the rest is easy."

Sometime in April, when I ran down the steps to go to the play field across the street from the lyceum building, a friend grasped my arm, causing me to fall and hurt my right leg. One of the bones in my lower leg was broken. This was traumatic for me. I suddenly remembered my illness from myelitis. Here I was again, crippled with a broken bone in my leg. It was extremely painful for about two weeks. Then I started worrying about missing classes. I even prayed that I would not wind up with a limp. I was in a cast for four weeks and had to walk with a cane about four weeks. I missed some classes, but the Easter vacation helped with time to recuperate. I started going to the gymnasium to see if I could do some of the exercises with care not to hurt my healing leg.

In the summer vacation, I was able to walk without the aid of the cane and enjoyed once again exploring the meadows and fields and swimming in the Crisus River, where there was no impediment to exercising my injured leg.

It was in this school year that my father suggested that if and when I had time I might attend the services in the Repenters' meeting house, in the suburban area which was not very far from where I lived. I had been attending the regular services in the Orthodox cathedral, going every other week with my class and other classes. I attended Sunday school occasionally. The teacher, George Mladin, a horse wagon driver, would at times ask my view on certain New Testament texts. I remember his saying, "That's a good viewpoint, Friend George." Then he asked me if I had read the text and when

I answered in the affirmative he wanted to know why. I explained that I was interested in the language of the New Testament as a literary language and I thought that the life of Jesus Christ was very interesting to me and his teaching made a lot of sense to life around me.

I discovered that I was the only boy enrolled in a liberal arts college and attended the Repenters' meeting house. People appeared quite friendly to me, offering me a ready handshake. The girl students and the boy students of the industrial school looked with interest at me and regarded me as someone special, according me special attention. I responded in like and accepted some of the invitations to garden and beach parties. I did not discuss my attending services at the Repenters' meeting house at school. It was said the Repenters were people who renegaded their ancestral Rumanian Orthodox religion; they were really lost people—some thought they were baptised again in the name of Satan.

At this time, my father was becoming more and more involved in the repentancy movement. People from far away places came to our house. I noted they were friendly, intelligent people, and I also noted that some of them dressed in white peasant clothes. They carried a copy of the Holy Bible wherever they went. And I noted that it was larger than the New Testament I was used to. I also found out there were very interesting stories in the Old Testament, including love stories. Many of the stories interested me.

On one occasion I had the opportunity to talk to the wife of the newly-appointed priest in the village. In the course of the conversation she asked me why the Repenters kneel and bend over the bench or chair when they pray. I thought I should express myself on behalf of my father, with whom she did not talk because of her husband, who constantly commented on my father's bringing strangers into his house and because many times he was on the road to the local court or other local county police or to the district court in Arad. So I tried to explain to her, "The Repenters bow so low because they repent of their sins, regret them, and they wish to humiliate themselves before God. They remind themselves they do not want to be like the pharisees who make great display of their prayers." Our conversation was not long but it had a very painful consequence for me!

In the fall it was school again. In the class of religion, our professor was a priest of the Orthodox church whom I considered a very fine man. It surprised me that some of the students, many of whom were sons of Orthodox priests, mocked him behind his back. One day he called me to his desk. His question astonished me. "Is it so that you try to proselyte people in your home village during the summer? I understand that you were preaching and even arguing on religion as the Repenters do. Is that true?"

"Oh, I have not done anything like that, Sir Professor. I did once answer a lady and some other people when they asked me why Repenters bow down so low when they pray. I was simply explaining that it was because they humble themselves before God."

The teacher replied, "Well, son, do not do anything like that again. Understand?"

"I will not, Sir Professor," I replied.

Of course, the boys in the class, about forty in number, were quite intrigued by this conversation. One, the son of a priest, said to me, "Well, Crisan, so you are a Repenter and even try to make proselytes!" I did not bother to answer.

I felt very humiliated, and for the first time realized why my father was often called to the court, to the police, to the county or state attorney. He was asserting that as a leader, a trustee, a cantor of the established church, he did not like what was read and was interpreting the Bible for himself. Instead of this experience causing me to avoid reading the Bible or going to the Repenters' meeting house, I was determined to get to the bottom of this—to find out what was wrong with my dad, or the Repenters movement or with the Orthodox church. So I began my own personal research.

Almost like a sudden realization, I noticed that the people from the meeting house were almost illiterate. Even so, they were always friendly and gracious. I never heard any sort of foul language from any of them as I did from classmates. Then I considered further why people used foul language. I had never spoken so and was entirely unable to proffer it. Sometimes I came to the conclusion that these boys were trying to play adult by using bad language, but then I doubted that such a language would bring any profit or make someone distinguished among his fellows. On occasion, while walking to the cathedral as a school requirement for the class in religion, I heard many remarks behind me that I was like a girl—I did not use any curse words, and it may be that I was a Repenter after all. I refused to let it bother me. I reasoned that I had been through several accidents—had survived a broken elbow, illness with myelitis, and a broken right leg—and restored to good health by God's mercy. I said to myself that God would judge me on my academic as well as my daily life record. I thought it was surprising that the sons of priests did not excel in their school work and that they used such bad language. I noted that there was little reading among them of the classics in French, German, Russian, Italian, and English. I realized I was singled out in some way, yet not by God, who gave me good health now.

Sometime later the mathematics class was taken over by the director of the lyceum, Ascaniu Crisan. He was a sober man, tall and commanding. He called me to the blackboard, probably because I had the same family name, but we were not related. I was able to get through the algebra problems to his satisfaction. I was up for assignment at the blackboard on several occasions and of course this raised my stature in the eyes of those who, behind my back, had said I was shy as a girl. Several of my classmates asked that I allow them to come to my room to work out mathematics problems. I was glad to do this, but few of them became close friends and I had no close or intimate friends.

My professor in botany was quite interested in my study. He called on me in class to explain something. He expressed his satisfaction with my explanations. I thought there was a logical sequence in problems in botany and geometry and algebra. The professor in botany never alluded to any reference that either I or my father was involved with the Repenters.

Here and there other boys would come up and talk to me who did not know who I was. My Jewish friend sat in the double desks with me in the class. Often we walked back and forth to school and even were able to converse haltingly in French. He was good in languages. Felix invited me to come home with him. I will never forget it. He lived in his uncle's home. I had never seen anything like this house. The huge leather chairs and beautiful furnishings took my breath away. Felix was studying piano, and his sister, one year older, played quite well. This was the first gentry-type of home I had ever been in, in my 16 years of life.

Other boys in time became interested in me or my friendship or my association. One was a son of a banker. He, too, played the piano and had a camera and a bicycle. They lived in a two-story house, and the second floor was their quarters. In the backyard they had a stable and horses. Zeno Antonescu was the first one who invited me to visit their farm. They had a home there and other horses for field work. They had servants and agricultural buildings and the like. I thought they must be very rich. *But how can they take care of all this when my friend's father works in a bank day by day?* I wondered.

Zeno invited me to join his Boy Scout group, but I turned the invitation down with the excuse that I did not have a uniform. Actually, I could not ask my father to buy a uniform for me for the sake of joining this group.

My professor in Latin seemed to become more and more aggressive toward me. I could not understand it. First, he refused to give me a B. The only C I received was in his class. I went to him and asked that he look at my other grades. "They are all As and Bs except in your class, Latin. I feel that I deserved a B."

He was furious and said, "I don't care what grades you earned in other classes. I am going to fail you if you do not give me good papers and good answers in class."

I felt that he was being malicious without reason. Then the answer to my puzzle was revealed. In my seventh year he one day called me to his desk, asking, "Is it true, Crisan, that you were sold to Beelzebub, that you even try to make converts in your village?"

I was stunned for a moment or so. I knew then why he was against me. It was because the priest of the village, who was after my father, put something in his mind. The professor was also the son of a priest. I answered his accusation, "Sir, that is not true."

The class became silent. After class the same boy who had asked me before came up and said, "Is it so that you are sold to the devil as all Repenters are?"

I turned my back and did not say a word.

The last three years, six, seven, and eight classes found me situated somehow among the same five or six students in my class. This was the class in Latin, where I did not get more than C.

During these years I frequently went to the Repenters meeting house. The Sunday school teacher was quite interested in my continued attendance. I was invited to small house parties where there was music and discussions on the Bible and its meaning to everyone, Christian and Jew alike, and the guidance it can give to all, both young and old.

It was at this time that the president of the Baptist community, as the Baptist churches as a whole were called, asked that I come to visit with him. This I did. He seemed to be a fine man, but his education left something to be desired, and it was impossible to have a serious dialogue together. He appeared to be a humble man and had the reputation of being a capable organizer.

My last year at lyceum was uneventful except that I met and briefly courted several girls. They were all pretty and charming at a glance, but I soon learned that conversation was difficult and dull to me, and there was no lasting interest. This last year brought the best recognition to me of my Lyceum years. Toward the end of the term we were examined on the subject of religion by a delegation of two high-ranking priests or theologians from the Bishopric of Arad joining the professor of religion. My turn came to be called to the platform along with three or four others. Dr. George Ciuhandu asked us the questions. The boys before me attempted to answer, but their answers were not completely relevant to the question. I gave very simple answers the best I could. Dr. Ciuhandu said to the amazement of the class, "Mr. Crisan, I heartily congratulate you for your answers. You gave me the clearest and most logical answers I've ever received. Thank you!"

Another unusual incident that boosted my self-esteem and enhanced my stature among my colleagues occurred in the Rumanian language class. The teacher, A. T. Stamatiade, a poet, lectured only occasionally when he had a certain inspiration or mood. On one of those rare occasions, he lectured for an hour on the style of classic literature, modern and classic poetry, et cetera. The entire class, with the exception of me, had not taken notes. He marked everyone, in the class catalog, with grade one, the lowest grade one can get. I got six, the only passing grade at that time. Then the next class was due. They arrived and got up in a body and left before the professor arrived. I did not want to leave. Two big boys took me by my arms and marched me out of the room. The class spent the hour in the park.

An investigation was made immediately by the director. One

by one the students had to give the reason for leaving the building. I told them I had no reasosn for leaving, but joined the class rather than remaining in the room by myself. I did not say that I had been removed by force.

I was puzzled by this strike against a professor. Then I considered the fact that even a small group can manage to carry the day with their idea. I did not like Professor Stamatiade, but I thought he was just and fair to us, and he knew a lot about literature and was quite an attractive speaker when he had his good days.

There were thirty-nine boys in the graduating class. All but a few were older than nineteen years of age. The test to graduate was the baccalaureate examination. Only those who passed were admitted to the university, namely to take law, medicine, engineering, teaching at the lyceum level, et cetera. All of us looked forward to it with dread. The examining commission was formed of one or two professors of a university. The others were professors of other lyceums. The commission examined candidates who graduated from several lyceums from the province. The total number of candidates for the June 1926 session held in the Moise Nicoara Lyceum in Arad, my alma mater, was about 110. It was a written and oral examination. I was always somewhat leery of a written examination because my handwriting was poor, meaning not quite readable.

I was happy when I learned I had passed the written examination. There were almost fifty eliminated by the written examination. The oral examination was given in the festive hall of the college. People had been sitting there for hours—some parents or other students waiting for their turn.

I was in a group of six students called for the examination on the platform. The question in any subject selected started with the first in line and went from there. I answered all the questions. The question on biological science was on plasmosis (or something like it) in the kidney. I made a simple drawing on the blackboard and explained how the blood exchanges the poisonous things, which are eliminated, and takes the clean matters for supplying the blood with new and useful matters. Well, to my real surprise, even astonishment, the president of the commission rose and shook my hand across the long table and congratulated me for the best answer he'd ever had, he said. He asked me what I wanted to pursue. I told him the school of medicine. He said he was sure I would do well and wished me the best luck in life.

This incident increased my self-confidence. I secretly thanked God that he had watched over me.

I met the daughter of a director of a lyceum in Brad, named Semina, an intelligent and very nice girl. We took walks along the promenade, usually winding up with a hot chocolate. That was all.

I was the first in my class to pass the baccalaureate examination, and I was third among twenty-eight successful candidates to the examination. How did this come about? I did not study harder than many other students. I always thought that whatever any other student in my class knew, I knew too. I never found my subjects hard or incomprehensible. Now, what should I look forward to in my life? I had no definite plans. I was ready to embark in the school of medicine at Cluj, but I had a mental reservation that I might not like it. I liked people and was ready to give a hand when I could—such as dressing a boil on someone's arm or back. But it took great effort for me to even kill a chicken or a duck. Back there, I had asked my mother to let me try. She allowed me to, but it required great effort for me to kill a beautiful fowl. The blood did not bother me, it was the thought of killing. But, of course, I enjoyed the delicious dinner Mom prepared from the fowl.

III

UNIVERSITY

Here I was a bright kid, as classified by the baccalaureate commission, who rated me the first of my class and the third on the list of about 40 passing the dreadful examination. *Of course I will make it*, I thought, since I knew more acceptable answers in biology and chemistry and mathematics and physics than the others. So my self-confidence grew.

I had never been to Cluj, the university city of my dreams. I went there in September 1926, with Sabin Veselie (Sabin "the joyous"), who also passed the examination with high marks and whom I had known since elementary school days. He was like his name—cheerful and of an outgoing personality. He came from a poor family, but because of his brilliant school record, his father did his utmost to help him to reach this point of embarking on an academic profession. He wanted to study French and Rumanian literature and to teach in high schools.

We traveled by train to Cluj, taking along certain provisions to start our housekeeping near the university. I remember we packed such things as bacon, dry sausages, apples, and walnuts. We found a room on Moon Street, a few blocks from the university clinics, where I was to attend classes, and close to the main university building, where Sabin was to go. Both of us registered. Because of our high rating at the baccalaureate examination and because we successfully passed the entry examination, we soon were enrolled as freshmen.

To say our living quarters were small is stating it mildly. I slept on a sofa and Sabin slept on a cot. The landlady owned this small house, which had a garden about twenty by three feet and a porch that ran along the living room—narrow but attractive. Our accommodations were limited. We did our washing in a basin, emptying the water into a bucket placed near the washing facilities. The toilet was located in the back of the house. Sabin and I agreed that it was probably the cheapest room in the whole city of Cluj, but it was clean and near our colleges.

We were able to get one hot meal a day in a private home along with about ten other students. There was a long table with benches on the sides. The meal was usually a bowl of soup along with beans or potatoes, which were at times cooked with a piece of cured bacon. Later when we stayed at the student dormitory we ate our meals there.

My classes started before I was able to get about and see much of the city, where there were wide sidewalks usually filled with students strolling up and down, discussing various facets of college life, including the voices they had heard the evening before at the opera. I learned that Cluj was the only city in Transylvania and the second to the capital, Bucharest, and had a theater and opera that had been quite well established before World War I.

The city of Cluj goes back to unwritten history—the Dacian period. It was an old trading point located between two rivers, the cold and the rapid Somes. It is only an educated guess that miners of gold from the mountains where the origins of the rivers were, were bringing the gold here to exchange for the necessities of life. The Roman interpretation of Cluj was Napoca (later named Napoca-Cluj) to ascertain that the city was an aboriginal settlement of the Dacians, taken over by the Romans in the early second century and remaining under Roman (or aboriginal) rule until the eleventh century, when the Hungarians increasingly expanded their occupation over Transylvania.

History tells us that there was a principality of Transylvania with a prince, who usually was elected, and his heir inherited the throne if he was worthy in the eyes of the electorate, which were the smaller nobility ranks and the priests. Then for almost three hundred years, Transylvania was an independent land under several princely dynasties. The Ottomans occupying all of Hungary were defeated at the gates of Vienna and forced to concede peace. It was in this period that Transylvania was a land receiving new currents from the west, such as Calvinism and Lutheranism, and it was at this time that the churches of Rome became more settled after the slowing down of the barbarian invasions. It was the era of rejuvenation in Europe, and the princes of Transylvania were receptive to the new, fresh air—at least, some of them were.

Transylvania was a microcosmos. There were the original ethnic people, the Rumanians, called *Olah* by the Hungarians. The Hungarians and the Germans, of course, were a small minority, but they had strong allegiances to both the Roman Catholics and the Protestants of Western Europe. Gradually the trade center grew into a political and intellectual center, which soon began to imitate Vienna or Budapest or both. The historians of the twentieth century looked over the past history of Transylvania as a miracle that happened—to see so many ethnic groups, different languages, varied religious customs, and usages all thrown together for such a long period of time.

General revolts did occur in the peasantry, however. In 1524, George Doja, a Rumanian, gathered together a group of restless peasants—of Rumanian and Hungarian origin—and started setting fires to the landlords' castle and barns. Why did this happen? More and more the landlords who made the laws in Cluj were encroaching on the small parcels of land owned by peasants, curtailing their rights of pasture, of wood granted for fire and building of huts, and of their hunting and fishing. The revolt resulted in bloodshed and revenge.

A more organized revolt, or rather revolution, occurred in 1780. Three landed peasants from the area of the sources of the three rivers carrying gold sands decided to do something about the plight of their countrymen. These three, Horia, Closca, and Crisan (my name derives from the river Crisus) were intelligent people but without extended schooling advantages. They looked at the plight of their people as insufferable. They saw how everything went to the hands of the landlord—the land, water, forests, the mining, the meadows. At such times, revolution was inevitable. Whether these three had heard of such things happening in Europe or America we do not know. Horia, leader of the three, went to Vienna to see the emperor to submit a complaint. His request was not considered and he was treated discourteously. This sort of reception made him quite angry, and he returned to Transylvania to organize a wholesale revolution. Nothing of the landlordships was spared. Everything was burned. No loot was taken. Then the emperor of Austria sent his army. Horia and Closca were executed February 2, 1781. Thousands of spectators were informed that the same would happen to them should there be any further revolt against the establishment. Crisan, one of my ancestors, had hanged himself in his cell in Alba

Julia. I believe he was a brave man in his struggle for justice. He had his small holdings in the valley of the same river as my other ancestors, the Crisans (in Latin *Crisanii*, meaning the inhabitants of the valley of the river Crisus).

That's Cluj, or Napoca-Cluj, history in half a nutshell!

There were about fifty students in the first year of medical school. Our classes were held in one of the amphitheater halls of the clinics. We could easily see our professors and blackboards in the classrooms. After two days of instruction, we received the first bone to study—a clavicular one. We had to pay a small amount for each bone. It became our property, a professional item in our professional stage of learning. I did not like the smell. It was preserved in formaldehyde. My clothes and hands smelled of formaldehyde. Next day, we got the femur, which was longer, larger, and smellier. Everything in our room had this smell. Sabin did not complain of the smell, but he did not look at the bones I had brought home. I began having dreams about skeletons and bones and would wake up in a state of perspiration. Then in about three weeks an incredible thing happened. We had a class in the amphitheater following the second year students who were dissecting certain parts of a human body for study. Parts of a female body were scattered on the table. The whole thing suddenly seemed horrible to me. That night I awoke from horrible dreams about it all. I could not sleep or even remove the odor or my feelings about it.

It did not take me more than three days to make the fateful decision: This profession was not for me. I must leave medical school no matter how much I had dreamed of becoming a doctor. I was obsessed with the thought that I must get away at once. Not even my father's pride in my endeavors stopped me. Perhaps it was my own philosophical and psychological feeling that helped me at this point. I spoke to the school secretary about leaving. I remember he was a youngish man and he called me by name, saying, "You are making a big mistake, Crisan, we all went through this same stage. Some started smoking to forget the smell. You were admitted here because of your high scholarship and you want to leave because of the smell, the bones, and seeing pieces of the human body. Some just looked at themselves as another human body, even as you and I. This is life. You will regret this step all your life if you withdraw now. Do you know that we have some of the most famous professors of medicine in Europe?"

I listened quietly. I stated I wanted to withdraw before it was too late to register in the school of law.

"Crisan, this is incredible! You will not be able to study law, which has to do with all sorts of theories. You are a scientist by nature and a born sort of doctor," the secretary argued.

"You are kind, but I've made my decision to withdraw from medical school. I'd like my withdrawing papers so that I may register in law school," I replied.

It was done. I expressed regrets to the young adviser, who was kind to me. I went to the law school registrar. I had to pay half of my tuition. The registrar asked me the reason for the transfer. I explained to him as best as I could. He smiled and said, "This is not unusual. Many students do the same, for various reasons. Also, students leave law school for other schools." He asked that I consider the school of biology and chemistry science, since I had done well in these sciences. I told him that my father would not be able to suspport me financially in this school, and I had not received a scholarship to it, and that it would take me another year or two to get one. Meanwhile, I would continue in the law school. I would be able to work full time and come for the examinations only. He agreed that this was so. But he cautioned me to remember that the examinations are difficult and many students had to take them over as many three times, thus losing time.

In the evening I ran into a classmate from Arad, Ilie Ardelean. He remarked, "I don't understand you at all. How can one who is good in biology and chemistry go to study law, which is a dry science? I would not study law for anything in the world."

I replied that I would try it.

Meanwhile, I wrote to my father that I was leaving medical school and would study law. I reminded him that I realized this was a disappointment to him and reassured him that I would not be a burden in a financial way as I was searching for a job in Arad.

I did some self-evaluation. Here I was, a boy of nineteen, with a good scholastic record, but no practical ability or acquaintance with the asperities of life, enamoured of nature, streams, and rocky hills around my home. What could I now do? That was the big question. Suddenly, I realized I must not go home in defeat, but from this time forward I would be on my own, earning my own way, no matter what.

Having made this momentous decisison, I considered the first step to take. I must find a job, and I decided to go to Arad. I would go to my former landlady at 31 John Calvin street and ask her for a room to be paid for when I landed a job. The old lady took me in but showed her disappointment in my predicament. She, however, encouraged me by saying, "Crisan, you are an industrious boy who made a good record in college. It will be to your credit to find yourself a job and work toward your professional training." Others however said, "George Crisan a lawyer? Unbelievable. He was the most silent boy in the class of 40. He never used bad language; he was always mild and shy like a girl." (I always hated that comparison.)

GETTING A JOB

What was the first step in looking for a job? Here, my good memory came to my assistance. Several years before I had been introduced to one of the fine lawyer friends of my father, Theodor Papp, who had been a lawyer in Halmagiu but who had come to the big city to become general counsel to the district government. I determined to go to see this man to see if he could help me.

I knocked on his door and then entered the room. Someone from the second room called, "Come in, come in," and then I saw a tall, balding man with blue eyes who was becoming rotund. I introduced myself. "I'm George Crisan, son of George Crisan, the miller; and the grandson of George Crisan, the old mayor."

He said, "Oh, yes, yes. George Crisan of Anischi." (My grandfather's mom was Ann, so in Romanian son of Ann.) Dr. Papp's manner of speech reminded me of my grandfather. He had been born and raised in Hungary before World War I, and his speech was a sort of modified peasant type of Rumanian language. I learned later that he had studied at Vienna and Budapest and Cluj and that he married late in life (age forty) to a widow of Serbian extraction whose husband had been killed in World War I. He had two sons of about six and four who were taught by a private governess to speak only German.

Dr. Papp said to me, "Well, George I'll see what I can find for you. I knew your grandpa quite well. He was a man of great intelligence; he helped me in my law cases. He knew everybody by name and every parcel of land by the right number in the land register. I have never met so intelligent a man as your grandpop in all my life. Though he was illiterate, he knew calculus better than I. Crisan, come by here tomorrow at this time and I'll see what I can do for you."

I went by his office at the set time next day. Dr. Papp was seated at desk shuffling a lot of papers. The papers were being arranged neatly and placed in folders. I thought he must be a well-organized man. I recalled that I had tried to organize my little library of twenty-five books; some of twenty to fifty pages—some larger. I had then numbered my books according to the date of purchase. Dr. Papp concluded the interview by instructing me to be on hand next morning at 7:00 A.M. at the office of the chief of police, Colonel Mutiu, at the police headquarters. I learned that Halmagiu was his birthplace and I seemed to remember hearing of him back there. The policeman at the door called me by name and ushered me into Colonel Mutiu's office. The colonel was kind to me and soon introduced me to the executive secretary, who took me into his office to do some paperwork. He asked me where I went to college and what I was doing as a student. He remarked that he had been a student in law school in Budapest, but the war interrupted his studies.

There were several papers to be filled out, which I signed. I was taken to the office of registry and introduced to two men there. Both smoked incessantly—one cigarette after the other. They were kind and courteous to me as the secretary explained who I was and that I was a student in the law school at the University of Cluj and would be taking a job there and would be a help to them, as it was known they needed extra assistance. So I went to work. I was to record petitions, reports, applications, and the like and index all correctly. My working hours were from 7:00 A.M. to 2:00 P.M. except on Saturday, when I worked until 1:00 P.M. I received the beginning salary for a policeman and classified as a plainclothes market policeman.

Dr. Papp had previously invited me to drop by occasionally to let him know how I was getting along. I saw him in about two weeks' time.

"It is good seeing you, Crisan," he greeted me. "Colonel Mutiu told me he found a job for you and that the people are satisfied with your work. You may be like your father and grandfather—plain, hardworking people who meet whatever circumstances come your way." He added, "Well, Crisan, I have a lot of paperwork to do and I need someone to do some typing for me. Do you know of someone who might help me?"

"Dr. Papp, I know typing," I dared to say. "My father brought a typewriter back in our village from a man who had brought it from America. I learned to type to a fair measure."

"Crisan, I need this work as soon as possible. If you think you can do it, come tomorrow in the afternoon and see if you can do it for me. I'll pay you, of course."

I was there before Dr. Papp arrived. I typed industriously for a couple of hours, correcting grammatical errors I noted as I went along. He was satisfied with my work and paid me as much as a professional typist would receive. He then asked me how I was able to correct the grammar, and I explained that I had a Rumanian language grammar and had studied it for some time. This created a trust between the young student and the old master.

It was late November or early December of 1926 when Dr. Papp called me in to discuss a plan he had in view. He started by saying that a job in the district government took a great deal of his time and the salary was small. He stated he would like me to take over the work as clerk in the counsel's office at the Victoria Bank in the city, beginning January 1927. I was surprised and elated at the prospect and then assured him that the job I had been doing was easy to learn and my replacement would be a simple act.

Shortly after January 1, 1927, Colonel Mutiu called me in and informed me that they did not mind my leaving to work for Dr. Papp and that I might start at once. I thought, *Here I am starting on new job after not more than two months in my first job!* It semed prophetic. As I look back over my life, I changed jobs at times when I did not see or predict such a thing happening!

At the Victoria Bank my salary was paid by the counsel, Dr. Papp, but we were part and parcel of the workings of the bank. I met many new people and I also met the general director of the Victoria Bank, a very important man by the standard of the place or of the society.

The pay was about three times what it was at the police office. This in itself had an enormous effect on my self-esteem. It all seemed more than I had ever dreamed of. I thought of my future—*Why the sky's the limit!* Then a little more soberly, I considered how I had arrived at this point. I remembered my mother's constant advice, "Do your best wherever you are and never forget your family background and your heritage." Then I thought, *I am here because Dr. Papp had confidence in my grandfather and my father and their qualities of character.*

Some said I was either lucky or a very hard-working fellow. I thought it was probably some of both. I had a natural inclination to tackle things. I was able to learn easily in the time allotted. I neither smoked nor drank alcoholic beverages. So what was the answer? Why? I don't know. But somehow I considered that God had been very good to me in the past: He had helped me recover from a serious illness, had helped me through accidents, had helped me through the grief of losing my grandmother, had helped me through a traumatic experience of being ridiculed by one of my professors in front of my class all because my father had become a Baptist—and I knew I must never forget God's goodness to me. Then I thought of good things that had come to me: I was first in my class when the chips were down, when the baccalaureate commission judged a student only by his answers and saw in me a good student. Then I thought that it was God who gave me intelligence and ability to think clearly and to form good working habits without getting tired easily.

Now I began to give some thought to the improvement of my social self—to develop an outgoing and pleasing personality. I had succeeded in overcoming my shyness around girls and could handle any conversation with ease. I continued to attend the small meeting house of the Repenters on Dorobantilor Street. I was more reserved now than when I had been going there previously. It seemed I was expected to counsel or speak as a lawyer right then.

I was never able to say no to anyone who I thought needed help and when I had time and ability to do something the circumstances required. I was the only law student in the entire country of Rumania (about 18 million people) who had ever graduated from a liberal arts school and enrolled in the law school, yet his parents had become Repenters, forsaking their mother church. *Ad astera per asper!!*(Through hardship to the stars!!)

I liked the Baptists because they are humble in their social situation, their education, and their real attitude toward things in general. That attracted me, because I felt I was needed, or wanted, or desired. Other associations with other people who smoked and drank or just plain did nothing were not attractive to me—I just did not feel at home.

One of the Repenters, about ten years my senior, became a friend to me. He was an industrious fellow, had been to the United States, and was anxious to better himself. He enrolled himself in a school of business and cooperative by correspondece. He wanted to stay in the same building where I was living and was interested in improving his vocabulary, writing, and style of living among people of good manners as the middle and upper level of society was called, in contrast to the peasantry.

He asked me how I learned such a beautifully spoken Rumanian language. I could not exactly explain but I said I just knew the language. It was he and other young Baptists who invited me to their Youth Fellowship and asked me to speak to them for about ten minutes. I made it five, as I remembered other talks that had been too long for interest. Many complimented me and asked that I come and make longer talks. Anyway, I thought of another of my Latin proverbs, *Non multa sed multum,* meaning,"Not many but much," in short!

I like the music the Baptists were using—good classic music. I liked the fact there was no discrimination as to background whether it be Rumanian, Hungarian, Serbian, or German. They called one another brothers and sisters in Jesus Christ. Of course there was here and there the question that I might request membership in the Baptist adroitly put. I felt that this was my own private business or conviction. My father and mother never hinted that they were hoping I'd request to be a member of their Baptist faith.

Kindly or not, I occasionally reminded myself that I had been baptized when eight days old according to the scriptures by being presented to the church and sprinkled with Holy Water in the name of the Father, Son, and Holy Ghost.

It was about this time (1927) that I was becoming aware of myself as a person—a budding personality—a promise. I took stock of myself: Here I am, son of a peasant from the Transylvanian Alps, now a clerk in the counsel office of the most important bank in the city and in the whole region—the Victoria Bank. I must see to my personal appearance. I ordered a good suit of clothes and shoes and other accessories and a university cap with the law school insignia. Of course, the girls took note of me and wondered who I was, where I came from, who gave me the position I filled, and other curious and interested questions about me. It was everyone's guess that I must earn a sizeable salary in the place of the office of counsel to the Victoria Bank.

"Who recommeded you?" seemed to be the first question a new acquaintance or friend asked. It seemed difficult to make it plain that there was no nepotism connected with my employment. Some even concluded that it was no doubt the influence of my grandfather, who had been mayor of the village. It was even more surprising that I could type.

I took all this and found that it must add up that I was a worthy entity—typing skill, my appearance, and my approach to other people.

It's true, I met attractive girls from good families but the extent of these acquaintances was a superficial friendship with periods of tennis, and ice skating interspersed with some conversation that did not produce discussion of the classic writers or of great music, and I did not come across any interest in church affairs of any sort. It just seemed to me that the girls were waiting for the right man to come along. We were a group of friends meeting at the tennis court, the ice skating arena, or the ice parlor Malka on the concourse facing the townhall or at the ice and coffee parlor at the Konigsdorfer. We had good times together. Sometimes I felt that some envied me and were curious about me. I was never able to retaliate in any way; it was not within me to attempt to hurt another by either word or act.

It was my job to go to the court each day to search the files and make excerpts from the land registry dossiers. I soon became an expert on these things. I liked my work. I would introduce myself to any clerk in the offices where I went. I received courtesy wherever I went; my work for the most important legal office in Arad was a sure-fire recommendation. The judges soon learned of the young clerk who was studying to become a lawyer, and I was welcome to visit their offices and make their acquaintance. I heard some friends saying that my modesty and humble encounter combined made a pleasing appearance.

I had heard that many lawyers took years to complete their studies because as students they had not worked but loafed. Since I was not planning my life work as a lawyer, I was eager to finish my studies so I could go on to something else like teaching at a college level. I was never attracted toward a clerical job with the central government or the city or the district.

The most interesting and, I was told, difficult subject was the Roman law. The instructor had just published a large volume on the subject. He was a graduate of one of the German universities and was already known as a scholar and researcher on Roman law.

I did considerable reading early in the morning as well as in the evening from various sources on Roman law like those of the copper tablets and the sayings of the great lawyers who were also judges, being elected to such positions by the Senate. Then later there was the Justinianus Compendium or Codex, or Novella. It seemed amazing how the rules of law were defined. I remember reading Ecclesiastes and Proverbs and Job in the Bible and could see a similarity in the concept of the law in the Bible and in the Roman law.

I bought two short books on personal rights and entities rights. They had to be handled with care, as they were worn and had been marked up by previous readers. I had to make out with these books as best I could, for no other new books on the subject had been published, and the teachers and instructors were demanding. Some students had memorized many paragraphs and definitions, et cetera. I hated to even think of memorizing something I did not understand. What I understood I was able to express in my own words and according to my own logic.

Sometime in June 1927, I went Cluj and registered for the first-year examination (there were to be three). I passed the examination satisfactorily and was glad to have that much behind me. Several students complained that the examination was very difficult and that the professors put in trick questions that only served to confuse the student. I felt that this was nonsense, no teacher would attempt to confuse a student.

The second year I took criminal law and civil law. When I stood for the final examination in criminal law, I was among ten other students. I answered the questions in my own way and thinking.

After one hour of examination, Dr. Aexander Pop turned to me and asked me several questions.

"Mr. Crisan, have you attended my classes?"

I answered, "No."

"Where do you live?"

"In Arad."

"What are you doing there?"

"Working."

"What kind of work are you doing?"

"I Work as a clerk in the counsel office of the Bank of Victoria."

"Who is your supervisor?"

"Dr. Theodore Papp."

"Mr. Crisan, you have given me the most logical and clearest answers I've had. Dr. Papp is one of my close friends. Give him my best regards."

Some of the students did not pass the examination and returned in the fall to do a repeat of the course.

A PERPLEXING CALL

One day during my third year in law school, a clerk from the bank came to me and informed me that I had received a call from Bishop Comsa requesting that I make an appointment with him at an early date. It seemed unheard of that a little clerk in an office would be called for an audience. I went to the bishop's office at the appointed day and hour and was surprised to see Dr. George Ciuhandu, the bishop's immediate assistant. He recognized me, perhaps because he'd examined me on religion at my last college examination or because I occasionally dated one of his daughters. I inquired as to the correct courtesy rules when having such an audience. He said, "We enter and say 'Good day, your Holiness,' and kiss his right hand. You may wish to follow such a manner or not. It is not required." I greeted His Holiness in this manner.

Without much ado, the bishop stated that he heard of my excellent record as a student and good work at the bank; that my father had left the church of our forefathers and joined a sect; and that if my father would return to the church, he would see to it that I get a scholarship to study abroad.

Many things flashed through my mind at this point. I had been involved with many cases brought before the state attorney to be

84

arraigned on a charge of disturbing the peace, or of a man in whose house a handful of Baptists had met to sing and pray without obtaining authorization to do so; and now, in so-called united Rumania, the police, at the instigation of the local priest, or of the bishop, arrested innocent people and eventually tried them for criminal offenses that did not exist in any book of law in Transylvania. I thought of my father's strength—that we must stand up for our faith in our savior who had suffered death for us. In most cases the judge dismissed the case with some admonition. These cases were forced on the judge's attention by the bishop, who claimed there were Communist stooges who were trying to destroy the unity of the church and these must be located. In these instances, the orthodox people did not care—they were not interested in such attitudes. They were Christians. They were baptized when infants in the church and attended two or three times a year to listen to the liturgy or went to attend a wedding or a mass for the dead. My father and all those Baptists did not believe in empty and unintelligible words and repetition of phrases repeated a hundred times during a liturgy.

I had read that those who worship God must worship in sincerity and humility and moreover in an attitude of repentance and that Jesus died for such repentant ones.

Now, I was almost at the point of becoming a lawyer, and for the first time began to understand my father's feeling toward his own salvation as a responsibility—not as an empty word. It was not a matter of just going to church, crossing yourself, and then forgetting about the meaning of the teachings of Jesus Christ, I began to realize. My father had been a cantor since he was a small boy, attending church regularly and giving the liturgical responses to the priest. Then I remember that he procured many different church books, such being obtained from the Archbishopric Printing Shop in Sibiu and from the Bucharest Patriarchate Printing Press. During World War I he obtained copies of the Bible and he became interested in reading and studying it more and more. It was this deep interest in reading the Bible that constrained him to "forsake the old religion and embrace a sectarian or protestant one, to repent, to be a Baptist in the name of the Father, Son, and the Holy Ghost and to live his life in accordance with the teaching of Jesus Christ."

Moreover, I realized for the first time that my father had a conviction that until one repents and forsakes his pagan ways, he cannot be saved. My father said the church cannot save a person, only faith in Jesus Christ can do this; as Luther said, it must be by God's grace through faith in Jesus Christ that one becomes a new creation.

Now, here was the bishop, trying to turn me toward influencing my father to "return to the fold." I felt shocked. Previously, I had not fully understood my father's position and the difficulty he was going through for his beliefs. The bishop's tone of voice was stiff and cold as he said to me, "Otherwise, Mr. Crisan, I will not allow you to become a lawyer in my diocese or in the whole of Rumania. I will not tolerate your becoming a Baptist lawyer in this country."

I do not remember what I said, but when I turned to leave, he reached out and shook my hand. I went to my office. My bosses were quite interested in knowing why he sent for me. I related the results of my visit and his threats. I was in tears; I had not wept since my grandmother's death. My boss did not try to comfort me one way or the other. He went immediately to the general director of the bank and then called me in. When the three of us were gathered in his office, Mr. George Adam, the president of the bank, said, "Mr. Crisan, you are doing fine work here. We all like your work. Don't be concerned about the bishop's threats. He has no authority over this bank. You just continue to do your work and your studies as you are doing and everything will be all right."

There I was, the son of a Repenter, from time to time attending services and Sunday school classes in the Repenters' Baptist meeting house. I was fully aware of the persecution initiated against my father by the local priest, who made public announcement that those who called themselves Baptists were sectarian stooges of the Bolsheviks, the gone-astray people who had forsaken the religion of our ancestors. The next time I went home, I questioned my father about his new religion, and he replied simply, "Son, I have read and studied the Holy Scriptures that we should not worship as heathens saying empty words and making no change in daily living."

Then I remembered that some of my relatives and close friends had further elaborated their own views. "What is wrong with us?" they'd say. "Why did your father leave the church? We've lived with it for hundreds of years; this is truly the Christian church because it is the oldest one; that Catholic is not, since the pope assumed supremacy; then the Baptist church was initiated by a blacksmith in England who did not know better. Our church tradition is the true one." The conversation would end with an added remark, "When we are dead, we are dead, so why antagonize the bishop or the priest when we can enjoy the life here and now?"

I discovered that this way of thinking was the thinking of the pharisees of Jesus' time: words without content, formalities without meaning, life without spirit, and care for the here and now only, nothing more.

With all these questions and thoughts in mind, I was convinced of two things: that Dr. Ciuhandu, assistant to the bishop, commended me on clear and logical answers, which had been due to my having studied the scriptures; and that Professor Pop commended me for my logical answers because I had studied with understanding, filtering the ideas through my own reasoning. I began to consider my father's freedom of thought and his independent conclusions resulting from his diligent reading of the ancient scriptures. I became more drawn toward the Jewish boy in my class especially because of his independent thinking on any subject discussed.

I soon became more involved in the youth activities of the Baptists. I also attended various churches and always found friendliness wherever I went. Eventually, I requested to be baptized in the name of the Father, Son, and Holy Spirit by Pastor Ioan Ungurean at the church in the town of Curtici. Now, I was greeted as Brother Crisan and not as Friend Crisan. Not long after this decisive event in my life, I heard that Bishop Comsa was very ill with a blood poisoning in one of his toes. He died soon afterward. I also heard that some of his church orthodox believers remarked that he was being punished because he had persecuted innocent people. I did not take any part in any such talk, but I felt that God's plans are above my understanding.

I discovered in my studies of Roman law that Emperor Justinianus thought that the old law and its customs and usages should be collected and revised. This thought fascinated me. I had learned from my grandfather, when he was justice of the peace, sitting under the mulberry tree in the front yard. When he imparted justice he would say, "Look, this is the usage or custom in this village since the dawn of history, it is so, it is good because all the previous mayors and justices of peace have judged the cases in the light of the customs, the local usage, and settled the case that way." He might have added, "You see the water runs in the same bed it always had. When the water was awesome, the river might have been swollen, but as soon as the storm quieted down, it went back to its usual run."

In my studies in civil law it was interesting to learn of the Austrian efforts to compile common law or usages and customs. It was Maria Theresa, empress of Austria, who had tried to codify old customs and usages, particularly those that pertained to landed property. However, they were never codified.

I became more and more interested in the study of law in general and felt no regret at having left medical school. I began to realize that this absorbing study of law was close to my own way of thinking, that every facet of law fascinated me except probably certain rules, which I had to learn and which were boring to me.

I figured I would be able to teach in a college or be an attorney for a bank or other companies rather than take private cases and collect fees, et cetera. I thought of the schedule of my former boss, Dr. Papp, which never included private cases. Along with this line of thinking, I remembered my mother and grandmother's commenting on my sympathy toward the poor and disabled and my interest in how they got along.

At the end of the year 1929, the bank debtors became more and more insolvent and the counsel office needed more lawyers to process and file proceedings. At one time there were fifteen people working in a three-room office. I had to supervise the work: purchasing stamps to apply on each case; filing in the court or in the office of land registry so as to register lien on the properties of debtors in sequence. I remember the attorney apprentices Moga, Faur, Suiaga, and Miron Butariu who worked there. I looked forward to becoming an attorney apprentice myself and getting a higher salary.

With this in mind, I felt it would be to my advantage now to take the final examinations. So I resigned my job and went home to Tisa to study for the finals. This was the end of December 1929. The finals were set for March 1930. I passed the examinations, and with my law license in hand returned to Arad to look for a job as an attorney apprentice.

IV

THE YOUNG LAWYER

I was admitted to the bar on April 21, 1930. I was prepared and eager to begin my apprenticeship, which, according to law, would last three years. There were no jobs available because of the depression. Neither the bank nor Doctor Papp was able to help me because the depression was so serious that even the bank was in danger of becoming insolvent. I inquired in several law offices about an opening. Finally, Dr. Orffy, an attorney with a bank, offered me a job in his office. He said, "George, I cannot pay you anything. My clients have no money and the bank has no money either. But you have good experience and background, and it's better than being idle." So I went to work without pay.

Aunt Anne and Uncle Stephen Albert asked me to stay with them, as they had plenty of room in their house, and I was assured that they would be glad to have me with them. I gratefully accepted and was soon settled there.

Within a month or so I was called by Dr. Sever Ispravnic, a highly reputable lawyer in the city and district of Arad, who said to me, "Crisan, I've been talking to Dr. Papp, who was an apprentice lawyer in my office once, and he spoke of you and your work background. He also spoke of your grandfather, George Crisan of Anne, from Tisa-Halmagiu, who is an old friend of mine. I understand that you are an industrious and ambitious young man. I do not need another clerk at this time, but I want to help you. You understand I am a very demanding man. You can learn a lot in my office. When you locate a better paying job, feel free to take it. If you want the job under these circumstances, come along."

There was a vast amount and variety of work in that office. The hours were 7:00 A.M. to 7:00 P.M. The old man came to the office about 8:00 A.M. and went to court or talked with his son, who was also a lawyer. At times I had to go to the court to do research in the files and prepare briefs or reports in writing for Mr. Ispravnic. The senior clerk, Mr. Anghel, was usually late coming in, and sometimes he did not come in at all. I learned that he was drinking heavily.

However, old Ispravnic relied on him and his memory—he knew the state of each case by heart.

A month later, my cousin Myron introduced me to Mr. John Hentiu, whose brother was a lawyer and who was looking for someone to maintain his office for the summer. This law office was located in a large country town, Chisineu Cris, a county seat, with a court with three judges, land records, and probate. This young lawyer planned to take the summer off for his wedding and honeymoon. Cousin Myron thought this would be an opportunity for me, so I took the job. I soon got acquainted in the town and fit in well in the community life there. I even received words of approval on my conduct of cases in court. The social aspect of my life there was somewhat unimaginative. Although the people were kind to me and I enjoyed the young crowd and met several attractive girls—I recall Mircea Popa and Andrei Grozescu among others—the small town atmosphere eventually began to pall. Once or twice I attended services at the Baptist church in town—a medium-sized meeting house with country folk for their prayer and worship meeting there. Somehow I did not feel at home in the town. I did not dislike it, but there was nothing interesting to do—the professional people had no better diversion in the evening than to drink wine and play cards. I simply did not fit into the country town atmosphere—so I was told.

By the end of August it was time to decide about the military year. Some of my Baptist friends suggested that I look into the possibility of studying in divinity school or seminary of higher education in Hamburg, Germany. I went to Bucharest to meet with the most prominent Baptist preacher in Rumania, Constantin Adorian, with whose son I had been corresponding but had never met in person. The Reverend Adorian knew me by name—there was only one young Baptist lawyer in all Rumania, and that was I.

He told me he had heard of my academic record and my association with the Baptist youth, I having been the first secretary of that organization. I stated my inquiry as to the possibility of study in a seminary. He said yes, but he wanted to make one thing clear; I would be asked to make a commitment to the task of ministry after graduation and to returning to the country from Germany. He said that he had had to bear the shame and disappointment when a student did not accept this responsibility but turned to other professions. I told him I would seriously consider these things and let him know my decision.

The next day, before leaving for my home in Arad, which is the most western city in Rumania near the Hungarian border, I talked to the Reverend Adorian again and told him I was thinking of our conversation but felt that I must first fulfill my military obligation of one year.

I enrolled in the military at the beginning of October. I was assigned to the artillery because of my ability in mathematics. I was sent to the city of Craiova to take the entrance examination in the reserve officer military school for artillery and passed the examinations satisfactorily. I was situated in the school dormitory for several days and nights in a room along with fifty to seventy other young men. It was crowded to capacity or more so, and we were uncomfortable. There were so many who passed the examination that some were asked to renounce to stay in school. I was asked whether I wanted to stay. When I answered no, I was sent to the military base within the next few days.

IN THE SERVICE

When the time came for the physical examination prior to recruitment into the military service, at age twenty-three, I found little comfort in my grandmother's assuring me, "My dear George, you will not be accepted into the military because of the trouble with your leg."

There were five of us from the village of Tisa. I remember there were five doctors checking us for various things after we had been stripped of our clothing. I was embarrassed and shy at first, but I soon relaxed when I saw the other boys being examined the same way as I was. The doctors concluded that the osteomyelitis with which I had been affected had long since completely healed and the other aspects of my physical examination showed good health. In fact, the doctors gave the unanimous opinion that I would make a good draftee and would be especially helpful in the artillery since I was skilled in mathematics.

Since I did not choose to attend the Military School for Reserve Officers in Craiova, I was sent to the Artillery Regiment Barracks for my military term. I attended the garrison daily, six days a week.

Spending the night at the home of Aunt Anne during this period brought a little bit of home into my time there. I would often commute by bicycle.

The military training started with horse care. Our regiment was a light horse artillery. The cannons used were of the old type, recalibrated at about nine centimeters. They were stated, at least theoretically, to be very effective weapons, shooting with good results up to eight kilometers. Our training exercises were conducted on plain fields.

The cannon was pulled by three pairs of horses and the caisson was pulled by two pairs of horses. The officers, sergeants, and all the "cannon feeders" (soldiers) were on the horses. We were instructed from the very beginning that the greatest attention must be given to the feeding and watering of the horses. Horse care came first, man care came second. Without good, well cared-for horses the artillery would be worth nothing. The power of the regiment was devised to follow the cavalry in its fast and quick moves to surprise the enemy; to breach the front and to enlarge it; and wait for the army to take over. Lieutenant Jacobini instructed us at the cannons, veteran Lieutenant Stefanovici was the instructor on horse care, and Captain Teodorescu was our battery captain.

As time progressed, I became more and more skilled in learning the instructions and the practice of them. Sometimes I had difficulty in mounting my horse, but once in the saddle there was no further difficulty. On one occasion Lieutenant Stefanovici ordered the cadets (about twenty) to form a circle around a horse. Then he called on me to brush the horse quickly with straw to remove any perspiration in order to avoid any danger of pneumonia. I thought he was joking. I said, "Mr. Lieutenant, I thought the job of brushing the horse is for the orderly."

"Do you have horses at home?" he asked.

"Yes," I replied.

"Do you know how to take care of them?"

"No," I answered, "my father has a servant to take care of the horses."

I thought this was the end of the conversation. Not so! The officer reported me to the captain as not responding to his order. The captain, in front of the other cadets, while we were at attention, told us that the military service was established by law and that a soldier, or cadet, must not question the order, but execute! That was the end of it. In the evening, again while we were at attention to disband for the day, Colonel Sion came around and informed us, "One of you has not yet understood that this is military service, not civilian life, that an order is to be obeyed and not discussed." He ended his remarks by ordering that Cadet Crisan was to remain at the barracks until further orders. This was an incredible blow. To have to sleep in the hall with about seventy people and to eat from the "common kettle" made me sad and mad. Such a fuss for nothing! Is it the punishment to stay in the barracks for the entire year? Incredible! I did not stay in the reserve officers' school because I did not like the dormitory sort of existence. Here I was, back in the same situation. After this, everybody left the barracks. I remained there and was soon called into the office. Col. Ion Sion, a strikingly handsome man of forty, talked to me privately. He explained that he had to make the decision he had in my case because "We, the armed services, are called to defend our country against the enemy. We cannot possibly take as a joke any order of our superior officers, but to comply."

I said, "I now understand, Mr. Colonel. Long Live!" I went back to my dormitory. It was a long night. There was no privacy whatever.

I had received a good lesson on several things all at once. One thing I now understood was why civilians often scoffed at military officers assuming that the military were "yes men" in ornate uniforms, with no thought of their own.

Among our group of cadets (about thirty in all) there were two graduates of universities abroad, one from Germany and the other from Switzerland. John Stauber was a graduate of a university in Switzerland with a degree in journalism. His father ran the daily news of the city of Arad. The Hungarian name of the paper was *Arady Közlöny* (the *Daily News*). Alex Bedeus was a graduate from the University of Yenna, in Germany, with a degree in engineering. These two and I became close friends although they were of other ethnic groups.

John Stauber and I often spoke to one another in the Hungarian language rather than Rumanian. He arranged to have his father's daily paper delivered to my aunt's home. I appreciated this kindness to me as well as his friendship. The newspaper helped me keep abreast of local and world events. He later invited me to visit his parents' home. It was a pleasure to be a part of a visit to this palatial home and John's delightful family. I discovered that John was indeed an educated man on a broad scale. In addition, he was an accomplished pianist and I came in for a treat to hear his music.

Alex Bedeus left Arad and Rumania and moved to Hungary. I never heard from him again.

Six weeks of intense training went by quickly, and another period in my life began.

Captain Vasilovici was searching for a secretary who could write and had typing skills. I had these skills and also was the only lawyer in the cadet group. I was asked if I would like to work in the office. I answered in the affirmative and soon found myself installed in the office, typing the colonel's reports and other papers. Later on, the colonel invited John Stauber and me to attend the officers' parties, which we did.

Gradually I discovered that the military service was not as awesome and terrifying as I had thought; it was just a period of time young men were legally required to contribute. I learned that officers were really nice people and some were far above the average in general knowledge and education and certainly had more to say than "Yes, sir" and "No, sir." I also discovered the workings of military law regarding marriage of the officers. They, by law, unless they obtained dispensation, had to marry a woman with dowry, either in money or an estate producing a certain amount of revenue per year. I have never learned the history of the dowry in the military.

It was during my "military stage," as we called the year in the military, that John Stauber wanted me to meet his friend Baron Francis Neuman (de Vegvar). The baron was the youngest son in his family. This family was the wealthiest, not only in the district but probably in the entire country, at that time. They owned a textile factory, a flour mill, and a yeast plant, as well as palatial homes in the city and other properties. They had impressive international connections and relationships with merchants and businesses abroad.

Family background had always held great interest to me. I soon learned the baron's family background was especially intriguing and fascinating. I found that the baron's grandfather was a plain Jew

95

from Galicia. He started collecting junk iron—all kinds of discarded material like horseshoes and old implements about the farm no longer in use. He collected all these things in exchange for ribbons or trifles of various kinds and delivered his scrap iron to the iron or steel plant. He became prosperous as time went on and finally came up with the idea that a title of nobility would add to his prestige. How could this be obtained in the late nineteenth century? He set about to gain a reputation that would gain him a noble title. He built a children's hospital with the latest equipment and the finest staff to make an outstanding example as an up-to-date hospital. It was set in an attractive park. The emperor of Austria-Hungary was duly impressed by the construction of this hospital and bestowed the title of baron upon the hospital's builder.

I remember once the young baron was reminiscing about the origin of the family title and said, "Well, we are not an old nobility but just the same we've fully enjoyed it."

I recall visiting in the baron's family home in the company of John Stauber, and we were deeply impressed at the opulence of it. There were rooms for dining, there were rooms for just sitting, there were rooms for music, rooms for various entertainments, et cetera. There was a walled garden. From the outside, the house was inconspicuous in appearance. It was just around the corner from my office at the Bank of Victoria where I was working as a law clerk before becoming a full-fledged lawyer.

After ten years or so, it happened that my brother, Titus, a textile engineer, was employed in the baron's business. In 1945 or shortly thereafter, the baron came to America. About twenty-five years after that, as an expert counsel with the Foreign Claims Commission of the United States, I had to study and make recommendations to the commission on what indemnity the baron was entitled to after the Rumanian Communist government took his Rumanian properties. It turned out that almost all his business stock was in American hands, and therefore he was entitled to compensation.

Various experiences of my youth in Rumania some fifty years ago come to mind. I remember one evening three of us, Stauber, Bedeus, and I were invited to the officers' mess for a party. It was a cold buffet. The main dish was rabbit with black olives around it along with a glass or two of good wine. A dance followed. I did not know what the black round fruit was and I did not like it. I wondered what it was but soon learned when Johnnie asked me how I liked the olives marinated. I replied nonchalantly that they were alright but I did not care for them. This was my introduction to the buffet party. Some had a drink of wine; others did not. I saw it was a personal preference. And of course the young men had the opportunity to prove their dancing ability and awareness in any social situation. I enjoyed dancing and never grew tired of this recreation. I even heard from Captain Vasilovici that the ladies approved my polite manners and commented that I was a good dancer, which, of course, pleased me. There were three or four such parties during our year of required military training.

One day late in the spring of 1931, I went by the home of my former boss, Dr. Theodor Popa (or Papp), to say hello to him. He seemed pleased to see me and was glad to learn that I was getting along well in the military. He said he would like me to work for him on Saturday when I had the time to spare as well as on other days when I had free time. He explained that he had a lot of work to do and he knew I was familiar with it. I immediately started working for him, and he assured me that when my military term was up he would be glad to have me work for him full-time. In August when I had a furlough I worked at the Victoria Bank Counsel Office, where I had started working four years earlier. Friends and acquaintances thought I was very lucky to find a good job in the depths of the economic depression.

When I was out of the military I decided I should no longer stay at my aunt's home but find a place of my own. I found one not far from her apartment. The landlady (herself a tenant) had a kitchen with an entrance and a bedroom. She rented me the bedroom. It was not an ideal situation. It was necessary to cross the kitchen and the entrance way in order to reach my room. At times she would be in the middle of dressing chickens for the market, and one day she asked me if I would like her to cook some chicken livers for me. I turned down the favor. It was distressing to see the butchered chickens.

EMBARKING AGAIN ON A PROFESSION

At the Repenters' meeting house I met a man called Nika Neta, who might have been in his early thirties. He had red hair, which was the first thing I noticed about him. He was an accomplished violinist, I soon learned. He was looking for a furnished room and I told him I, too, was looking for another location. I called to see my former landlady with whom I had stayed the four years of college life and also inquired about the boarding lady upstairs. I soon learned from her that she could accommodate two more persons and that we could move right in. Shortly, we moved into the basement apartment, whose entrance was through the narrow kitchen.

I began to learn something of the red-haired man's background. He had been in America ten or twelve years, spoke English well, and was active in the Rumanian Baptist churches in Cleveland and Akron, Ohio. He told me his Rumanian was poor since he had never attended a Rumanian school. He had attended a Hungarian school, which at that time was part of the Austro-Hungarian Empire. He was deeply involved in reading the Bible in Rumanian (a translation in the Old Rumanian language of the nineteenth century) and he also kept up his regular reading of his worn English Bible. He was the first man I ever met to tell me face to face that I was "the most intelligent and well-educated young man he had met among the Baptists." He also commented at length on my skill in Rumanian pronunciation and stressed the fact there was no regional or countryside slang in my speech.

I remember that at times I felt rather bogged down, but at the same time I was pleased at his high evaluation of my "talents," as he put it in a sort of biblical jargon. He worked for a cooperative society in the city. He was enrolled in cooperative studies by correspondence in a school in Bucharest and often came to me for advice in preparing his lessons. He learned rapidly. I encouraged him as best I could and assured him that he would have no difficulty in learning the Rumanian language or in accomplishing his assignments in the cooperative association.

Nika (pronounced by us as Neeka) wanted me to go with him to meet his brother Theodor in a suburban community of our city. I met his brother and his brother's wife, in their beautiful home with a large garden of fruits as well as a vineyard of fine grapes. I felt they had all the goodness of the earth; things I especially enjoyed. Theodor's very young daughter Emma was destined to become the wife of my brother John some fifteen or more years later.

Nika reminded me from time to time in our evening chit-chat

that I was equipped to do just about whatever I chose to do: practice law, be a senator of the Baptist Union in Rumania, or other things. In a word, he was sincere, I could see, and it was a boost to my self-confidence. He further reminded me that there were Baptist folk who might turn to me for legal help or other counsel in their times of stress. In reality, these times of stress were soon to come.

The Baptists were considered sectarians. In some villages, at the instigation of a bigot priest, people who had been Baptists were stoned and expelled from the village as having sold themselves to Satan. My father, still a prominent man in his community, was subject to indignities such as suits in court. But his constant reminder to his listeners was, "Our Lord was crucified for our sins! He saved us! He made us worthy of eternal life with him! We must withstand all for his sake! Trials and tribulations were forespoken by the prophets and by Jesus himself. We must never be afraid of losing our lives for him who saved us for the eternal life with him."

Through Nika Neta I inadvertently became involved in more things than I wanted to handle. Many of Nika's acquaintance in the world of business administration and accounting and such were apprised of the fact that they could turn to me for help in any legal matter. About this time, the Baptist students organized a meeting in Oradea. I was invited to attend, which I did, and was asked to act as secretary of the meeting. I became the first executive secretary of the First Baptist Union of Rumania (with some reluctance, I might add). I had to draft some bylaws and have some minutes done as well as have correspondence with some of the other leaders. At times I felt I had been drawn into more activities than I needed that were outside or not related to my own personal activities or profession.

Being involved in sports activities at the River Bank "Strand" swimming and sundeck facilities led to my meeting many people—lawyers and businessmen who attended the Strand regularly. I remember playing chess with some judges and others while staying in the sun or in the shade for hours on end.

Someone in this group got the idea that because of the varied interests in sports and hiking there should be a tourist club. It was further remarked that there was such a club in Bucharest, which was recognized by law as promoting physical fitness, interest in nature, and general sports. So, a meeting was called by Brutus

Pacurariu, the executive secretary of the Chamber of Commerce of the district. Among those attending were lawyers, judges, businessmen, and city and state employees, for the purpose of discussing the establishment of a tourist club of Arad, possibly an affiliation with the National Tourist Club of Bucharest. We met in the evening at the Chamber of Commerce with a considerable crowd of people attending. Brutus called the meeting to order and called on me, asking me to be the secretary of the meeting. I did not like the assignment, but how could I refuse the executive secretary of the Chamber of Commerce and Industry, who, I was told, was the most powerful man in the city of Arad? Of course, others mentioned that this was just a shrewd approach to me, as he had a young daughter! I simply shrugged off such an idea. I commented to myself that this, too, would pass and I would go along with the whole thing.

Not long after these organizational meetings and after the New Year, a beautiful booklet appeared in the bookstores. It was the *Yearly Tourist Club of Rumania Almanac*, a volume of about 150 pages, illustrated with pictures of various natural sites in Romania. My friend, Peter Ciumpila, an attorney, mentioned to me one day, "George, have you seen the almanac for the year? Go buy a copy; your name is in it."

I was astounded. There was a write-up connected with the establishment of the Sectional Tourist Club for the district of Arad and area and mentioning the first secretary, George Crisan, attorney of the Bank of Victoria. Of course, I was pleased to read the write-ups, but I did not speak of it to any extent. But when I mentioned the notice to Nika, he exclaimed he was right in stressing my capabilities and added, "We, the Baptists, will make you our senator in Bucharest in the Parliament of Rumania."

The years 1931 through 1939 covered the period of the great depression and recovery. During this time I was forging a profession, becoming more involved in Baptist affairs, and becoming more involved in the affairs of the Rumanian authorities. In addition, I was acquiring a reputation as a lawyer of the Repenters. Among other recreations, I attended several balls in the season between Christmas and the first Sunday of the Easter fast. This time was also the season of the marriages.

SOCIAL LIFE

I always enjoyed dancing, and my dancing partners commented favorably on my skill. But some of my Repenter friends as well as my father had something different to say about the dancing. I became somewhat of a black sheep in their sight. A young preacher among the group even remarked to me, "Brother George, you are a fine fellow, a good lawyer—in fact the only Baptist lawyer in Rumania—now, why are you not a more exceptional Christian?" I was surprised. I did not smoke, drink, or use any form of foul language; my recreation consisted of attending the theatre, opera when it came to Arad, movies, and balls. I never attempted to explain either to my parents or friends or clients my views of my personal faith.

I enjoyed meeting the girls at the Baptist Youth Fellowship and attending the social parties in their homes. There was singing together, and they usually ended in a discussion of the present Baptist plight—the struggle to be recognized by law as a denomination, which we were not at that time. We were only tolerated on the grounds that the former Austro-Hungarian laws acknowledged the existence of the Baptist followers and by international rule of law set out in the peace treaties at the conclusion of the First World War guaranteeing civil liberties. While such Baptist Fellowship sect has been recognized in Transylvania, which became part of the kingdom of Rumania after the First World War, in the other provinces of Rumania (Moldavia and Valachia), there was no recognition by law or otherwise of the Baptists. It was unheard of that Rumanian-speaking folk could be "heretic," or worse, "Bolshevic" or "Communist," an agent of some foreign power such as Hungary or Russia.

First as a lawyer apprentice and then as a lawyer on my own at the Victoria Bank Counsel Office, I had the liberty to work in my spare time on my own cases, whatever they might be. The counsel encouraged me in this part of my work, because eventually I would have my own office and the experience would be of benefit to me. My being a lawyer or associate counsel in a bank's legal office was a great advantage to me. The bank's clients were often looking for a lawyer to help them with their problems—the purchase of lands and houses, the matter of wills, or the matter of border disputes. There I was, an expert on real property matters, moreover, knowing the land registry and mortgage or other encumbrances and being readily available to render any assistance needed. While the counsel and practically all the offices of the bank were either Orthodox or Catholic of Byzantine rites, there was no discrimination against me. I did not make an issue or create any discussion regarding my belief or my adherence to the Baptist folk.

There was a pretty young woman called Smaranda Ciuhandu who had just finished her business management course in school. I enjoyed taking walks with her, and we would often stop for ice cream in the neighborhood shop. Smaranda was the daughter of Dr. George Ciuhandu, the highest ranking priest next to the bishop. On one occasion Dr. Ciuhandu had an open house, and many young people including me were invited. I was introduced to Smaranda's parents, and Dr. Ciuhandu remarked, "I am quite sure we've met before." I replied in the affirmative and reminded him that he had held the examination on religion in my last college year and that he had complimented me on my examination write-up. I could never forget that! He then remembered the occasion and said it was the clearest answer he had ever received from the students. He added that some questions in religion could prove to be intriguing or confusing, but he recalled that I had expressed clear understanding of the questions.

I remember all through this period I met many girls but no serious feeling evolved. I enjoyed their friendship and wanted to know the individual girl and she me a little bit better.

Miron Butariu was my cousin and closest friend since elementary school days in Halmagiu. He worked in the same office with me and in like capacity. He often teased me about my dating and asked me just how long would the new date last and so on! I did not have a ready rejoinder for him at the time, but thought about it later.

For a short time I dated a girl who was a student of law and philosophy. She was attractive and intelligent and impressed me by her two major studies. Years later, when I returned from the war about 1945, we met on the sidewalk and renewed acquaintance. She invited me to visit in her home—that we would enjoy talking over old times. She reminded me of the letters I had written her in the past and intimated that they were loving letters. She went on to sum up that now that our mutual studies and war experience were behind us we might take up our personal living once again. She was rather forthright, all in all, and finally assured me that she would be receptive to any serious commitment. She invited me to visit her next day for further discussion. I had not up to this point contemplated marriage. But the next day when we met it turned out that we were mutually serious as to a permanent commitment. Her father at that time was ill in the hospital and her mother was sitting with him. We went to the hospital to visit her parents. Without further ado, she introduced me to her parents as her fiancée!

That night I came to face some serious thinking. I tossed around the thought of marrying a fine girl. I did not know much about her background and beliefs and so on. I did not know her church affiliations. Her parents spoke to one another in Hungarian. My thoughts were in turmoil. What would my bride talk about with my parents and my brothers and my sister? There was nothing of common interest. I finally arrived at the decision that I must get away for a few weeks and do some serious thinking about it all. I left for my factory at Dobra,* about one hundred miles away, but at the railroad station I changed my mind and went instead to a hot water spa, Herculaneum (the ancient spa where the Roman emperors went for their recreation or cure). From there, I wrote to my fiancee to the effect that I might have been somewhat hasty in the decision for an early marriage. The fact was I had a mass of financial and economic problems with my factory, where about 250 people worked producing lime and bricks. I seriously felt we should postpone our plans and let the matter rest a while. My cousin Miron came forth with his kidding and teasing me again, "Yes, you were engaged once before, from sunset to sunrise."

More than twenty-five years later, my wife and eleven-year-old son George Stewart went to Rumania to meet my parents and brothers and sister. My wife met my cousin, George Motica, who related that the wife of a former attorney now working for him in Timisoara was once my fiancée. When Eunice returned home and mentioned the incident, I added my own story of my short engagement.

*Uncle Stefan Albert had persuaded me to become one of the partners of the lime and brick factory at Dobra.

103

Two amusing incidents come to mind both to do with my friend Paul. He asked me to learn from Mrs. Negus whether he might propose to her daughter. Mrs. Negus, who knew me quite well from her business with the bank, said she was surprised that this serious question should come to her through a friend. She replied, "No, I do not have a daughter who is ready to get married," but she added, "If you were asking for yourself that is another matter!"

It seemed that my willingness to do something for whoever asked me got me in unwelcome predicaments at times. The second incident also had to do with Paul's desire to get married. Maria's father was inclined to drink on occasion, and I elected to approach the mother instead. She was eager to know the reason for my visit, as I had made the appointment several days earlier.

"I come on behalf of my friend, Paul." I became hesitant then, thinking back to my previous rebuff. Then I went on. "I've known Paul for a long time. We are good friends. He's studying to become a lawyer. So, to make a long story short, he wants to marry Maria."

"Mr. Crisan, we appreciate your advocacy for Paul, but I would not consider saying either way until Paul is a lawyer, moreover until our Maria wishes to consider him as a serious suitor."

I realized that my good offices were a flop. But when I thought about it I came to the conclusion that things do not always turn out as we desire or plan.

I was Paul's godfather, which explains why he consulted me about aspects of his social life and sought my advice. He later married, and there were two children in this happy marriage. He completed his law studies and became a successful lawyer in the city of Arad. It was reported that he charged exorbitant prices for his services, but this phase of his life did not come within my jurisdiction.

I remember one time I met an attractive girl at a Baptist youth party who possessed a beautiful singing voice. We had several dates later, but I soon discovered, to my disappointment, that she was a high school dropout, and I suspected that the study workload was beyond her capacity. Her older sister also had a beautiful singing voice, and my friend Macavei liked her at once. They eventually eloped to another town and were happily married. A girl in our group remarked to my aunt, "George is just like a butterfly. He is ready to break a girl's heart and goes away and forgets all about it. He is interested only in himself."

My aunt related this conversation to me and I said that I was not interested in marrying any girl just because of a beautiful voice or any other physical beauty.

Somehow, I concluded that indeed there were girls of my acquaintance who were ready to accept proposals of marriage, but it was I who was not ready to propose. I was not interested in getting married just to be married. That much I was aware of and felt strongly about. I considered my status in my profession and in my life otherwise. I thought about the support of a wife in daily living. I even thought about some of the parables in the Bible, such as, stories of the talents or the ten maidens or the rich ruler who wanted to keep it all, his wealth as well as assurance of eternal life. But I did not think of these things at any great length. I just considered the compatibility of interests and likes and dislikes when I met an attractive girl. And my cousin Miron never failed to argue, "What's wrong with so and so, she's very attractive," and so on and on.

BECOMING A FULL-FLEDGED LAWYER

Being the only young attorney of Baptist faith in a country of 20 million people may have been a drawback or stigma, especially at times when the government changed; when the student movement to the right was almost alarming; when my father was carrying his cross with faith and was of such endurance that he felt he was suffering for his saviour. I was not afraid to defend Baptist folk. I asked Miron to defend my father.

I came to realize that the populace as a whole were tolerant and some even interested to find out more about the Repenters—that they could go to jail and still could sing and read the black book (the scriptures) and carry on the baptisms in the river. On several occasions I was asked by Baptists from certain communities in the district to go and try to make peace among factions in a church. I accepted these requests and did my best to clear up any points of dissension. I enjoyed being called upon with or without any thought of remuneration.

Once Miron said to me, "I don't understand your father. Why does he ask for trouble? Is he better off as a Repenter when the priest tries to accuse him of everything: strangers staying overnight in his house; meetings and singing in his house without legal authorization; going to meet other Repenters miles away to sing and talk from the Book? Well, George, he was a cantor and your family built that church more than a hundred years ago and supported it in every way. It was good for his ancestors; what is wrong with the church today? Is he going to reform our centuries of tradition?"

"Miron, I can't answer these things. But if you know me, you know that I have gradually come to the conviction of my own thinking and my own way of worshipping and praying to God. I don't agree with the idea that the priest has charge of everything like the incenses. We do not accept such a posture. We think we are personally responsible to God for our conduct; we do not believe that we only go to church and give some money and consider ourselves Christian and then go out and act as we please the rest of the time."

I did not discuss my religious concepts except with only a few friends from among the Baptist people and with practically none of the orthodox tradition. I considered it entirely useless. Somehow, I realized that if my deeds and the deeds of my Baptist brothers did not make our faith relevant, no words would!

Then Miron added his thinking on the subject. He said, "It is, of course, a beautiful attitude to keep such ordinances and commitments, but who can? We are so weak, are we not?"

Baptist folk from the vicinity of my city, Arad, whose properties were enrolled in the land registry at the court, came more and more to see me about such matters as drawing up a deed for them or making a division of property, or writing a will. At the same time I was working as a lawyer in the counsel's office at the Victoria Bank. One would bring along another, and at times they came to see me on matters not related to the law. I was happy to talk over any matter—I was never ready to say no!

In my law practice among the farmers and the big and not so big landowners of Baptist faith, I met many in the faith that I might not have had the opportunity of knowing otherwise. Some of the farmers had two homes, one on the land and another in the village. Usually, the family lived on the farm to take care of the cattle and pigs and farming the land. These families made a better living than many who were living in the city.

Sometimes I became the lawyer for the entire clan. I met many young people, both boys and girls. I was amazed that they did not seem willing to pursue higher education. This ended any interest I might have had in any lasting friendship with any of the attractive girls.

In a village about nine miles from the city of Arad there lived a brother called John Bocsa. I remember him as a man short of stature who expressed clear thinking and good judgment on any subject. He had come from Hungary to settle in Arad. He had seven sons who were of his faith and beliefs; they all attended church regularly and took an active part in the church activities, such as singing and reading the scriptures. I recall the father had the plan to build a house for each of his sons and to divide his land among them. I worked for Bocsa for many years. He would come to my small efficiency apartment on occasion and many times early in the morning, asking whether such and such a procedure would be right and acceptable under law. After these forty years I returned to Rumania as an escort interpreter for Rev. Ed. Plowman, senior editor of *Christianity Today* (a Billy Graham publication). We visited many Baptist churches in Rumania, in Bucharest, Brasov, and Arad and vicinity. These visits were arranged for Ed and me by the Baptist Union leaders with the authorization of the ministry of denominations. We were scheduled to go to Sofronea from Arad. A young driver was assigned to drive us to Sofronea where we would speak to a congregation there. Ed asked the young driver his name and profession. "Octavian Bocsa, artisan" caught my attention, and then I remembered John Bocsa.

I spoke up that I had been a lawyer in Arad and among the many clients from the neighboring towns and villages I had a client by the name of John Bocsa for whom I did a lot of work and had enjoyed his friendship.

"For goodness sake, that must have been my grandfather," the young man exclaimed.

That evening after the church services for Ed's and my addresses were over there were hundreds outside to see and hear the American Baptists. We were invited to dinner in a Baptist home. The house, though large, was full of people. The young car driver said to us, "You are in my father's house. He wants to talk with you, Mr. Crisan." There he was!

"Do you remember me? he asked. "I was about twenty years old when you were here. I had been married only a short time, but we decided to get a divorce and you completed the divorce for us. I later remarried and now have several children including Octavian, who was your driver. Let me tell you, Mr. Crisan, all the houses on this street belong to our families and it was you who made the divisions for us and made up the deeds and recordings in the land registry. How could we ever forget? You were our father's best and trusted counsel! We always thanked God for your coming our way or our father's way."

In working with the Baptists there I discovered that some of them had been in America for some time or had relatives there. The relatives in America wanted to send money home to buy land either for themselves or relatives. There I was—an expert in real property since I worked as a clerk in the office of counsel at the bank, at which time it was my responsibility to see that a mortgage was set at the first rank in the land registry books.

At times during the period from 1930 to 1939, the Baptist faith was severely restricted not so much by a written law than by the local authorities prompted by the central government, which had been prompted by the Orthodox hierarchy. They believed that the Rumanian folk who left the national and ancestral mother church were heretics who were ignorant of the true religion (Orthodox), but most likely were stooges in the hands of foreign powers as Hungarians or Russians or Bolsheviks.

In 1968, I accompanied my wife, eleven-year-old son, and sister-in-law from our home in America to Brussels, Belgium. They left me in Brussels and they traveled on to Rumania to meet my parents and brother and sister. I had been advised by good counsel not to go into Rumania as I was a political refugee and my name might appear in the Rumanian criminal books as an escapee from the law. My wife, American born, and my son went, believing there was no possible danger to them in Rumania.

I traveled to Germany to meet a friend I had known since high school and who escaped with me from Rumania, V. Tulescu. He was previously the cultural attaché of Rumania in Berlin. We had many things to talk about. Vasile said to me, "George, I want to tell you something I was not able to before. I never dared to back in those days. But I don't want this on my conscience any longer. I remember how ostracized you were by Professor Albu and then derided by some classmates of ours because you were a Baptist and because your father was a Baptist. When we were in the seventh and eighth class of lyceum I was called in by the president of the college, Ascaniu Crisan, and ordered to spy on you to see whether you were a Communist or had any connection with communism. I reported back that I had not found anything like that. Now that you are in America and the Baptists are many and powerful there, I dare tell you this thing."

On our second trip to Europe in 1970 I went to Rumania for the first time since my escape in 1948. We visited in Germany and again met my friend, Vasile. I was able to do something for his old mother: to give her some money. Vasile had given me this in German marks. I have not heard from him since. He seemed to have aged early. He had been in Berlin during the heavy bombing but survived without any mishap.

My counseling of my Baptist friends was at times both ridiculous and incredibly sad. Once early in the morning about 5:00 A.M. there was a loud knocking on my door. There in the street were two gendarmes and several people, among whom was Rev. John Socaciu. It was explained that Reverend Socaciu and the others had held a meeting in the open air by the river and several had been baptized in the White Cris River. They had been seized and driven from station to station to the prosecuting attorney at the court in an effort to be released. They went on to say that it was their understanding no crime had been committed under the law. I went out and joined Reverend Socaciu and learned the group was from the town of Talagiu, not far from my village of Tisa along the Cris River. As soon as the district office opened at eight o'clock, I was received by the chief of security. He informed me that he had nothing to do with the case except to process it and suggested that the matter be referred to the prosecutor. I then went to the prosecutor, whom I knew, and shortly thereafter the group was released pending their appearance in court, when a hearing would be held before a judge or three judges.

It must have been sometime in the midthirties when I received a letter from America addressed to me personally and even containing the title attorney at law. Even the mailman was reluctant to put it in the mailbox but delivered it to me personally! It was the first such letter he had ever seen. The writer of the letter, Stanley Catana, wrote the letter on his personal stationery as notary public and insurance and travel agent of Detroit, Hyland Park, Michigan. He apologized for the letter to me, a stranger, but mentioned that his wife, Ecaterina, had been in teachers' school with one of my aunts. She had been in Rumania a year before, asked about my aunt and the Baptist affairs in Arad and had been informed that I was well and busy in my profession—and that it probably would not be proper to just drop by to meet me. Now her husband "dared" to write me to see whether in my busy time I could tend a case for one of his friends and clients. It was a divorce case. The man in the case was in America and the wife was in Rumania. They had been separated for twenty years and both wanted the divorce. Stanley had sent papers previously as well as money to a lawyer in Timisoara but heard nothing from him. So now he wondered if I would see what was involved and let him know the charge for the case.

I wrote back to my American friend immediately, telling him what was necessary. First, it would be published in a local paper and after six months the court would enter a final decree of divorce. I made no charge to Catana for this service. Ten days later, I received a letter asking me to proceed and telling me that one thousand dollars were sent to me through the International Bank. This was astonishing to me. A thousand dollars was a considerable and important sum of money in Rumania. In fact, I could have built a comfortable family house with it!

After this interesting incident, and agreeing to work for Catana's clients, he was sending money to distribute to people in Rumania, to buy a house or a parcel of land, or just help from the "American rich uncle." In fact, in some of these cases, I had to travel to some remote village to deliver the money or to prepare a deed. Once I went to Catana's father and mother-in-law to see that they had the necessities they needed since they were old and somehow unable to take care of themselves. I always let Catana set the fee. It was always beyond my expectations.

As Nazism in Germany increased, so in Rumania a movement of students called the Iron Guardists spread. It was alien to the Rumanian spirit of tolerance. Yet Rumanians were advised by the Orthodox priest in their villages that whatever is not of Orthodox faith is an enemy of the Rumanian mother church and other Rumanian folk as a whole. There were even songs containing such sentiments as, "Whoever loves the aliens, may the dogs eat his heart," and so on. Some youth looked at the Jews with envy and jealousy because they were merchants or lawyers or medical doctors or engineers—that they were "better off" than many of the Rumanian peasantry. But nobody asked or tried to understand why they were better off. They did not attempt to understand that it was because of hard work, attaining a good trade and educational tradition, traveling, looking for new ideas and new things, and realizing that the Rumanian village was not the beginning and ending of living for a Rumanian.

King Carol tried to cope with the problem of these citizens and their Iron Guard movement. They were not numerous but were bellicose and troublesome. Then the prime minister of Rumania was murdered on the street on the way to his office. King Carol executed a thousand or more students between the ages of twenty-one to twenty-five years and their bodies were left at the crossroads for several days as a terrifying example. The Iron Guardists could be seen as the Rumanian breed of Nazis who looked at any Baptist or sectarian as a renegade, a "worst enemy of the Rumanian church" because they became Christian and they were looked upon as turncoats and heretics, joining hands with the Masons and the Jews.

The Baptist churches, though few and small, were ordered to be closed and sealed with red wax. The Bibles were to be turned in to the police stations. One of the most incredible and sorrowful cases I ever had was when two people in their seventies were put in jail. The gendarme had discovered them reading the Bible and singing in their own home. It was against the order, the police informed them. I defended them, but not successfully. The wife was sentenced to three years imprisonment, but was allowed to stay at home because of ill health. The husband was sentenced to three years to make the term.

With the movement of the Iron Guard going on, we were called in the service as reserves. There was a young lawyer in my battery, several years younger than I. He was a quiet young man who talked very little and seemed to avoid me. I heard from others that he was a member of the Iron Guard and as such he did not have anything to do with Jews or their friends the Baptists or renegades. Well, my friend got a furlough. He went to his home near my village and never came back. He was among the number killed and left at the crossroads.

I began to hear rumors behind my back that I had "connections" with the Americans and even with the Francmasons. I had nothing to say to such rumors. I was never a member of a Francmason lodge. It was considered a secret and dangerous society. I knew some very nice people who I understood were members. I knew where the lodge was located. It was a large building with no windows. I never knew who the members were and was not interested to learn. But it came back to my mind from my college days that because I was a close friend of the only Jew in our class I was looked upon with some suspicion yet with a degree of admiration. People described me as "trusted by the Jews and by the Francmasons."

Among my friends was an older man by the name of Peter Ciumpila. We had hiked and skied together in the past. Once he asked me whether I would be interested in buying eleven parcels of land close to a railroad near Tisa, my father's village. I said I was not interested—that I would not know what to do with it. He called me obstinate and said that my father could see after the land and resell it for me. He went on to say that his private railroad company wanted to sell these preferred properties and they might be bought for a bid. I was taken by surprise. What did he mean by bid or offer?

Uncle Stephen explained that such large companies wanted to have several offers and then they would select the best offer to close the sale. I made an offer after I had asked the bank if they would grant me a loan to have a mortgage on the land I considered buying. They agreed that it would be a good investment both ways. The deal went through. In a few weeks, a neighbor to my newly acquired property called me by phone, which was quite unusual for that time and place. He wanted to have a courtyard built and wanted to buy a parcel of land next to his property. He offered me more than one half of what I had paid for all the parcels. I repaid the mortgage within a year.

The word spread around that I had been born with a silver spoon in my mouth; that I was a lucky young lawyer; and that I was wealthy. I thought of all this as nonsense. I was not wealthy.

Not long after this, Uncle Stephen came to see me. He told me of a large plot of land in his neighborhood in a suburb of Arad that the owner, a member of the Hungarian gentry, wanted to sell for cash, as he planned to leave Rumania and go to Hungary. He wanted a quick sale. I was not interested in a quick sale, which was to my dislike. He replied, "George, I and Aunt Anny live there and we know it is good land. Animals lived on this land for centuries. It would be fine land to own. You do not have to do anything. I will take care of the deal."

Well, after all this talk, I inquired about a loan to be mortgaged for five years. The bank was ready and glad to grant the loan. Then I learned that the seller had already made plans to parcel the land into thirty-six plots. This development was not yet approved by the city. The division of the land into plots and two cross streets were approved by the city after the sale went through, and in about a year and a half the lots were sold and the mortgage wiped clean. Here I was, a partner with my uncle and aunt.

Twenty-two years later when I returned to Rumania I wanted to see what had taken place with this property. It was an incredible sight! There were five apartment buildings of fifteen stories. They told me the housing was for the workers. I met the mayor of the city, an ardent Communist dogmatist. I said to him, "John, don't you think that now since I am a friend of the Rumanian government by your Ambassador in Washington, I should be compensated for the loss of my property?

He replied, "We could do that, but you would not accept the compensation. It would amount to a few dollars altogether, as we pay less than one cent per square foot of land."

I laughed and dismissed the subject.

It seemed that my colleagues and others really thought I was hiding something—some secret relationships or connections, that only such things could make me a wealthy young lawyer. I never thought I was just lucky; I felt that such things gave me more re-sponsibility. But I did feel good that my father was ready and able to administer those parcels of land and that my Uncle Steve was an excellent administrator. I never thought of myself as independent of my family regarding whatever I might have acquired.

The anti-Semitic movement took on some proportions, not be-cause it had a large membership in Rumania, but because it was vociferous. It was sort of reverberation of what was happening in Germany under Chancellor Hitler.

Again, Uncle Steve came to my apartment one day, trying to

interest me in buying a brick and lime factory in Dobra. This factory was owned by Brothers Stern, Henry and Sigmund. They were considering selling their business because they could not obtain sufficient credit to carry on. Also, Brother Henry was in ill health. Uncle Steve maintained it was a good property to invest in and assured me that I would not be required to take any active part in the negotiation, but I was needed to obtain the proper credit at the bank. So once again the deal was put through and I became a one-third partner in the factory and land. There was an acreage of one hundred acres of land, stables, and living quarters for the administrator, manager, and even for the owners. There were warehouses and brick shelters and the plant itself with its high chimney. The narrow gauge railroad led to the quarry from where the limestone was extraced. That was about eight kilometers upstream.

On one occasion Uncle Steve concluded that I knew how to handle the workers. Many of them I considered my personal friends and not my employees or laborers.

THE WAR APPROACHES FAST

Who would believe that the fire started by Hitler on the Danzig Corridor would quite quickly spread over Europe? After all, Ribbentrop had made a "smart" pact with Stalin and with France and England. Poland's allies would not be able to stop the Vermacht. Rumania had her own pact with Czechoslovakia and Yugoslavia. But Austria's Anschluss made possible earlier the establishment of a so-called friendly government in Czechoslovakia. In fact, it was occupied by Hitler's forces.

Events at this juncture moved rapidly and with most dizzying effect. The Russians gave an ultimatum to Rumania to give Besarabia and Bukovina to them because Besarabia was within the Russian Empire before First World War. The fact is, it had been a territory inhabited 100 percent by Rumanian ethnics and had been an ancestor province of Rumania since Herodotus was traveling along the Black Sea shores. The Bukovina province was sometimes under Austria but Russia asked for it, and how would Rumania dare to say no to Russia, the colossus leaning on Rumania from all eastern borders? Thousands of Rumanian farmers, government and city employees, and others took the way to exile from their country. Some, like myself, asked, "How can these things be tolerated by the great Allies, who at the end of the First World War declared that *all peoples are free to choose their destiny*—so said President Wilson of America."

When a wolf becomes incapacitated or wounded or becomes weakened, the other wolves may devour him if he is completely helpless, said some old saying among the Rumanian folk. So Bulgaria asked that a good portion of Dobrogea be returned to her. Why? Because it was acquired by Rumania in 1912 in a war and the accession was not fair to Bulgaria, they said. This case was negotiated between the Rumanian and Bulgarian governments.

The war broke out in a fury in September 1939. Poland was defeated quickly by Hitler's storm troops and Russia, on the other side, took a slice from Poland's body. Rumania and Poland had a mutual defense agreement. But Poland refused help. More than 200,000 Poles, military and civilian, all who were able to carry arms, escaped through Rumania and found their way to England through Egypt—most of them joining the British army or their own units in Africa to fight the Germans.

About twenty years after this Polish bloodbath, I met one Paul Zaleski in America. He had just graduated from law school in Poland. He had been among the number who had migrated to England. We have remained good friends to this day. He never forgot with gratitude the Rumanian hospitality to the Polish refugees.

Rumania mobilized all the active forces possible, including men my age, thirty-two. My bank tried to have me mobilized for work, but to no avail, since there were older men who could keep the work going. In November 1939, I was sent to Timisoara, where my regiment was based. I was allowed to stay outside the barracks and I took a furnished room. I was a sergeant with a connotation (TTR Cadet—one with higher education). In the spring of 1940 my regiment took a position on the border of Yugoslavia, as the Germans might try to take Rumania from that side. I had the most unusual experience—living in a ditch or in the fields of wheat or corn. It was a rainy spring, and the ground was wet most of the time. There were hundreds of frogs underfoot, and one had to be careful to keep from stepping on them. I remember the place in the Bible where I read of God's sending frogs on the Pharaoh's land when the Egyptians did not let His people go to freedom.

In the fields I met a young second lieutenant, Macavei Nicoara.

115

G.C. as second lieutenant, 1942.

We had met before at some Baptist youth meetings. He was a cousin of my friend, Macavei Slev. He was a great help to me by encouraging me with his view that I was really better off as a commissioned officer and for this reason could take advantage of extra training, and become a reserve officer.

As the storm was gathering in Western Europe, the Rumanian Iron Guardists began demonstrating by marches, singing of death to foreigners and of their destiny to save Rumania. The cross they carried was a symbol of patriotism. Many youth joined either from curiosity or a wish to take part in organizing demonstrations in the towns. I thought, *How foolish they are, being carried away by words or singing marches and not being able to think for themselves.* The marches here and there became larger.

Being mobilized in the spring of 1940, I was qualified to attend a short-term military school or artillery for the reserve officers in Craiova. In June 1940, I with hundreds of others throughout the country were commissioned reserve officers with the rank of second lieutenant.

I spent most of my time in the Operation Zone, facing the southwest of Rumania close to the Yugoslavia border. At times I could take three or four days each month to go home to see my office, which was closed.

116

As an officer I felt closer to the people than to the higher ranking officers. Several times I was cautioned by my captain that it was not good to be friendly with the soldiers, that they must respect you and that it was only necessary for you to give them orders—nothing else. That was difficult for me because there were people I enjoyed talking to and I learned that there were one or two Repenters among them.

In January 1941, several second lieutenants from my regiment and I were sent to attend a school on mining roads, bridges, buildings, et cetera. I well remember Sabin Pop, who later became a judge, and Demetriu Codrean, a lawyer in a country town. I stayed in one room with the others and went to the barracks to be taught the mining techniques. While there, we heard that the Iron Guard had taken over the radio station in Bucharest and were broadcasting messages that the "leader" Antonescu had been deposed or arrested by King Michael. In our city, Alba-Julia, we heard that the state attorney for the district, who under Rumanian law is the prosecutor of any crime, had jumped from his window of his second floor office and was found dead.

These things were not confirmed and I, in the military, could not go anyplace to learn what the situation in Bucharest was at the time. We were summoned to the barracks during the night, and the commanding officer of our school told us that it was necessary for the post office to be protected or defended against any intrusion. He asked for volunteers of a sergeant and two soldiers to protect or defend the post office of the city. For an incredibly long minute none volunteered. I felt ashamed of myself and all of us. I rose to my feet.

I went to the post office and stretched out there on the desks and chairs. In the morning, twenty or more peasants (or dressed as such) came toward the post office building. I took my sergeant and soldiers and went to meet them about a hundreds yards away. I suggested to them that if they wanted to enter the town they would have to take another route. They informed me they were Rumanian, "the same as you, officer," and wanted to go to the post office. I informed them this was not possible as we had orders from my superior that no one was to approach the telephone and telegraph building. I realized that they had been ordered to come and take over, thinking that everybody would rejoice at such an action now

117

that the Iron Guard was in power in Bucharest. I was there about three days, during which time there was no news from Bucharest. A week or so later, I heard that the Iron Guard group with leader Horia Sima (the previous leader had been shot while King Carol was still in the country) had butchered many prominent Jews and Rumanian politicians of democratic persuasion and attitude. I also heard that Nicolas Iorga, a foremost historian of the times in Europe had been taken away and stabbed to death and that some of the assassins had been his students. Why? Really, nobody asked such questions. Some of us were thinking that if man was created in God's image, how could such a massacre occur?

Later, when asked why I volunteered, I replied in candor that I was ashamed of us all and could not bear the shame. Still later, they agreed that most of the officers (about sixty) were guardists themselves, and of course could not volunteer to oppose the Iron Guard. Then it all came clear to me! The fact that I was the only Baptist (no one knew who I was and did not know I was a Baptist except my roommates) explained my courage. I also discovered there that something entirely unexpected can be accomplished.

We heard on every side that "we the Rumanians" are different—we are not like the Bulgarian people who are in constant turmoil, killing the political leaders, murdering their own king, the King of Yugoslavia. No, we were of a different strain. What a strain! Thirty years later I was invited to lecture at Carnegie Hall in New York City one hundred years after the birth of Nicolas Iorga. I spoke of his visiting America. I spoke of his visiting Rumanian Baptist churches in Akron and Cleveland, Ohio, and in Detroit, Michigan, in 1929–1930. In my research here in America I found comments about the fact that among his assassins were some of his students, who later became Iron Guardists. Then and there I concluded that no matter how wrong a parent or a teacher might have been, it is even a greater offense to the law of God and of man that one should raise his hand against the teacher who might or might not have been a source of enlightenment.

MEETING FOREIGN PEOPLE

While in college, I met John Socaciu, Rumanian by birth and educated in America. I learned he had been a classmate of Dr.

Edward Hughes Pruden, former pastor of the First Baptist church in Washington, D.C., now pastor emeritus of that church, and later connected with the Southern Baptist Theological Seminary, Louisville, Kentucky. He was the one who talked to my father regarding the idea that I might come to America to study for the ministry. I had rejected the idea at the time.

Socaciu was the Rumanian counterpart director of the Rumanian Baptist Seminary in Bucharest while the American Southern Baptists were the real directors and mentors in Rumania. Most of the Baptist folk were found in the city of Arad and in the surrounding areas. That is to say, in Transylvania where the Austrians and Hungarians ruled since A.D. 880 or so, after the Hungarians had established themselves in the Theis and Danube plain—the Hungary of today.

Transylvania became a part of Rumania in 1918 after the break of the central powers, Austria-Hungary and Germany, and the Rumanians in Transylvania joined their sister provinces, which were already united in the Kingdom of Rumania since 1866. But the old Kingdom had not encountered the western sectarian movement. The church had been the ecclesiastical authority ever since the time of the Byzantine Empire and ever since the church of the Eastern Roman Empire became the state church with the emperor the head of the empire and head of the church. The Orthodox church was the only church known. The priests were mostly either Greek or educated in Greece. They were suspicious and jealous of their *Orthodox* faith, which means the "true one."

The little kingdom of Rumania became Greater Romania. The government, by the International Treaty of Peace of Versailles and Trianon, is bound to keep the civil law, the usages and local rules of law in the land that were added to the old territory of Rumania. But the government and the officials who sooner or later were appointed in the new province had no idea who the Repenters were and had never heard of Baptists. Once a young lawyer asked me point blank whether it was true that the Baptist movement started with a Blacksmith (probably because of John Smith (?)), who just revolted against his "God-foreordained priest" and in his dissatisfaction went to the river and baptized himself.

"Are they heretics, George?" he asked.

I did not answer directly. There was no sense in arguing on things not quite familiar to me and even less to him concerning the beginning of the Repenters' movement.

I was well aware that practically all, if not all, the Baptists in Romania I had met before meeting Socaciu were either entirely uneducated or self-educated, like my father, a little more than the elementary six grades. I was somewhat embarrassed to be considered a Repenter, for none of them had a secondary or professional education. At the same time I gave credit for this to my father and grandfather and the members of my family and other relatives who one by one became Repenters after my father took the lead. The Rumanian authorities could not comprehend that there were Repenters in Transylvania who looked in the Black Book, the scriptures, as a sole source of guidance and faith in a Christian life.

Because of Socaciu, who was educated in America, a group of American and English Baptist leaders came to Arad, at a "sort of convention" of the Baptist community, as the Baptist group was called. I met Dr. Truett, Dr. Rushbrook, and two others. I even took some pictures of the group. (These were lost when my belongings were ravaged by Political Security after my escape from Romania in 1948.) Lo and behold, I was told (because I did not know how to speak or understand English), there were Baptist lawyers in America who were much respected and some of whom freely spoke of their dependence upon reading the Bible before going into court or before starting a day of work.

At that time, I heard that there was another lawyer of the Baptist faith in Oradea (about two hundred miles from Arad) whose name was "Hungarian George Simonka" and who said he was of Rumanian origin. However, his wife and children did not speak Rumanian. Who was he? I did not know.

My own outlook on foreigners or local Hungarian, Jewish, or Serbian ethnics was favorable. My father's father was mayor of Tisa for twenty-five years and my father twelve when there was a Hungarian administration of the country, and they realized the Hungarian, German, and Jewish people were good people as well as honest and were often better off than the Rumanians, who constantly worried that their children might leave their village and never return or might become bewitched by strange beliefs and customs.

Historians of the past and some today are still pondering on how the Rumanians preserved their identity—language, customs, and laws—for just less than two hundred years under Roman rule.

Then the Eastern Roman Empire was pressured by the constant migration of warriors from the east. The Rumanians withdrew into the Citadel of Carpathian Mountains of Transylvania into pastoral living for more than one thousand years. German colonies established themselves in Transylvania. Hungarians from the Theis Plain continued to nibble more and more of the tableland and mountains in the western triangle of the Transylvanian Alps.

Even today, if one travels from Vienna, Austria, to Bucharest by train, one would unmistakably recognize the great difference in the style of living, housing, and even customs as soon as the train passed the Carpathian Mountains on the eastern slopes. A newspaperman by the name of Ed Plowman, with whom I traveled in Rumania in 1977, asked me how come before crossing the Carpathians everything looked like Austria or Switzerland, but after passing Predeal (the highest point of the pass) everything resembled Greece or Lebanon or something like that? I explained to Plowman that for more than one thousand years Western Europe stopped at Brasov, the city established by the Teutonic knights in the eleventh or twelfth century as a watch post against new invasion from the east upon Vienna and Western Europe.

Some of the historians call the Rumanian provinces of Moldavia (to which Bessarabia belonged), which is again under Russia, and Wallachia the boulevard of migration tides, and so it was and may continue for some time to come. This is because Rumania is a romance country, an island among slavonic peoples, with some Hungarians on the western rib.

Another question comes up—is it proper for Rumanians to marry foreigners; that is, Hungarian, German, or other such nationalities who have been enemies of the Rumanians for centuries? All such "barbarian and heretic" people were looking for the Rumanian lands inherited by the Rumanians from the dawn of the world or from prehistoric times!

Since being in America, I have discovered that in present-day Rumania and in parts of Hungary and Yugoslavia, German archeologists have found pottery and some bricks containing strange designs, and some believe these are inscriptions something like those of the Sumerians. The pottery resembled that of a Middle Empire of China and may be as old as twenty thousand years. To sum up, it may be, some say, that it was somewhere here that the European

121

man *Homo europeus* surfaced and this might have happened long before the ice cap of the north withdrew some fifty thousand years ago (or God knows when, for sure!).

I, like any other Rumanian, was apprehensive of any foreign-language-speaking fellow. Here's my approach to the matter. I remember that even when I was a small child, on occasion Hungarian officials came to my grandfather and later to my father's home looking for the sport of hunting boar, reindeer, or plain foxes. The impression at the time was that the Hungarians were peaceful, were not savage in any way, and were not trying to do away with the Rumanian peasantry.

When I was in college one of my valued friends had been Felix, a Jewish boy. Because we were good friends and got along so well, other boys hinted that I was a "Jew lover." Why? I could not understand such a thing.

I continued to have good Jewish friends when I became a lawyer.

As a young lawyer I courted for a while a young German girl who spoke fluent Rumanian and German without a trace of an accent. The story went around that she was the daughter of a Catholic priest, who deserted her. Her mother took care of the Catholic priest's household in a town next to Arad.

I befriended young Hungarian Baptists and occasionally attended their meeting house services. There I met a beautiful girl who was a talented violinist. My romance did not last long. She left to marry in America!

All these minute incidents in one's identification are too numerous to list but demonstrate that when encountering each unit of experience, a person's appraisal of it goes into the development of his mature outlook on life, on his neighbor whoever he might be. Then one may be able to rise to assess himself as a person, an individual who can stand on his own wisdom or outlook as to various ethnics and various faiths or formal religions.

Thus, the impact of meeting Rushbrook and Truett in the mid-thirties left a most lasting impression. It was the realization that my Romanian-stern-Orthodox friends and people, most of whom rarely attended church except on Easter Sunday or when a friend got married in church, were much behind the times, not to say entirely ignorant of the western cultures and western religions.

122

It may be it is historical destiny (or fate) in these days (1982, as I type these lines) that the communistic dogma is not far from the Orthodox dogma. The first thing the Rumanian Communist government did was to "abolish" the Catholic church in Rumania by law, under the guise that in 1699–1700, when part of the Rumanian people joined the Catholic church of Rome where their priests were educated, it was against the Rumanian national church.

I felt, after meeting the foreign Rumanian leaders, that I belonged to an international society of man. But that was another anathema for most of the Rumanians. The strong overt belief was that when one is in contact with a foreigner he must be a Francmason and this was prohibited by law because it was said that the Francmasons wanted to dominate the world, through commerce, religion, or promises of money.

Now it was suspected that I must have been drawn to such a formation, which was at once feared, envied, and despised. I have never been a member of any lodge. As I learned of such organizations, I realized they were made up of people who elevated themselves above the level of narrow ethnic chauvinism.

A new "ideal comes to the Rumanians through the Iron Guard" to purify the Rumanian ethnicity, freeing the Rumanian people of schismatics and heretics—"all these being in the service of aliens." The more this movement moved on, taking adherents here and there among the students in the universities, the more I grew in doubt of "Rumanian purity." I came to the conclusion that it was an antediluvian concept, unbecoming any man, less for so-called intellectuals. Nevertheless, the Rumanian students who had joined the Iron Guard, who had one of the university professors, Cuza, among them, proffered that whatever was not orthodox was anti-Rumanian and should be extirpated from among nationals.

Again and again I heard on every side the discussed question of why I was a Baptist. It was said the Baptists were of foreign origin and that they had nothing to do with Rumanian tradition (the Orthodox church). They could not account for my beliefs. Some hinted, "You are a likable fellow, the judges like you, you have a good presentation in court, or even in other encounters, you are liked by most people although you do not take part in drinking or the card playing parties and such." Then some who knew my family said probably my father had not liked the village priest, resulting in my turning to alien sectarianism. These observations only served to increase my own faith—that man was created by God with intelligence, wisdom, and understanding and that the more one looks to the Bible showing how people of God journeyed in their life pilgrimage the more it was realized that people who sought understanding from God were always criticized. Then I recall my father saying that the Lord himself was despised.

It annoyed me no end when some friends would say, "Don't take your father's attitude. He should know better. One just cannot stand against the whole hurricane alone." I did not try to argue, and this disarmed my friends.

One thing I did, which in the sight of my "lower-educated" Baptist friends did not appear to be Christian conduct, I learned to dance, which I enjoyed immensely. I attended theater performances, operas, and movies. It was my view that I was not violating in any way my commitment to a life dedicated to Christ and his way by getting involved in "world's affairs of pleasure."

Because of the Iron Guard's getting more support from Hitler's Nazis, or for some other reason, I was told my father was put on the list to be one of the first in the community to be shot as the worst traitor to the Rumanian nation. In other towns there were others in the same category as my father. I might have been on the list—I do not know—but I was not alarmed. I talked to my father and he said he had heard one of his young neighbors had turned in his name to be added to the list; in fact, it was a teacher in the local school whom my father had helped to go to school in Arad because his father had died in the war. The Scriptures alone sustained my father. I looked at the teacher with pity. He would avoid me when I was in the village, and for a time I avoided him. But soon I just greeted him and said, "I trust you're doing fine!"

About seven years later, when the Communist party took over Romania, I was told it was John A., chief of the party cell in the village of Tisa, who put my father first on the list to be done away with because at this time my father was a capitalist. Yes, he had a mill—a water-powered flour mill. At that time my father had already fought in the war, and was not concerned about losing his life. His many brushes with death and threats made him immune to any life and political changes and only served to deepen his faith. His Bible reassured him that the reward for faithfulness is eternal life. His faith was not shaken by any adverse happening. His only concern was that his faithfulness remain till the end.

I saw in my father a fearless, unperturbed follower, a real man. I agreed with his philosophy that tragedies would come and they must be faced. But Jesus taught his disciples that he would be ready to help them in any difficulty. Also Paul stressed that this life is only a very dim mirror view of life in eternity in the presence of God.

The incident that occurred in one of my college classes when I was called before my class and told I had sold out to Beezlebub and the time I was told that I would not be allowed to practice law in the city of Arad and other hints here and there either as a joke or as a warning that I may be in trouble did not bother me. They instead made me realize that my friends were really ignorant as to what comprised a thinking man, a man of conviction. The only explanation they could come up with was that I was born a Rumanian Orthodox Christian and how could I betray my birthright? To me this was a very narrow and childish approach to thinking, to faith, or to some solid principles in life.

My meeting American Baptists and finding that there were other people who take their faith seriously was like a ray of sun in my grey habitat. In the early thirties a group of American girls was sent to our western province of Rumania by the American Southern Baptist Mission Board. They were intelligent, well educated, and easy to talk to. I enjoyed my friendship with Miss Smith. We were able to correspond about one year in the French language. One of the other girls married a Rumanian man by the name of Dr. P. Trutza. More than thirty years later, Peter asked me if I remembered my little romance with Miss Smith. I did remember quite well. I was still unmarried at the time and here in the States. He said she had married long ago and that her husband was either a minister or involved in denominational affairs. On meeting the Trutzas, she ventured to learn about George Crisan, the young Baptist lawyer in Rumania.

All these little incidents served to make me feel closer to my fellow Baptists. In 1936 or 1937 I took my first long trip abroad. I went to Zurich to attend the Baptist World Youth Conference. As a delegate of the Rumanian Baptists, I was able to make the trip, having room and board offered. In Zurich at the concert hall, which at that time appeared amazingly large to me, I met a young German girl at the registration desk. I learned she came from Dusseldorf. I thought she was one of the most attractive girls I had met among the Baptists. For about a year we corresponded and I proposed to her by correspondence. She tactfully declined, saying she could not consider going to live in Rumania. That reply set me thinking. It was made clear to me that Rumania and even a lawyer in Rumania both are far away from the life and interests of a German, English, or American girl.

From Zurich I went to Paris and London and I met many other Baptist brothers. I gradually came to the conclusion that Baptists may be as universal as the Catholics, who I admired for their outlook on man—not parochial like the orthodox.

It might have been I was the only lawyer in Arad who had traveled extensively, going to Paris, London, Switzerland, Venice, and Milan as well as other places. Some of my friends questioned the wisdom of spending so much money on trips. Some even questioned whether I was receiving remuneration or promises because I was a Baptist. They could not conceive that one could stand simply on faith. Money must be involved or some other benefit. I felt sad at hearing such conclusions.

It was not easy to start any type of profession in Rumania. I considered that I was just lucky to have accumulated some property and have a lucrative profession. But I did not consider myself wealthy. In fact, the factory became a burden: the time, concern for the labor, taxes, et cetera were arduous details.

V

THE WAR

From the city of Alba-Julia we went back to the town of Varias, a German settler town, in the rich farmland of the district of Timis. We were in constant readiness to defend the Rumanian borders on the southwest against any Nazi invasion from Yugoslavia. It was expected any time but, although as officers or soldiers we did not make comments on the war conflagration in Europe, we were half-assured that Hitler would not occupy Rumania by war, since Rumanian oil was badly needed for the Nazi tanks and Stukas. Hitler was happy with the French government of Vichy; the war in the African desert was not going bad for Hitler thus far; and day and night bombs were falling on great Britain and it was expected from day to day to hear that Hitler had crossed the Channel and landed in England.

As a reserve officer and a professional lawyer, now in readiness to defend the "sacred borders" of our motherland Rumania, from time to time I was allowed to take a furlough and tend some of the cases pending in my city courts in Arad.

My office and living quarters were located in the very heart of the city, across the plaza from the town hall, an impressive building with tower and columns in a combination of Greek and renaissance styles. My apartment was on the second floor of the building owned by the Victoria Bank. During the day when on furlough I went to the court, but at night I slept at Cousin Myron's apartment just across the boulevard. We played chess in the evenings and listened to the Voice of America broadcast. All the windows were covered with blue paper so that no light could stream through, thus avoiding the possibility of any Nazi recognizance planes.

During such a furlough, I was visited by Mrs. Marioara Pascu. Her husband, the Reverend Danila Pascu, had been the minister of the Baptist church in Buteni. The Buteni Baptist congregation was the largest in Rumania at that time. Reverend Pascu was not only the minister there but also the itinerant minister for the small Baptist churches in the villages along the Crisus River Valley. Among such churches was the church at Tisa, my native village. This church was built by my father. All these small churches had an ordained deacon or elder but no ordained minister. Each church, however, had a very active youth group in music and brass bands. In May 1939, Rev. Danila Pascu, together with two other young preachers, Luc Sezonov and John Cocutz, went to the United States to attend the Baptist World Alliance Congress in Atlanta, Georgia. Cocutz tried to persuade me to join them for the trip to the United States. Since I was still in active military duty and, with the threatening war situation in Europe at the time, I was not able to obtain a passport. On September 29, 1939, the war situation became even more dangerous when Hitler crossed the Corridor to occupy Danzig (Gdansk, Poland). Reverend Pascu was offered a church in America with the option to remain until the war was over. His wife and two young children had to remain behind. He tried in every way possible to get the documentation necessary for his wife and children to join him in the United States of America, but how could a young woman with two young children attempt such a trip across a continent under fire?

At the time I was amazed at the brave decision of this young woman. I realized anew that in human behavior the mother displays a courage and determination that is even greater than in the man. Marioara, with a boy of two years and a girl of four, made ready to leave Rumania for the United States to join her huband in Cleveland, Ohio. I succeeded in obtaining the passport for Marioara and two young children. I was the last Rumanian to hold the little boy, Dan Pascu, in my arms before the mother and two children took the train which would go through Yugoslavia, Italy, Southern France, and Portugal. From Portugal she would take the ship across the Atlantic to New York. The Atlantic was swarming with German U boats, and we heard daily of ships that were intercepted or even sunk.

But Marioara made her trip safely—without knowing any other language than Rumanian. We felt again that God's people make it. That little boy of two is today Dr. Dan Pascu, astronomer with the Navy Observatory in Washington, D.C. He is married to a wonderful woman, Julie, and they are the proud parents of three adorable children. They attend the First Baptist church, called the Church of the Presidents, in Washington, D.C. Such are the ways of the Lord! Miraculous!

Our "waiting" for something to happen lasted for almost two years. On June 22, 1941, Rumania declared war on Russia and the United States of America. During these years the boundaries of Rumania were chopped on the East, and on the West, according to Hitler's secret agreement with Russia, Rumania was losing Bessarabia and, because of the Hitler Diktat of Vienna, more than one-third of the province of Transylvania was ceded to Hungary. "Divide and Impera," said Julius Caesar. How true. From a medium-sized power in Europe, Rumania became a small power, almost, if not totally, powerless without a great ally, the Hitler's Reich.

By this time, the Baptist churches were closed, Bibles were confiscated, the Baptist folk were considered more unreliable than the Jews because they were "Rumanian ethnics." They were considered as having betrayed the mother church, which was treason.

I realized that it was better to keep quiet than to discuss Hitler's new conquests or victories or to comment with people you did not know quite well about the United States' response to Rumania's declaring war on it. Much, much later we understood that the United States did not accept the Rumanian ultimatum until December 1941, after Pearl Harbor.

Why should Hitler take Rumania as an ally to fight against Russia? Some promises were made: "When the war is over, Rumania will get back Bessarabia, which Russia took from Rumania following the secret agreement between Russia and Germany." It must have been also, "Come with me, Hitler's armed forces, or we will crush you down as we did France and Poland—England will follow." Then, as always, Rumania had been at odds with Russia—for many reasons—for a thousand years or so as near neighbors.

But I thought at the time, *It may be a real joke to join Hitler's victorious armies in Russia.* Hitler's armies were encircling Leningrad, Moscow was almost at cannon's reach, and Ukraina was almost taken. This section was the granary of Russia. Then we thought the Ukrainians might be happy with Hitler's delivery from Stalin's communism. All these things I was able to toss about in my mind, but I very seldom exchanged views with anybody.

Most of the active officers were eager to go right away into combat. Those young officers might have been entirely Nazified under the Rumanian Iron Guardist philosophy, "Rumania to Rumanian," meaning no to Jews and the sectarians, as the Baptists were considered by the Rumanian Nazis. These officers were looking for promotions, military awards and decorations, and even a lot of good-sized rich farmland, when they received high valor decoration.

The plain soldiers, all recruited from the peasantry, were neither enthusiastic nor defeatist. The Rumanian peasant is a fellow of long endurance. For thousands of years he lived in constant adversity: adversity of nature; adversity of the invasion from the East and West; despoliation by the landlord; and suppression by the Orthodox church, which is very fatalistic in outlook—"This too will come to pass." Some of the soldiers thought only of their wives, parents, small children, and their patch of land somewhere on the slopes of the foothills of the Transylvanian Alps. Their individual patch of land had been in their family since the dawn of history. Others did not seem to be restless or worry about the welfare of their families or their farm: "This will come to pass!" was their best "hope."

My orderly, George M., was a farmer from a little village in the higher hills. He had three children back home and once in a while he cried to me, "Mr. Lieutenant, will we ever be back home?"

"Of course, Mr. M., it may be over by the time we get down there in Russia." I comforted him with the thought that Hitler was almost occupying Moscow, and then the whole thing would be over. My orderly was not assured with this reasoning.

Over one night we embarked all our fighting equipment—cannons, horses, and all—in rail boxcars. Our men were to stay with the horses and equipment while we, the officers, had a third-class passenger car. We settled ourselves on one wood bench. We were not told where we were going, but evidently we were going eastward toward Bessarabia. After three nights we arrived at the banks of the river Prut, which divides Moldavia from Bessarabia, which was already liberated by the Rumanian armed forces before our unit arrived.

We dispersed throughout the houses of a small village. I was quartered at a small peasant hut on a mild slope with a fruit orchard on one side and a vineyard on the other. The woman of the house had two small children and spoke Rumanian with the mild Moldavian accent or dialect. She offered me a small cup of hot milk, which I accepted.

We had been ordered to refrain from fraternizing with the civilian population wherever we were for fear that they had been left behind as infiltrators or guerillas to destroy our lines of supply or blow up our ammunitions.

In spite of this, I did exchange a few words with this simple woman. She said she would rather not talk with me or any Rumanian military man. She said her husband was in the Russian army. She said when the Russians returned and heard that she had talked to the Rumanians she would be in deep trouble. But what really impressed me was that she did not seem happy to be "liberated by the Rumanian armies." She knew "The Russians will come back" because they were much stronger than Hitler, even when his forces were combined with Antonescu's.

The next night we advanced toward the capital city of Bessarabia, Kishinew. On our way we crossed the fertile farmlands of Bessarabia. The mild, rolling hills of this province, long renowned for grain, wine, fruit, and cattle, were indeed a prize gain for Russia. I was traveling through Bessarabia for the first time in my life. I had traveled as far as England in the West but not in Bessarabia when it was a Rumanian province. But so be it—as the French would say, *"A la guerre comme a la guerre!"* Meaning, when you are in war you must conduct yourself as a soldier, or, as we lawyers said in Latin, *Mutatis mutandi*, meaning *Be yourself in whatever circumstance.*

Kishinew looked deserted in the large streets. We passed by the building of Provincial Parliament where the first Bessarabian Congress had met in 1917 during the Russian Revolution, before the end of the First World War. That Congress followed President Wilson's principles of self-determination of the nations involved in the First World War to declare their independence from their centuries-old regimes, like the czar of Russia, and ally with the country they chose. The Congress of Bessarabia declared Bessarabia a free and independent country and then passed a resolution to join the Rumanian kingdom for "eternity."

I met one of the delegates at this historical congress in the United States in 1959. At age seventy he took refuge in France, a refugee from Bessarabia and from Rumania. He then came to America, and I met him as one of the members of the Rumanian Committee of the Association of the European Captive Nations. If he still lives somewhere in Missouri, he must be close to one hundred years of age as I write these lines (March 1982).

The next night we approached the high banks of the river Nistru, a large river bordering Bessarabia from Ukraina. I had not seen such a high and abrupt bank since the seashores near Constantz. We found our way in the valley and again we crossed Nistru River on the pontoon bridge, the horses and cannons and all.

We were then in Ukraina. The farmlands resembled that of Bessarabia but with less trees and vineyards and villages. We advanced quietly on wide dirt roads which had high telephone poles with the lines broken here and there. We reached a small town and dispersed ourselves among the houses and trees to camouflage our presence against any Russian spying or bombing planes. The woman of the house spoke Rumanian. I was amazed. She told me she was a Rumanian gypsy and that her husband was the blacksmith of the town, and he withdrew with the Russian army. She encouraged me by saying, "The Russians will be defeated because they are godless." She pointed toward the little church of wood on a hill, saying, "They made a warhouse of the church and God will punish the Russians."

I hoped for more encouraging words from her. But then I thought, *How much more are the Germans God-fearing people?* There was no priest in the village. The land was all worked in communes and at the end of the season each worker received something from the Russian supervisor appointed by the central authorities. She said it was hard work and one never knew whether he would get anything at the end of the harvest season. I thought to myself that the Russian army was not supported by the populace. The Ukrainians were deprived of their farms and of their livelihood and were enrolled in Kolkhoze. There was no church and no priest and there was no freedom to work when the time was proper, but at the time as "planned" or ordered by the unseen boss.

The next night we moved forward, coming closer and closer to the "engagement" in the "fire baptism," as we were told. We arrived in a larger village—a country town. There were large houses of brick, wide streets, and well-built barns and stables. But the entire town was deserted and it did not seem to be a recent happening but at least a year old, judging from the weeds that had overtaken the courtyards and streets. What had happened? Shortly after the Ribbentrop-Molotov agreement, Stalin had ordered that all German towns established in Ukraina by the Empress Catherine the Great (a German by birth) be evacuated and the population be moved somewhere in the interior of Russia on the river Volga. Nobody can tell where they moved to or were settled or dispersed. Stalin feared that the German population in Ukraina after two hundred years still preserved its culture and language. The German population had been a model to the Slavonic people in the way they built towns and farmed the land. They were evicted overnight by Stalin and deported to God knows where—perhaps to the immensity of the Russian steppes.

Later in 1945, when the tide of the war turned against Hitler and Rumania, we faced such a deportation. Russia occupied Rumania. After the war was concluded, the Russians asked the Rumanian government to gather two hundred thousand able-bodied German ethnics in Rumania and send them in boxcars to Russia to rebuild the devastated towns, industries, and mines. How many came back and how and when is the question? Nobody kept any account.

In September 1941, here and there I noted sheaves of wheat and even uncut fields of wheat. The straw appeared more like reed. I was amazed at the fertility of the land. Later, I understood the wheat was a hybrid form of wheat brought from Poland, resistant to drought and high winds, to which the Ukraina's steppes were exposed no end.

We were steadily marching southeastward toward Odessa, the city harbor of Ukraina on the Black Sea. Then the order came that the next night we were to take positions to support the cavalry and army in the assault of the city of Odessa. We marched through the night and arrived near a tree curtain, one of many that served to break the winds and keep some shade on the lands. We found our division sector. I had to place my two cannons on a little wallow. The Russians threw lighting rockets. My people and myself were almost mute! But we were at war and must proceed according to orders from the captain and from the colonel and ultimately from the army commandant in our sector.

I, as commander of my two cannons and in conjunction with the other two, was ordered to go forward with the telephone and two men, at a highest point, from where to direct the fire of the cannons. The area was quite abrupt with ravines and wallows here and there some bushes. The air was still except when machine guns were firing at some distance, probably four or five kilometers. But the lighting bullets were somewhat scary before I realized that they came and went unexpectedly and there was nothing to do about it. I had to move forward with the wire and be ready for the next two or three hours to direct the fire of my cannons.

I directed the fire as well as my knowledge of artillery was at that time. (I was knowledgeable in mathematics and in trigonometry.) The fire was supposed to be concentrated on a narrow sector. There was a repeat answer to my fire by the Russian cannons or machine guns or both. In the early morning the Russian planes flew over us. One came lower and fired on our encampment. Two horses were killed and one wounded. Only one soldier was wounded.

I stayed in this location for three nights. My orderly did not come with any food for me and my two telephone operators.

One night I got the order from the captain to come to my cannon and attempt to withdraw both cannons from that place because the cavalry and the army of my sector had withdrawn and I was in no man's land. The problem was how to disengage myself, as the Russians might come at any moment and take the area, including me and my cannons and my men. It was clear that as an officer I would not let the cannons fall in the enemy's hands but would blow them apart. As for me and my men, we would have to destroy my identification as a Rumanian officer.

Lo and behold, my soldiers, or horse servants we called them because they managed the horses, arrived with two pairs of horses for the two cannons. With my thirty-six men in all, using our hands and shoulders, we helped the horses to pull the cannons from the embankment, which was wet and almost muddy. This was accomplished by moving backward. We learned that day that we had been in no man's land for almost twenty-four hours. We succeeded in saving the cannons and most of the horses. As a result the unit was decorated with the second decoration for valor. We became heroes without really meaning it!

The battle for Odessa appeared to be at an end. We moved closer to the big city. Some of my soldiers were getting anxious to see the city, but no artillery man is allowed to go with the cavalry and army from street to street and quarter to quarter to be sure the enemy had been eradicated. I remember my orderly brought me a little pancake of sweet crackers. He got it from other people. This was my emergency ration—I had eaten once in three days. We had to move forward, this time northeast. Some news trickled through that the Germans had broken the Russian resistance and had conquered or occupied the other large harbor of Ukraine-Stalingrad harbor on the Volga River (formerly Zaritzin). The fall season was almost passed and the winds were blowing colder as we were going north.

At Christmas 1941 we were somehow settled in the town of Balta, meaning "the pond." It was a small town, a single large structure in which we settled. It was my first Christmas away from my parents and brothers and sister. I shared a room with my fellow lieutenant, who was a better friend with the captain. My roommate, being married, was allowed to go home to Rumania for Christmas. I remained and took my turn for a short furlough at a later date.

I discovered that my two sergeants at the cannons were Baptists and one of them had a pocket New Testament with him. He was anxious to share with me some thoughts concerning whether this might be the last war and so on. Moreover, he asked me when this conflict would end. We found maps of Russia. I was able to read in Russian and even understand it. Jokingly or not, I was able to show him just where we were on the map. I ventured to say, "If the Germans along with us move forward in Russia at the pace we were doing at the time then maybe in fifty years we will arrive at the other end of Russia at the eastern coast at Vladivostok."

In a joking way the sergeant told my estimate to another comrade and somehow the word reached Captain Groza. Well, it was a miracle that I was not sent up for court martial for my defeatist attitude in the time of war.

That incident made me more cautious in writing home or to my cousin Myron to whom I had written, "If there is a hell, I'm in it right now. This morning I woke up and discovered I had been leaning my weary head on a bunch of dry bones—probably of a German soldier—now completely dried by the sun of July. I had rested well because it was a night stop after too many miles riding my horse." My cousin Myron destroyed the card immediately. He was aware that such imagery was not to be expressed as it meant defeatism. This could be punishable by even death. Well, I realized that my slowly developing humor was not acceptable in time of war.

In the move toward the North, I met an old friend, Macavei Slev, who was with a cavalry regiment. We talked for almost an hour on a bright, sunny day. Someone snapped a picture of us together. This snapshot is the only one I have taken in Russia. In 1980, when I traveled in Rumania with my wife as guest of the Rumanian government, we met Macavei Slev in Bucharest. We learned he was seriously ill, and in 1981 I received word from my brother John that Macavei had been called home by his Lord. He was my age.

It was evident the Germans needed more support from the Rumanians. For a time we were led to believe that once Bessarabia was recaptured and even TransNistria taken under the occupation, our involvement would be at an end. Not so! The stubborn Russians would not ask for peace even though the Germans were shelling the suburbs of Moscow, or so we were led to believe. We must have been very close, but we did not know it.

My brother Titus served as sergeant in our twin regiment. The twin was originated when we declared war on Russia and the United States. His regiment was ahead of mine and paved the way for the march toward Stalingrad where carnage was at its peak. My brother, Titus, was a student when he was mobilized. One of his instructors

November 1941, meeting of friends on the battlefield in Russia.

had urged him to remain in school until graduation and thus become an engineer; then he would become a commissioned officer. A telegram was sent to him with the colonel's approval of a furlough to take the final examination. Titus returned to Bucharest and passed his examination with honor. He was not sent back to the regiment because the regiment had arrived at Stalingrad in the meantime. There was little information as to the real situation of the regiment. We learned it was completeley decimated and a few were made prisoners of war. One of the prisoners was a close friend of Titus's, and we learned he was enrolled at the Lenin Institute for Marxism Studies. Paul met me in Rumania during my first trip to Rumania after the war in 1970.

My turn to go on furlough came in February 1942. I recall the parting words of my sergeants, "Lieutenant Crisan, shall we ever see you again? Who knows, we may fall before you come back or you may never come back." It took me about a week to reach home traveling by horse and wagon, by riding and by train.

I discovered that life was moving along as usual at home. The news of a fallen friend or a relative brought its sadness and regret, but in general the main stream of life moved on. Life was moving on! I began to realize and feel within that somehow all must be a matter of conjecture. I could see around me the evidence of life's moving along from day to day in the same orderly fashion as usual; people were getting married, material businesses were prospering, attorneys had more business than they could take care of, and so on. It was bewildering to me. Cousin Myron, not included in the military because of a limp, became the attorney of a big company and eventually handled some of the king's matters in connection with the property he owned in our district of Arad. My conclusive private thinking was that the meaning or effort of war is not easily understood at any time. It is illusory and therefore difficult to be enthusiastic about participation when there seems to be no purpose and no gain—either personally or in behalf of the country. Again and again, words from Ecclesiastes came to mind, "Everything in due time." And God only knows that due time. No Hitler or Antonescu can know it!

Uncle Stephen was an excellent businessman, but this acumen did not extend to any degree in the area of public relations. He was too often rigid in his views regarding working conditions and labor relations, particularly at the factory we owned, Albert, Stern, and Crisan. Sigmund Stern, a Christianized Jew and a Catholic, along with his wife and children, was very cautious about doing anything new, as he was afraid someone might raise the question regarding his share in the company and there would be trouble from the Nazis.

Uncle Stephen tried to persuade me at the time to become the manager of the factory (bricks and lime), whose product was important for the national economy during the war. I told him this would be very difficult for me at the time. The rigors of the war were very difficult to bear. In addition, my leg, in which I had suffered the effects of osteomyelitis years before, was bothersome again. My uncle took me to a military doctor, Dr. Klein, for his opinion and treatment. The doctor said I should never have been drafted into military service because the bones in my leg were not strong enough to undergo the effort of mobilization. As a military doctor, Dr. Klein made his report to his superiors. I was called to report to the military hospital in Sibiu, where I was examined by nine or ten doctors. I did not hear the opinion of each, but the conclusion and summation of the examinations was that I could remain in the military but serve at the home base of my unit. I became the adjutant of the homebase commandant major in Timisoara. In addition, I had charge of the management of the factory, which had to produce its maximum for the national war efforts.

In March I learned that my regiment had moved forward toward Stalingrad. The regiment was destroyed by the Russians, who encircled the city after the Germans and Rumanians occupied it. General Paulus (if I remember his name correctly) wanted to surrender, but Hitler sent word to "stand fast." I do not know whether he was captured or died. But I do know that from my regiment, the Sixth Light Horse Artillery, only a dozen came back.

At that time, my homebase commandant, a major, was at the age to be either promoted or retired. He wanted to be colonel or lieutenant colonel. According to the rules, if an officer served at least six months on the "firing line" he was in a position to be promoted. So the major went to defend the position of Germans and Rumanians in Crimea, a peninsula on the Black Sea. His promotion went the "way of no return!" as a Rumanian saying goes. He was a very fine fellow.

At the homebase, I had occasion to befriend a Capt. John Bogdan, a former congressman from my district, Arad. He was an honest, likable man but somewhat cynical and a convinced democrat. He was a member of my party, the National-Peasant party, but we only tacitly recognized this fact, since no political parties were allowed in Rumania.

In 1968, when Eunice and our oldest son, George (aged 11), visited Rumania, John Bogdan went to see them and sent me his regards and love. He related that he had been in hiding since the Communists had taken over the Rumanian government in 1947. In 1948 he sent word to me that he wanted to meet with me. We met at the home of his sister at night. He said he was too old to attempt to escape across forbidden, mined, and dog-watched borders, but he said if I could send somebody or organize something, he might be able to fly or go by boat to Turkey. He said, "George, please do not forget me." He thought there were many possibilities and so many ideas for his escape.

It was learned that later, when he could no longer endure to remain in hiding, he gave himself up. He was sentenced to years of hard labor as an enemy of the working people of Rumania. He, himself, was the son of a worker. In 1965 Dean Rusk, secretary of state, stated that the United States would not consider better relations with Rumania when its government kept hundreds of thousands of its people in jail and labor camps because of their former political views. More than two hundred thousand prisoners were set free, John among them. He was free, but without a piece of paper in hand. He worked as a waiter in Timisoara. In 1968 he went to Arad to meet the wife and son of his American friend, George.

At the regiment homebase, routine activities moved along in a normal manner and were even enjoyable. We instructed recruits in the military techniques, preparing them to be sent to fight in Russia. All the news from the battlefront appeared to be encouraging whenever I went home. I would join my cousin for dinner at a good restaurant downtown in Arad. There we enjoyed good food, good music, and ersatz coffee, and we jokingly assured ourselves that soon we would have ersatz everything. There was dancing on these occasions. It was rumored that the *stukas* (Hitler's airplanes) were dominating the fields of battle—nothing could withstand the *stukas*!

But the Rumanians were somewhat cynical in their views; there was considerable doubt concerning all Hitler's claimed victories.

The Rumanian people had been under foreign rulers and domination for thousands of years. Here and there they succeeded in gaining a little independence but for only a short time. Rumania had been "an apple of discord" (something that is a subject of division) since prehistoric times. Rich in forests, wild fruit, hunting, mountains, rivers of fish, tablelands of grain and vineyards, plus the richest gold mines in Europe, Rumania had been exploited probably since about 1500 B.C. It is a historical educated guess that the Romans fought the Dacians in A.D. 107 and eventually overwhelmed them. The reason for the conflict was that the Romans needed land and the emperor needed gold and grain for the plebes in Rome. The Rumanians summed up by saying, "The Visigoth and Ostrogoths' migration eventually ceased. The Russians were defeated by the Ottomans, then the Ottomans were defeated by the Russians and French; the Austrians diplomatically gained or lost some of the Rumanian territories, so . . ." the word was going around, "This war will end sometime, and we Rumanians will not be forgotten by the French or the Americans or the British because we are Roman (meaning West-European culture and civilization) and are their cousins in one way or another—JUST WAIT AND SEE—the key word."

The Rumanians went along with the Slavonic people because they shared the same Orthodox, the true Christian religion; nevertheless, the Rumanian thought of himself, for reasons of his own, as superior in comprehension of the world or local problems, of political outlook, and even of the realm of culture. Why? Well, we continually claimed, whether jokingly or not, that we were the true descendants of the Romans, even of purer origin than the Italians and French.

Here was something I observed at the time: The Germans, our old friends who had settled in Rumania hundreds of years before, keeping their ethnicity, and some Catholics and some Lutherans, were now looking down their noses at their Rumanian neighbors and fellow citizens. It might have been a temporary abberation because of Hitler's racist dogma, but I thought any condescension was an incredible attitude.

Here we were, Hitler's allies, but not his friends or not the friends who would put life in danger. How could this be? Rumanian provinces had been given away by Hitler to Russia—a big part of ancestral Rumania—which we called the Cradle of the Rumanian nation, Transylvania. Hitler had chopped it up and given a big slice to Hungary, then turned around and asked the Rumanian dictator General Antonesc to fight with his Germans against Communist Russia and reconquer Bessarabia from the Russians, the province he had given to the Russians. Could there be any plausibility or sincerity in such a gimmick? Such was the atmosphere in Rumania among the intelligentsia while I was carrying on my responsibilities as adjutant to the commandant of the homebase regiment in Timisoara. I had long discussions with my friend, Captain Bogdan, sometimes frivolous, though meaningful, in order to keep our sanity. He reminded me, "We have to abide by the idea that now and here the Germans are masters but this will pass in due time!"

Thirty years later, John Bogdan, the self-made scholar and archaeologist, published a book on the prehistory of Rumania and the origins of the Roman (possibly Greek) alphabet. It's a very interesting study leading to the conclusions found in Ecclesiastes that "Whatever it was, it is now and forever shall be!" How is this statement explained? It is whatever interpretation each person finds for himself. It is a mental support and sustenance needed for finding a solution for every problem and difficulty.

On my trips to the factory at Dobra, some of my men there were anxious to know when the war would be over. No one knew the answer to this, and it followed that my assurances were somewhat evasive—"It will last to the end!" The peasant worker, with his philosophical outlook of life, accepted my answers as quite truthful. Life would go on as usual in good times and in bad, in war and in peace. This had always been so since the dawn of mankind. There's nothing new under the sun.

I stopped regularly at the legal counsel office of the Victoria Bank, as I continued to be considered one of their lawyers. I had good relations with the directors: Joseph Albon, Oliviu Sirbu, president of the bank, Dr. Nerva Iercan, and, of course, my old boss and friend, Dr. Theodore Papp, now Popa. There was business as usual there, if not even better during the war. The Albons had only one son. At eighteen he was drafted and selected to go to Germany for training. Hitler sent them into Finland to fight. They received news that he had been killed in fighting. One cannot find words of compassion to parents at such a time. He was a handsome lad, good and intelligent and with a promising future.

The balls and parties were many and social events filled our leisure time. We lived one day at the time. There were parties for card games, prohibited by law. There was the "running for the skirts" by the men—any age and any time, like the gossip of the evening. Some of my Baptist friends, more modest in their social status, and people from the countryside discussed among themselves and once in a while asked me, "Is this the world's end? We live like the people of Sodom and Gomorrah!" It seemed that everyone tried to live each day to its fullest extent, that tomorrow we may die! Or be mobilized and sent to Russia—a route with no return! Skeptic or cynic? Both.

Gradually and steadily we realized that the war with Russia was to last longer than we thought. Hitler did not invade Britain, either because he could not or was afraid of a fantastic defeat right on the shores of Britain or France.

The general mood began to change. We were saying, "The Americans will come—that will end the war."

VI

THE AFTERMATH

The American bombers came! My hometown, Arad, felt the damage. The railroad station and surrounding area were severely damaged. That night I was at my factory. People were saying, "The end of the war is nearing." Then Ploesti in the foothills of the Carpathian Mountains and the oil fields were heavily bombed, if not razed. The Rumanians in their hearts rejoiced. They sensed that the war would soon come to an end and that the Americans would not allow Russia to take over Rumania. Why not? No one could say for sure why not, but there was a feeling that Rumania, a Western people and country, with its politics formed an important buffer between Russian expansion toward the Dardanelles, the Bosphorus, and the Mediterranean.

We trusted American might and had not forgotten that there was a Greater Rumania because of Wilson's pronouncement that every people may determine its destiny of independence (1917).

The Germans were withdrawing with immense losses. Even today we do not know how many Rumanian soldiers perished at Stalingrad, at Odessa, or in Crimea.

I was awakened in my apartment in Arad on August 23, 1944, by the cry, "The war is over." It was not quite over, but everybody thought that for Rumania it was ended.

That night, the Rumanian dictator, General Antonescu, while in audience with King Michael, was arrested. The king asked for an unconditional truce with the allies: Russia, Great Britain, France, and the United States. Rumania accepted. It even turned to fight against the Germans, who were withdrawing through Rumania, in case they refused to withdraw peacefully.

I was in Arad when the Germans with their new allies, the Hungarians, occupied Arad and raised the Hungarian flag on the town hall across the plaza from my office.

As a Rumanian officer, able to carry arms, I was subject to immediate arrest and internment or worse. My brother, Titus, ten years younger, came to spend the night with me. The Hungarian army was swarming over the city's main street. An elderly German lady and her daughter lived in the apartment above me. They were staunch Hitlerites. I was in a precarious situation and must move quickly or be caught like a sitting duck. I said to my brother that we must leave the city at once. I went to the tobacco shop next door and bought several packages of cigarettes, speaking only in Hungarian with the lady behind the counter and appearing to be in the happiest of moods that we were back with the Hungarians, since the Rumanians took over the city in 1919 from the Hungarian Bolsheviks of Bella Kuhn. Meeting Hungarian patrols, I tendered them cigarettes, which they gladly accepted while I welcomed them in Hungarian, saying it was a great day of deliverance.

How were we to get out of the city? I made up my mind immediately that the shortest way to leave the city and toward the foothills of the Transylvanian Alps was through the leading artery, where the electric train was running. We encountered full battalions in march. We went on small and unpaved streets. About two hours later we found ourselves on the outskirts of the city and in the fields. We went toward the corn fields, not walking too fast as to attract attention—not too slow either. There were other people in the corn fields. Lo and behold, there was one of my clients, a Baptist fellow. "What are you going to do, Brother Crisan?" he asked.

"We are going to get through to the mountains," I answered. The foothills were occupied by the Russians and now probably with some of the Rumanian army.

Brother John M. joined me and my brother. The stretch of fields between the city of Arad and the town of Siria is about twenty kilometers. Siria is situated in the foothills and is one of the most delightful towns in Transylvania. The fields were not only of corn but of wheat, which was already harvested. How to get from one corn field to another was a matter of good or bad luck! The foothills were occupied by the Russians or their advance patrols. We were in no-man's land. So be it! I did not talk, but rather led by marching on. By the evening we had arrived at the outskirts of Siria, meeting no Hungarian or Russian soldiers, only once in a while did we hear distant machine guns firing.

My friend John proved to be better acquainted with the town of Siria than I was, although my brother John had lived there and served as the chief supervisor engineer on agricultural and winery matters.

John M. guided us to a house where one of his friends lived. Only his friend's wife and child were there. She did not know whether the Russians had or had not occupied the town. She was able to send someone to my brother's place to see how he and his wife and two small children fared. They were not in the house, and the doors were unlocked. Later we learned that they, too, were in hiding in the hills while the Russian and Hungarian armies were in the town.

We stayed overnight in the stables. Next morning before dawn we left and started our climb up the hills. We took the narrow and sharp-rising footpath toward the citadel of Siria (built probably in the twelfth century on the highest peak as a lookout for any enemy coming from the plains—like the Ottomans in the fourteenth century.)

We reached the wooded area, and we did not know just where the path would lead us. By late in the evening we arrived at a little village with not more than a dozen or so of little, thatched, one-room houses and with a larger stable next to them. The first woman to greet us did not appear friendly and hesitated about giving us direction toward my home village, Tisa up the river Cris. I had some money and bought some eggs from her. She agreed to boil the eggs for us and allowed us to sleep in her hay loft in the barn.

Next morning we proceeded farther along. The woman of the house where we stopped was unfriendly, though she realized we were Rumanians, gentry by our clothing. Mountaineers do not trust gentry or dark-clothed city people.

By the third day evening we arrived at Buteni, a larger town in the Cris Valley. I had friends there whom I had not visited before, but they had been in the home of my parents many times, being merchants of dry goods at the country weekly open markets.

We located these friends and they were happy to see us. After a shave, food, and a bath we were all tired. I really had not closed my eyes since I left Arad. The lady of the house then offered a bedroom for our rest. About an hour later she knocked on the door, crying, "Mr. Crisan, you must leave immediately. The Hungarians are fighting for the railroad station. They could be here in no time and catch you here. I will not be able to help you if they find you."

We left at once and took the narrow but practicable road along the Cris River and by next morning arrived at Gurahont where I had another Baptist friend and client. He had been in America and had come back home to be a merchant. Here we felt safer. My friend John left us here to go to his home village, which was not far from Gurahont. Titus and I took a train to Halmagiu. The train was not able to go farther than this station, because the bridges had been blown up by the Hungarians to forestall the advance of the Russians. The train consisted of the engine and several freight cars. It was traveling slowly, and we could see the Russians advancing cautiously. Soon they were coming in swarms from every direction, it seemed. It was the most amazing thing I had ever seen. An ocean of people marching! Early in the evening we arrived at my parents' home near the mill. The courtyards were jammed with carts and wagons and horses and oxen. These people had left their home villages, which were exposed to either the Russians or the Hungarians, and had taken refuge, looking toward the mountains. They felt somehow that at the place of George the miller they had a haven if even for a short time.

World War II came to an end May 9, 1945, by the German surrender to the Allies. In August 1945, there was a conference at Potsdam, Germany, between the leaders of the allied nations: President Harry Truman, Winston Churchill, and Stalin. It was the breaking point between the Western Allies and Russia's Stalin.

I was active as a young lawyer and still considered so in local politics. I was ready to do some of the chores that other party members higher on the political ladder would not do. The whole activity, in fact, was to go occasionally to the club and read some newspapers sponsored by the National Peasant party. Juliu Maniu was the president of the party.

In August 1945, shortly after the Potsdam Conference, a client of mine, a Baptist fellow who escaped from Arad with me through the mountains from the Hungarian occupation, brought me one typewritten page. THE RESULTS OF THE POTSDAM CONFERENCE was the title. It read, "The Russians are to withdraw from Rumania and other occupied countries; the Rumanians are entitled to have their own armed forces; the Jewish people from Russia and from other countries are free to immigrate to Palestine; that there will be free elections so that the people may choose freely their own system of government; that such elections will be supervised by the Allied Control Commission."

I was elated with this rewarding news. As a liberal-minded member of the democratic party, National Peasant party, I felt I had the right to distribute the good news to my friends. I typed this one page, made about twenty copies of it, and distributed these to a few of my friends. I did not get back any special comments.

IMPRISONED

Shortly after this distribution, while in my office, two men appeared at the door. I invited them in. One of them said, "We are officers of the security police. At this moment you are arrested. Do not make a move or shout or make a sign or even turn your head. You are to follow me."

I thought it was a joke. I did not take it seriously at the time but followed the instructions, since they were husky men and appeared to be rough characters. The offices of the secret police, or the National Security Police as they were called, were in the next block from my office. I had not known this before. It was in the largest apartment building in the city—the Newman Palace. I was taken there and shortly introduced to my investigator. He told me his name and I answered that I had a client by that name. He answered that the client was his father and made no other comment. He showed me the printed leaflet, copies of which I had distributed. He asked me if I had prepared it and who had given it to me. I answered that I had prepared but I did not know who had given it to me as I had many friends and clients, being the lawyer of a labor class of people who came to me even for counsel in family matters. The investigation lasted a long time, going along very slowly. Then one day a guard was called and ordered, "Take Mr. Crisan to the 'Politics.'"

So I had made an acquainance with a jail—an empty room facing the courtyard. There was a single wooden bench like those in public parks—nothing else.

The guard at the door apparently knew me and said that I might send word home to bring me a blanket and food. I sent word to my cousin Butariu, who sent his housekeeper, an elderly lady who started crying in the courtyard below my iron-grilled window. She brought a blanket and food for me. Next day I was taken back to the investigator, who asked me whether I remembered who had given me the leaflet. After my negative answer I was escorted back to jail.

Some of my friends heard of my being in jail and came into the courtyard and talked to me. One, a bold man, said, "George, you are a hero—the Americans are coming to deliver you and us all from the Russians and their stooges—your jailers."

That lawyer was Theodor Barbatei, whom I had met in one of my trips to Rumania. He said he remembered well when I was quietly planning to escape from Rumania. Barbatei recalled my saying, "The Americans would never come to deliver the Rumanians from the Russians," but he could not attempt to escape because he had two small children to consider.

He recalled, "It may be that you can do more for them from the free world than from here. How right you were, George. I was in jail and as result my daughters had a terrible time in school and in finding any place to work."

After about ten days, while at the daily investigation, the investigator, Aczel (Hungarian name meaning "steel") shortly brought in another man. I recognized he was my friend and saw that his face was badly bruised. The investigator asked me, "Is this the man who gave you the pamphlet?"

I replied that I had so many visitors and clients I was unable to say for sure. "You see, I am a lawyer of the Baptist folk, and they are many in number." Then Aczel turned to my friend and asked him in my presence whether he had given me the leaflet. He answered yes. That afternoon I was free. Not so my friend.

I felt that it was certainly a bad humor to have me detained and then dismissed without any prosecution and without being brought before a magistrate. I had to learn gradually that only one department of the Rumanian government (the Interior or the Security Police) had a Communist minister, Russian imposed. I thought justice was still in good hands. The Justice Ministry was headed by a Socialist party man, Patrascanu, who was later condemned and shot by the Communist justice on allegations that he was sold to the Western powers. Ten years later, while a legal analyst with the Library of Congress, I wrote an article on that man, Mr. Patrascanu. My supervisor got a special note of appreciation for my article from the Department of State.

It was during this period of time that somehow I discovered again some of my characteristics and the meanings of my destiny. Not concerned about tomorrow! Not afraid of what tomorrow brings! *Que sera, sera!* Now, I believed that since God had protected and watched over me thus far bringing me out of Russia and out of confinement in jail, surely there was some purpose for me in the future.

Stanley Catana, my correspondent friend in the United States, wrote me and invited me to come to America, either to see it or to study or even to remain there. At that time, I was becoming more solidly established in my business and profession, and I replied that I would think about it. He continued to send me all sorts of business for his clients in America to help their relatives in Rumania.

In April 1947, my brother Mircea married. Cousin Miron attended the wedding party with me in the town of Plescuta. It was late in the night when we left the little village by train to Arad. On the northern side of the sky there suddenly appeared a curtain of light, sort of shivering like from high up down to the earth. It was

Three generations of Crisans, Tisa, December 1942.

spectacular. I learned later that it was the aurora borealis. Those who saw it thought it was either a sign that the war was not over or one of peace.

My cousin was arrested the day after his arrival in Arad. I tried with difficulty to locate him, which was impossible. He was in jail for about three months. In another place in my memories I make mention of his tortures.

General elections were scheduled for August 1946, in which the country would choose their free Congress and Senate and get rid of the Russian stooges imposed on Rumania by the Russians.

I was a delegate of my party to supervise the Central Precinct with the balloting place in the town hall. The people came to vote in numbers like never before. We had not experienced free elections since the early thirties. The voting started at six o'clock in the morning and ended at six the next morning. We, the judge and delegates, were worn out physically, but the ballots were counted according to the rules. There were about 2,800 ballots cast for the National-Peasant party, and about 350 for the Liberal party and about 35 for the United Workers party. I asked the judge, who was a friend of mine, to sign the certification of results. He said he was so tired he could not lift his hand and that he must sleep or rest and then he would sign it. He went into the next room. In less than five minutes he came back and from the threshold said, "These are the results of the elections for this precinct: 3,200 ballots for United Workers party, 100 for the National party, and 100 for the Liberals."

I asked, "Are you joking? What is this farce?"

Suddenly behind him appeared the chief of the Security Police, Rafila, who said, "Mr. Crisan, if you disturb this session, I will have to arrest you." Nobody said a word.

I said, "I will see to it in court."

During the next few days, I realized that the Communists had falsified the elections throughout the country and the judges who presided were threatened with dismissal if they said anything about the forcing of their hand and heads.

RUSSIAN OCCUPATION

We lawyers, including the whole of the intelligentsia of Arad and indeed all of the country of Rumania, were waiting and watching the Communist movement under the Russian occupation. There was marching in the streets, put on by the local Communist cells, by order of their central organization or by order from Moscow. Continuous shouts were heard in the streets: "Down with the Nazis" (meaning any who was not a Communist sympathizer); "Away with the Allied Commission" (because it was supporting the former Nazis). They said, "In the election the people have expressed their will for a communistic government." Confidently, certainly not defiantly in any way, we looked forward to a time when the Russians would withdraw their occupation armies from Rumania, since Rumania had made a truce with the Allied powers.

The battle to join the party was enthusiastically high. The party was the Workers Block, the Communist front show, as inspired by Moscow. According to the top Communist leader in Rumania at that time, Anna Pauker, there were at the most about one thousand party members in the whole of Rumania. She was of Jewish background, had been a teacher in Bessarabia and had attended the Lenin Institute of Marxist Studies in Moscow, later returning to Rumania. She stated she had the confidence of Stalin and openly added that it was the duty of the "faithful" to recruit and enlarge "the cadres," which so far amounted to very little in a country of 19 million people with a peasantry of 80 percent of the population.

I hoped against hope, reminding myself again that there must always be hope in the heart of the Christian, that there could not be a communistic regime in Rumania. The party was practically or theoretically nonexistent and no mass expectation or desire for a radical change from an established peasantry-type society to a totalitarian one—communizing land holdings—changing radically a society whose usages and mores go back for five thousand years.

It was a typical Rumanian attitude—persistently hopeful, yet fatalistic, too. "Something will come to pass in some mysterious way to give us aid." "Surely the Americans will not give up Rumania, when they have economic interests here, e.g., telephone companies, oil refineries, and such." It must be remembered that Rumania had been a stumbling block to the Russian drive for open seas; it was the so-called window to the oceans, since she was a landlocked empire. All that was in the past the Roman luck—that Germans, Austrians, English, or French were interested in this land with a Latin background situated on a Slavic sea.

Something continued to bother me. In my thinking as a student of history and because of historical events that I had lived through, I was under the impression that Americans with their allies would not start a new war against Russia, their former ally. In Rumania or any other country I thought that wars just do not follow one after another without at least a generation between, which meant about twenty-five years. So I resolved to continue to do my best and wait and see what would happen. I felt it would be a good joke on the Communists when they would be overrun and wiped away like an annoying itch.

We of the intelligentsia were not ready to "rise to arms," nor were the peasantry, whom we claimed we represented. After the election people were disappearing in the dark of night without any trace and the families were not even daring to investigate. Only the Ministry of Security was Communist. There were other ministries that were entrusted to people of democratic concepts, former members of the Democratic parties in Rumania, the National Peasant party, or Liberal party. The prime minister was a general of democratic persuasion, the king was still there; Rumania was still a kingdom: how could it be communistic?

In the fall of 1947 mass arrests took place among the leaders of political parties under the allegation that they were plotting with the Western capitalistic countries to overthrow "the people's legitimate government." During these times, slogans were being posted and were emphasized in marches and song. There were special hosannas to the liberators, to Tovarisch Stalin, and to the glorious red (Russian) army. None would dare to speak any ridicule to such happenings. Your neighbor or your brother or even your parent might have had already disappeared in the dark of night. The most prominent of the Workers' Block advocates appeared to be of Hungarian, Jewish, or Slavic stock. There were many of the former Iron Guardists (formerly in the Nazi movement) who were either planted there or were looking for any party allegiance where there were strong leaders who would command others to go, do, shout slogans, sing, and so on, which I thought an average Rumanian national would not be found doing unless he was some sort of emotional person and not be able to judge things coolly.

In my father's village, the teacher who had been the head of the Iron Guardist movement became the chief of the Communist cell, together with the least reasonable people there. My father was put on the list to be eradicated first because he was the best known well-to-do man. Our family had owned the only flour mill in the town for the past eighty years. My father's affluence and influence went back many years. He had been mayor of the village and was the mayor who had built the bridge over the Crisus River. Because of his position and background he was considered an enemy of the people. My father built the largest house, of stone and mortar, in the town and donated it to be the first established school in Tisa. The village of Tisa was in existence as far back as 1436, according to a Hungarian chronicler. This same teacher had been recipient of my father's aid in receiving his education. It seemed unbelievable that when the time of crisis came he was found to be a person easily deceived by the enemy. He proved to be gullible to their every suggestion; another parasite to be absorbed. The faith of my father and my mother, and my faith, too, only deepened. We had only to remind ourselves that our Lord suffered many things and that our way would not be without difficulties. But according to our Bible we must continue to carry our cross daily and, as Paul put it, continue "to run our course and keep our faith."

The amazing thing was that some people of fine education and intelligence, who had held high positions in former governments, now were courting the communistic leaders, though imposed by Russia. Some of us, jokingly and privately, were saying these were "profiteers or parasites of fawning or ingratiating characteristics." Also, we sadly reminded ourselves there would always be turncoat people in whatever government.

The democratic newspapers were censored or suppressed because they were against the great liberator Stalin and his Red army. Who would raise a fuss about that? If one did, he might disappear in the night without the slightest trace. The cynicism was rising higher and higher! To save your skin you collaborate with the enemy in every way! What's wrong with that? You save your life!?

When my cousin was freed after three months in unknown places of imprisonment, he went to his office. The first day he received a phone call. When he inquired the caller's name, the reply was, "The police." He dropped the phone. He could not understand why the police called him. He just was not able to make it. What did it mean? Apprehensive, he left his home and stayed for some days with one uncle and then with another in the valleys of the mountains. I asked him to stay for several days with a cousin in the city of Timisoara. This put Cousin George in danger; he was jailed because he did not report to the security police that Miron was in his apartment.

I was trying desperately at this time to make some connections with the "black guides" people, who for big money would undertake to cross you over the border in Hungary and from there eventually help you cross into Austria and then, somehow, by God's mercy, to get you to the American zone. I went to Satu-Mare, the farthest north corner of the Rumanian town, which was only some miles from the river Sommes and, at that point, the borderline between Rumania and Hungary. There I met with a former girl friend of my cousin, who was now married. She was not able to help me. Then I returned to Arad, where I learned that a friend wanted to meet me. He was Miron's friend, too. He informed me of a certain young man who was willing and able, for a price, to take Miron across the border into Hungary and to help him to find his way into Austria. (The young man was about twenty-two—I failed to retain the name.) Miron had some gold coins, which he had not turned in to the National Bank as ordered, and two gold watches. These were offered and the deal was made.

Miron was still in hiding in the Cris Valley villages, where I arranged to stay until I would find "the way"! The weather was excellent in the fall of 1947. The grapes in Uncle Steven's vineyard produced a plentiful crop that year. I visited my uncle and aunt every week and during these visits little was said about Miron being a fugitive or of my having been in jail in 1945. The National Peasant party leaders had all been arrested at that time for subversion.

IMPRISONED AGAIN

On November 17, 1947, about 1:00 A.M., there was a knock on my door. I left my bed to open the door and there were two men who announced, "We are security officers—don't make a move and don't say a word. If you do we are authorized to kill you. You follow us. Do not look from side to side but keep your head down. Leave everything as it is." The men had very rough voices and attitudes.

I had never met such people, even in the military. I followed without hesitation and even without trembling.

Again, when I think about this incident I remember that I was not afraid; I was thinking, *This is going to pass, too, by God's grace.* I was taken about five blocks to the home and office of my former doctor, a Hungarian fellow whom I had befriended some time ago and who, in 1944, had gone to Hungary when the Germans and Hungarians withdrew from our area. I did not know that the Security Police of the city and district of Arad had its headquarters in my doctor's former home.

I was kept waiting only a short time and ushered to Rafila. I knew him by name but had not met him previously. Rafila was about thirty-five years of age, had sort of blondish hair, and was of average height, well built, and muscular. I was told later that he had been born in Russia and was brought to Rumania by his father, who had been a war prisoner in Russia in the First World War. His father had married a Russian girl and eventually, after the war, had been repatriated. What strange coincidences, that under the Russian occupation I was now a prisoner in the hands of a Rumanian (but Russian-born of a Russian mother in Russian Siberia) security officer, the chief of the security police of the district of Arad.

I greeted him, but he did not answer except to tell me I was under arrest because I was subverting the National Security and the Allied Control Commission (which in fact was Russian—the English and Americans were not taken into account by the Russians, since they were the occupying power).

"Are you a member of the National Peasant party [Pres. Julius Maniu]?" I was asked.

"I am, but I am really not at all aware or informed of the party leadership activities which were done in Bucharest—if at all."

"Do you know Marseu?"

"Yes, I have met him several times. Marseu was an elderly lawyer, the president or senior leader in the National Peasant party; formerly active in the National party in Transylvania, which brought about the making of Greater Rumania after the First World War. I have never been invited nor attended any meetings at his home or elsewhere. I have never talked with him about the party activities. I was a delegate of the party at the elections (where I saw Rafila from a distance in the mayor's office)."

After several moments of investigation, I became calm and relaxed before my investigator, Mr. Rafila. (I do not remember his first name, if I ever knew it). In Rumania one was usually called by the family name.

The interrogation was held in the chief's office, he, sitting, and I, standing. There were long pauses between questions. Once he turned to me and said, "Do you know that I have the authority to shoot you dead here and now?" He pulled out of his back pocket a hand gun and laid it down on the desk.

"Of course," I answered. "I suppose you can do whatever you want to do, I am in your hands. I cannot say more than that I am a Baptist believer. I am not concerned about dying. I do believe in the eternal life with God and Jesus the Christ in Heaven." Then I added, "I am the attorney for the Baptist people; most of whom are poor workers or poor farmers. I was defending them in the court under the Nazi totalitarian regime of Marshal Antonescu when they were accused that they were Communist inspired. I am interested at the turn of events now. I am accused by a Communist officer of conspiracy against the socialistic regime. I was persecuted during my student years, both at the college and as a law student." There was no answer to my words.

About 2:00 P.M., a guard came in and asked him to answer the phone. He went into another room to answer the phone call. After the phone conversation he said he was going to a soccer game and would be back later. I was left in the cigarette smoke-filled office. The guard came in and opened the windows to let in fresh air. It was a glorious fall day. Alone in the room, I went to the window and looked down into the street below. I realized my location was across the street from a lawyer's office. He was an elderly lawyer who had been dealing in cases involving towns, grazing pasture lands, river beds and so on. He had been a recognized member of the National party but presently was not actively engaged.

Standing there by the window, I mused, *If only some of my acquaintances would pass by on the other side of the street and spot me here and tell others of my predicament! Otherwise, I'll just disappear like many others.*

At this moment a man appeared on the other side of the street on the sidewalk. I recognized him—a Baptist fellow, who had had an arm amputated because of an accident in the stone quarry at Virfuri Quarries. He knew me quite well, as his home village was near my father's village, Tisa. Many times we visited his Baptist church, and the brethren from Virfuri also visited our church at Tisa. Then, on several occasions I had assisted him in some legal problems. He entered the door across the street from my window. I was sure he was going to the old lawyer, who dealt with communal holdings, including the communal stone quarry. Should he come out soon, he might glance toward my window and see me. But if his visit were long, my investigator could return and close the window, and I would just "disappear into the night," as many of my friends. There was no way to discover the places of detention, as I knew from my experience with my cousin Miron Butariu in the spring and summer of 1947. Was this to be my turn now?

Shortly, the small gate in the building across the street opened widely and my Baptist friend came out. He glanced up toward my window, spotted me, and called out, "Hi, Brother Crisan, what are you doing?"

I hastily put my fingers on my mouth and only answered, "Pst!"

He cried, "What is it?"

I whispered, "The secret police." He looked stricken. I mentioned Paul and Brother Dragan. He understood and started up the street, almost running.

I moved away from the window and sat on the chair and moved about. The guard came in several times but said nothing and neither did I.

Evening came and it got dark. It must have been 9:00 or 10:00 P.M. when the investigator returned. In the next room he answered a phone call. He came into the room in a rage. "With whom did you speak in my absence?"

"With nobody," I answered.

He said, "Don't negate! Here is the pistol on the table. I can kill you right now and here!"

"Of course you may, I am in your hands" was again my answer.

Again he spoke, "Look, I am not kidding. This is a matter of life and death. With whom did you talk?"

Again I answered, "With nobody." Then I added, "It may be that someone might have seen me in your office while the windows were opened. I have so many acquaintances, Baptist laborers, and many more Orthodox Hungarians, Germans, and Serbians who are the bulk of my clientele. Someone might have seen me. How can I tell who he might have been? They all know me quite well, but it would be incredible for me to say that I know each of them."

He moved about the room like an enraged tiger (amazing grace)! I was quite calm as I remembered I was in the thick of the fire in war. He kept repeating the question, "Who was he?" and this went on for about two hours. Around midnight he said, "I am letting you go free under certain conditions. Find out the man who saw you here." Then he gave me a blank sheet of paper and requested me to write as he dictated: "I will find out who saw me. I will report to you when I receive any word from the party's [National Peasant party] headquarters in Bucharest; I will report to you when I receive any news about anything told me by YMCA in Bucharest [I thought he knew of my being a member of the local board of YMCA some time before the war and then shortly after the armistice in 1945]; I will report to you any meetings even if only two people will meet and any other thing of interest."

In other words, I was committing myself to spy on my party members or divulge anything they might have done. I signed the paper. He put it in a folder and said, "See this as I put it in the safe. And you watch out! Anything you do against this signed paper, or that you do not disclose, will be counted a crime."

I assured him I would be willing and ready to report anything I saw or heard. But again I reiterated that I had never been a member of any committee because I was a Baptist and the senior members did not want to have sectarians among them.

It was late in the night when I was freed once again! It was a great feeling. Somehow God was working in a mysterious way to help, I felt. I went home walking along on dim lit streets to my apartment and office. I soon fell asleep and next day went about my business as usual. Of course, I said nothing about my being almost two days in the clutches of the secret police.

With extreme caution and great care I set about to travel to see Miron, still seeking a way to get out of that tight jail, Rumania. With a little money he had left and with a few French gold coins (francs) I located a guide (so-called "black guide") who on December 24,

1947, took him from Satu-Mare into Hungary, crossing the river Somes at a point the guide was sure it was not watched in the night of Christmas Eve. The river was frozen but not to the extent not to be able to wander about between the larger blocks of ice. That was it. But now how about my own skin now that Miron was gone?

A YEAR OF FATEFUL DECISION

I was anxious to learn whether any of my friends would be able to help me. I was extremely discreet in my every movement. I found that my Baptist friend who saw me in the window had gone to Brother Florea Dragan, who was the chief accountant of the city of Arad, a Baptist fellow and close friend of mine. Florea went a block only to tell my godson, Paul Tiurbe, an attorney whom I had helped to enroll and finish law school and become a practicing lawyer. He went to John Palincas, close friend to us both. John had, for "political reasons," spent a couple of months at my father's home in the Transylvania Alps. He enjoyed his stay there very much and it was a time of refreshment for him. My father did not know him previously, only knew that he was a friend of his son John and probably of George. And, too, he was an attorney.

John Palincas became mayor of the city. His friends and acquaintances were much puzzled when he was "elected by the crowds" gathered in front of the Town Hall shouting, "down with the Nazis." A friend of mine was the mayor of the Liberal party persuasion, and his deputy was a former classmate of mine, Octavian Lupas. People were saying, "Well, well, so John was elected mayor by a bunch of gypsies." Some of us who were a little closer to John thought he was a National Party fellow. He might have been. Again the idea of saving one's own skin occurred; for a bowl of "lentil soup" one easily trades his birthright.

Whenever that transformation was of John from a Democrat to a Communist or to Workers-from-Party member took place he must have remained faithful to some principles. Otherwise, I cannot explain why he came to call on Rafila, my investigator, the dreaded chief of the secret police, to speak in my behalf and to persuade Rafila to let me go free that very night.

After King Michael resigned and left, many of the intelligentsia

159

were thinking that now one must join the party or else he may be lost forever in the night. There was still some wishful thinking expressed that now King Michael was out of the country there would be opportunity to talk to the great Allies and persuade them to order the Russians to get out of Rumania. After all, Michael had asked for a truce and Rumania had fought with the Russians against the retreating Germans.

After these happenings, I did not dare to stay even two nights in the same shelter. Too many of my old or young friends had been taken away just as I was in November, with no trace of their place of detention.

The Corso was no longer the place to walk and meet your friends. Nor was the restaurant at the Dacia or the coffee shop at the Konigsdorfer or Malka frequented by anybody. In fact, they were closed most of the time. But they were opened once in a while to appear that they were doing business as usual. This was not the case. There were no goods to be sold—no coffee, no pastries!

At this point, I realized that there was no hope that Rumania would revert to some form of democratic regime or that the Russians would just go! I thought that with my factory and the money I was earning I would be able to secure help in obtaining a passport to leave the country by train and then, once in France, to stay there. I had traveled to Bucharest several times seeking assistance and I had some good connections, which I thought would help. A friend of mine from the military, Redis, was a cousin of the chief of the National Security, Bunaciu (I understood his mother was a Baptist). I even offered my factory "to the nation" in exchange for a passport, but this was tactfully rejected. I remember I went to Bucharest five times that winter of 1948, but to no avail. On March 30, 1948, I went to the court to attend my cases. The custodian of the building barred me at the door with the information that I was not to be allowed to enter the court and that I was on the list posted by the door. And he added, "You have been disbarred from the bar organization by the Ministry of Justice." I was shocked, but not for long.

I went to my friend the mayor (president of the local bar) and he told me, "Ghitza, this is not within my authority or my doing. I received my orders from Bucharest."

This only added to my understanding of the communistic rule of doing things, that one individual, regardless of his place in the administration of government, was only a little cog in the wheel, moved by another and by another and all in turn by someone at the top of the pyramid. He suggested that I write the bar office and request information about why I had been disbarred. I did so and in a few days received a card authorizing me to get in the courthouse and go to the bar organization office. I found a piece of paper ready for me that read, "G. C. disbarred because: (1) he is a member of the National Peasant party, which is anti-workers; (2) he had an undemocratic attitude during the elections in 1946; and (3) he has other means of existence." (The last statement probably referred to my lime and brick factory.)

I filed an appeal against such a removal from my profession. It was denied in a few days with the comments, "Unwarranted" and "The decision was not appealable."

I did not sleep even for one night at my place any longer. Good friends of long standing who happened to see me on the street pretended they did not see me. In a very short time I realized I was a "stigma-marked" man. Marked for what? Marked to be removed "from the march to victory of the workers' liberation movement"? Such slogans were posted everywhere—the town hall or the treasury administration building or the two district executive buildings or on any private buildings. No one would dare deride these things. In fact, there were no more jokes at the corner of the Corso or at home. It seemed that everyone lived by himself, having no communications with his neighbor or even members of his family. It seemed that now "even the stones, the walls, or the trees might have ears or eyes."

I spent my nights at the home of Aunt Anne and Uncle Stephen. My uncle only said, "This is coming to pass," but he would not elaborate even among us three. They welcomed me to spend my nights in their home but said it was not the most secure or safe place, as everyone knew we were close relatives and it would be easy to locate me.

Several times during the day time I went to see my closest friend, Aaron. Now I found the big gate with the small door carved in it locked. His mother-in-law asked me to stay to dinner, remarking, "You will eat what we eat."

I accepted and asked if I might sleep on a sofa in my friend's office. This was allowed, but little was said. I could see that they

161

were more scared than I was by their sheltering me.

Several times I went to my godson, Paul Tiurbe, who had helped me get out of jail in November 1947. He now had two small children. He said to me, "Godfather, as long as I have a piece of bread I will share with you. Please do not be concerned about your 'tomorrow.' "

While I deeply appreciated his care I also realized he knew more than I did—that my fate was more seriously in jeopardy than some others. (Paul was a Baptist from a Baptist family from the district of Bihor.) It was said of him that he was clever enough and had the faculty of turning the sails according to the winds! I knew what the saying meant. Because things were changed politically, it would be well that I mold myself accordingly. The Communists demanded submission and praise for their work for the people; there were shoutings against the "workers' traitors," meaning that whoever stays aloof from the communistic demonstrations day in and day out was a traitor.

I remember many things about that time. Every day it was a problem to find an inconspicuous place to sleep. There was welcome, but I felt I might be putting in danger those who took me in for even one night. Several times I went to my parents'. I slept in the old house in the Big Run Valley where I was born or I went to the home of Aunt Betty at the Youga Run or to the home of Uncle Alexander. None of these relatives, including my father and mother, asked me why I was running like a hunted animal. They were all aware of the reasons and their only comment could be, "We have you in our daily prayers."

On two occasions I walked from Tisa to Dobra where my factory was. I crossed the Moma mountain range accompanied by another man my age and my youngest brother, Silviu, from Tisa, who knew the way better. We stopped on the very top of the mountain where the forester's lodge was located.

The forester, Ioan Darau, was my parents' godson. In fact, he had been my father's servant for many years. He had learned to read and write from my father and was hired as a forester later. He was from the same hamlet of Tisa as my grandmother, and we were far-distant cousins.

We were royally treated at the lodge. I remember there was honey freshly taken from the beehive. I had not had such a treat

162

since before the war. They did not make any comment on the route we had taken through Dobra. They knew very little of my situation at that time. They rarely descended into the valley to the town, which was about twenty miles away.

The forester's place was in the center of beautiful surroundings. There were, in addition to the beautiful views of the mountains, spring water, walnuts from the forest, unlimited firewood, and mostly clear skies. Living there was like a retreat from daily life and its involvements; a sort of withdrawal from life. They had a patch of land in the clearing where they cultivated vegetables such as tomatoes and potatoes. They also had crops of hemp and linen, and even a patch of corn.

After descending the south slopes and once reaching the run, a footpath led to the next little town of several straw-thatched houses. Farther along the run became deeper until after another forty kilometers it emptied into the river Mures, which connects many districts in Transylvania. It goes through the district and the city of Arad, my home town, and eventually crosses into Hungary and empties in Theis. This range of mountains makes up a part of the Transylvania Alps. It is also called the Metallic Alps, because from time immemorial there were open mines excavating gold, silver, and copper. At that time the mountains were covered with virgin forests of beech, ironwood, oak, and in several south slopes, wild walnut. The meadows were surrounded by hazelnut bushes. It might have been that the Romans, like many conquerors following, were looking for timber or gold and copper mines or open meadows to supply the necessities of the increasing population in Italy or elsewhere, and once the area was conquered they distributed large estates to the legionnaires. This apparently is the explanation for the development of the lordships and *latifundia* (large landed estates) that developed in the Dark Ages and flourished up to the Renaissance. Not far from my limestone quarry at Dobra, there was a slope about 6 to 10 miles long, covered with wild walnut trees.

The question to be settled now was what to do with the plant at Dobra. The factory had stopped at the time of the currency conversion because there was no money to operate it. In August 1947, the currency was converted into a new currency. One new unit, *leu*, was equal to twenty thousand old *lei*. But the capitalist people, bourgeoisie, got nothing for their old currency. We had several

163

billions in the bank for operating the factory and for paying the workers, taxes, and so on. We received nothing except a piece of paper acknowledging that we had deposited the entire amount of our money in the National Bank.

However, the slogan was, "When a bourgeoise stops producing, he is counted a criminal, a despoiler of the people, and worthy to be eradicated, a parasite which must be disposed of."

My administrator at the factory said to me, "Mr. Crisan, these people do not know what they are doing."

He was of German extraction, a fine man and a faithful administrator. I had known him as a clerk in the orphans' court in Arad, and when he retired I hired him as administrator at the factory.

Time seemed to pass slowly in the circumstances then, but in looking back it was only a short time from the date of March 1948, the date of my disbarment, till May 30, 1948. Living the two months seemed an eternity.

On the night of May 30, 1948, my administrator at the factory called me by phone. Sobbing, he informed me, "A group of several people came to the factory and said they were taking over the factory and everything in it and on the premises. They also informed me in specific terms that you or your partners would not be allowed to enter the factory area to take anything from it, even personal or professional items."

I thought this must be a prank. There was no law that private property could be taken from the owner. On the contrary, the owner was ordered to keep production in force at his plants.

I called on the district of Hunedoara executive, a former lawyer whom I had met only once before. I gave him my situation and he replied, "It is now no longer necessary to have a decree or enacted law in order to take people's property. These things are not well understood at this time, but please be assured, Mr. Crisan, that the party's only interest is the good of the working class."

He did not say, but it was clear, that there was no recourse against the "people's action" in taking my property.

I faced my plight: barred from my profession; not allowed to collect fees owed me; my bank account liquidated due to the fact that nothing was returned to me after the conversion of the money; and my factory taken. Job's story in the Bible came to mind—"Naked was I born into the world, naked shall I return."

Even now a peace of mind came over me. I thought of all the things that had happened to me in recent months. I had been concerned with collecting fees due me; finishing my clients' work in courts; concerned with my factory and its ongoing existence. I considered further persecution. Then I reasoned within myself. The Lord had given me much and other "lords" had taken it all away. I could only say in my heart that the name of Almighty God, in Jesus Christ's sacrifice, be praised. There occurred to me that this was the amazing refuge in the time of need. I also realized to the fullest extent that now there was nothing to bind me to Rumania, to Arad, Dobra, or Tisa. There was nothing except my parents and my brothers.

I thought back over my life. I had started working at the age of nineteen and by God's grace had amassed a fortune. Now it was all gone. At forty years of age I was the "poorest of the poor." I was also a marked man. I was not allowed to take a job because I had been an "exploiter of the working class!"

I felt that my time of freedom was running out and what could I do? First I went to a town near the Yugoslavian border to seek a way to flee through Yugoslavia. There were several Baptist brothers there. I had met two of them in the military and I looked them up. They were not happy to see me in their town. They kindly received me as their brother, however. I left on the next train. Otherwise, they would be forced to report to the secret police that they were sheltering a stranger in their home.

What little information I had been able to obtain from one of them revealed that trying to escape through Rumania in the Yugoslavian border had two dangers: (1) the border was well supervised by the Rumanian border police and by the Yugoslavians (the relations between these two countries were at odds since Tito had broken away from the Socialist Russian bloc); and (2) equally important, I only knew a smattering of the Serbian language. I knew a little Russian, which might have been detrimental. Also I was told that there were rumors that the Serbian border police would shoot, point blank, any trespasser without questioning. Furthermore, those who were captured were put in jail or sent back to spy for Yugoslavia. Then somehow in conjunction they were just "felled" or "exterminated" while forced back into Rumania.

There were rumors that some tried to swim the Danube in

Yugoslavia. But once captured they were treated like those who passed the borders. Another escape possibility was to go to the Black Sea shores and hire somebody to take me to Turkey. But nobody could be induced to do this unless you had a lot of money—enough to buy a boat—and then try your luck to escape through a very stormy Black Sea.

I had helped Miron escape through Hungary. He had arrived safely, according to word I received by word of mouth (always dubious) and now was in Austria.

I went to Oradea, a city very close to the Hungarian border, to try to make a connection of escape but had no success there. I then went to Satu-Mare and learned that the connection I had made for Miron had moved. I was really afraid to talk to anyone about my desire to escape from Rumania. Now the area of my freedom was closing in.

I did not dare to talk even to my brothers John, Titus, or Silviu (who was seventeen and in industrial high school). I had been looking after him and was concerned with his finishing school and eventually being admitted to the School of Engineering.

In July 1948, through very devious maneuvering, I was told that the mayor of the city, John Palincas, wanted to see me. I went to his office and he received me immediately. After shaking hands with me and saying *"Servus"*—a Latin word for "your servant" or "salutation," used only between close friends on a first name basis with *thou* instead of *you*—he opened the door of a little room next to his office. He invited me in and, while standing, he said, "Ghitza, I wanted to see you and tell you that I do not understand why you are still here. You have friends abroad."

He said nothing further. This was the last conversation I had with him since he became mayor of the town. (I have since returned to Rumania twice—the first time in 1970 and the second time in 1972.)

This visit to the mayor's office was an eye opener to me. I now realized the precariousness of my position. I must act now. But how? *How, where, and when?* was my every thought. On every hand there were constant incidents of somebody's being caught trying to cross the border by the police or police dogs, tried in a summary fashion, and sentenced to life or years of hard labor.

There were rumors that people like me looking for a way out

of the country were trapped by former friends, made to pay or give anything of value such as a watch, a ring, a few silver or gold coins, and then security was alerted and they were found to be guilty of high treason, of possessing gold (which had been ordered to be turned in, even a wedding ring or family watch).

Many stories were heard of those who attempted to escape and were caught. But there were a few stories of incredible flight and safe arrival in a free country in the West or even Turkey.

One day on the street I came upon a friend, Nerva Iercan, the former bank president, who in the course of our conversation said, "When you escape I wish you could put me in your suitcase and take me with you."

I had no way of knowing why he thought I was trying to escape the country! His wife was Jewish, they had friends outside the country as I did, and they knew I was a Baptist. Whatever the reason for his statement, I did not dare to enlighten him that I was indeed trying to find a way out of the country.

My godson Paul wanted to give me his version of sound advice. He reminded me that a lawyer in Rumania might find it extremely rough going in another country where he did not know the language and could not become a lawyer in another country. He also reminded me that as long as he had a crust of bread it would be shared with me. He went on to say that his lawyer friends and other intellectuals shared his views. They felt that their future in another country would be bleak because of the language barrier and because they had no training except for writing papers and so on.

When I was five or six years of age I remember my grandfather loaned money to some young peasants, enabling them to go to America to work and to return home with enough accumulated funds with which to buy a piece of land and even a yoke of oxen to till the land. While in America they did not learn the language but worked in the woods, or on the railroads, or roads and came home with enough money to establish themselves and even acquire a home and family. But what can an intellectual do in France, Germany or America? Beg, starve, die?

I felt that these alternatives were quite clear: that a lawyer of any worth is valuable only where he speaks the language of the country. I considered my own case: I was a lawyer, not trained in any other profession. Although I was the owner of a factory, I did

167

not work with my hands in the lime or in the brick making.

I enjoyed gardening, but had done it only superficially and occasionally. I had planted trees at my factory, but only in a supervisory way. I had gathered apples and pears and plums and peaches in my father's orchards or on my factory grounds, but only for my enjoyment. So at that point my mind was in a whirl: considering my present situation and my immediate future, should I stay and run the risk of the same fate of so many others or persist in pursuing ways of leaving my country? I remember that many nights at the home of my uncle or my brother-in-law's I hid out in the stables so as to be undiscovered in the night.

The story of Abraham gave me encouragement and comfort—why had I not thought of it sooner? He followed a word of God heard only by him to leave his home and country. He did not hesitate, but went! Then think of the story of Joseph: one of twelve children of Jacob who was sold into slavery by his brothers and because of his complete trust in the providence of God's leading became prime minister of the country. The paramount principle in the life of these men was deeply impressed upon me: they dealt successfully with new situations, a new life in another country with a people unknown to them, and they not only survived but prospered.

I thought back over my life. I had prospered in the country of my ancestors, but now my country had been conquered militarily and politically by Communists whose god was the party, ruled by the great liberator Joseph Stalin, who showed neither pity nor mercy to one who would escape this steel cage, socialistic Rumania. I thought of my own difficulties because of my allegiance to a new sectarian religion, the Baptist way, and I thought of my father who had had hardships beyond description and who did not falter in his personal beliefs.

I had helped my brothers obtain their training for the profession of their choice: one was an agriculturist now transferred to the other side of the country; another, a textile engineer; and the third, at seventeen a student in the industrial college (high school).

A former classmate, Vasile Tulescu, stopped by for a visit one summer day. I remember that he was an excellent student when we were in school together. He was now far up the ladder of success. He was the Rumanian cultural attaché in Berlin, where he had remained during the war, and the rise and fall of Hitler's empire. Vasile told me that he was jailed after his return home. His wife divorced him and his children were with her in Bucharest. He then lived with his mother in the little town of Firiteaz, Banat. He spoke perfect German, probably more accurately than the native-born.

To what extent could I divulge my present situation to Vasile? Could I trust him implicitly? Could it be possible that he might be an agent of the enemy? It seemed that all was in chaos—there was no order or trust in one another even down to the members of one's own family. It was a time of turmoil personally and nationally. Which way could I turn? Whom could I trust? I was discouraged to the point of questioning whether I could trust anybody at all. I had hit rock-bottom.

So the summer passed swiftly and the days began to give cool nights after the warm days. In August a message was passed to my aunt that Annie Moraru, a girl a little younger than I, wished to see me. I wondered what she wanted. I recall that I had been in the same regiment as her brother. There was another brother who was in the twin regiment.

I met her at her job, where she was employed in the Workers' Welfare Office. I was in agreement that this was the best way to communicate where nobody would suspect that I was a "pariah." I knew a little of her background. Her brother Pete spoke excellent English, her parents having been in America, where their three children were born. Pete knew that I was a Baptist. Also I knew that Pete was an ardent Hitlerist as a Rumanian Iron-Guardist. Pete, fearing that he might be captured by the Communists, disappeared from sight.

Annie had very little to say at our first meeting at her office. But she invited me to meet her at her cousin's home in the suburbs of the city where we would be able to talk at length of "something which would be of great interest to me." She was waiting at the door when I arrived. Shortly she said, "There is someone here whom you know," and when she opened another door Pete stepped into the room.

Of course I was surprised because I thought he had left the country, but I managed to hide my astonishment of the moment. After his sister left the room, Pete explained he had returned from Germany to help a certain well known and well-to-do doctor get out of the country. As it turned out, the doctor was afraid to attempt to leave.

Now Pete informed me he was ready to help me escape. What

strange things and circumstances! I had known Pete somewhat casually as the brother of my closer friend Aurel and his sister, with whom I met occasionally in a social way.

How could Pete be so open and casual in making such an incredible proposition to me? Had he really been to West Germany, returning through the Iron Curtain? And now, having arrived in Rumania, was he truly planning to make the return trip? He hurriedly explained that his time was extremely limited and that his offer to me was also very limited. I asked if I might consider taking Vasile along with me also. He agreed to this plan but said I would have to pay for both of us. It was a question of money and had nothing to do with friendship or of my past friendship with his brother when we were in the military together. In my desperation in this short time of decision I knew above all I must make the attempt to escape. "To be or not to be free" was uppermost in my mind and heart.

Pete gave me his brief and sketchy plan with little detail. I eagerly accepted his curt instructions. I was to get in touch with his sister Aurelia. This I did within a few days, meeting her in another relative's home. She was ready to give me directions as well as the cost of a "black guide" to lead me out of Rumania and across the Hungarian border. The amount of money asked per person was enormous. I trusted Aurelia that this whole thing was not a hoax or a trap of any kind in order to extort money from me. I had heard that people had paid phenomenal sums of money to procure a black guide out of the country and that some had put their entire fortune into gold, which had a great value at that time.

My brother John had his property at Siria in partnership with Ilie Motu. I wondered if they could or would consider to help me. The amount of money needed would be about the market value of a carload of grain. I went to Siria and talked to my sister-in-law. My brother was at work quite a distance from home. She said she would call on Ilie Motu (a Baptist brother) who would do for John or me anything possible. When I met Ilie he quickly informed me that he had just sold a carload of barley and had the amount of money required and would let me have the money to carry out this unique opportunity to leave the country. He advised me to leave at once. Within a few days I had a brown bag of *lei* (Rumanian currency) which, if I remember correctly, must have been about twenty thousand dollars.

With the money in my attorney briefcase, I was to go to Pecica, a large town bordering Rumania and Hungary. I was given the street number where to go and ask for a certain feminine name who will answer, "Yes, I was expecting a package from my sister at Arad." She instructed me to just talk from the street and not come into the house. She took the brown bag and told me to wait for further instructions, which would be sent to the home of Aunt Anne in Arad-Sega (a suburb).

I took the commuter train to Pecica and visited the town office of Aaron Ponta, a lawyer and former classmate of mine. He had accepted work in the County Executive Office to be near his parents and his wife's parents. I had luncheon in their home. His daughter, not yet a teenager, played the piano quite well. I did not give Aaron any details of my visit there or why I stopped by his office to say hello. But he gave me the needed directions without question and I carried out the instructions given by Pete's sister, Aurelia Morar.

When next I saw Aaron 28 years later, he told me that he felt sure at that time I was trying to escape from Rumania. He said after I left he was interrogated on several occasions about my visit there but finally he was let go. Of course, he was telling the truth, for I had told him nothing of my plans. Aaron shed tears as we talked over these things when we met in Arad at the college for the fiftieth class reunion in 1976. We became close friends and still correspond.

As I write this recollection, it seems a century, not like eight months, since King Michael left the country, and since I was at the Security, since. . . . At that point I made the final, irrevocable decision—I was getting out of the country as soon as possible, and I hoped to take Vasile with me and to be guided by Pete Morariu and his connections in accomplishing the whole thing. Vasile was as anxious as I to get out of the country but was assured that we would have to wait for word from Pete.

I spoke to no one of my intentions but did mention to my father that I was taking a little trip and did not know when I would return but was leaving it all in the Lord's hands. My father bolstered me in my faith, saying that the Lord would guide me in all things. My mother added that their prayers would follow me wherever I might be. I also mentioned to my young brother Silviu that I was considering leaving, but gave no explanation of details.

171

VII

ESCAPE

THE word came that on September 18, 1948, which was a Saturday, we should be ready to leave. We were instructed to also take bacon and bread to last for a few days. No other instructions were given. When I arrived at the home of Uncle Stephen there was a carriage drawn by two horses in front of the house. The driver, a Hungarian peasant, told me that he would wait there awhile, but that Vasile and I should walk on and he would catch up with us after leaving town where the road leads into the fields.

I thought of my young brother, Silviu, who with tears in his eyes had begged me to take him, too. But I explained patiently that I could not attempt such at the time but that he must finish his schooling and I would be in touch with him later. It was about thirty-four years later that Silviu arrived in America. He arrived with his wife as an immigrant on June 28, 1982.

As I write these lines I remember that I was not frightened as I prepared to depart my country, but felt somewhat as I did at the time of war: This is my "fate"—I am leaving to attempt to reach West, God willing!

Vasile bothered me a little. He was practically deaf in one ear, which resulted from the incessant bombing in Berlin during the war and before Hitler's surrender. He was no longer the young and best athlete in our class of 1926 and the star of our soccer team in college. Yet he had the daring and bravado to start out with unquestioning faith in my arrangements and in Pete's integrity.

So I walked out of town, with Vasile walking some distance ahead of me. I never looked back to see whether I was being followed. And Vasile never looked back to see how far behind I was. The road left the city and turned into the cornfields. When I reached the cornfields, the carriage soon arrived and the driver casually inquired if I wanted a ride. I climbed in and soon he picked up Vasile, and after another stretch he stopped to pick up Pete. This was about sunset, and soon it was getting dark. We entered a rough, narrow road leading through a field. Not one word was spoken!

After about fifteen kilometers we arrived at an isolated farm-house in the middle of a field. This was in the Theis plain of rich farmland. The corn was tall and healthy and green.

We were offered hot milk to drink, but I remember I did not take any. We were offered a place to sleep on the floor on a sheepskin mantle such as is used by the shepherds watching their cattle and sheep in the fields. I could not sleep, but Vasile soon dozed into a nap. Pete told us that the farmer would awake us shortly after midnight to go through more fields and reach the border into Hungary. There were no lights. The wartime order of no lights at any time was still in force.

FIRST CROSSING!

We were awakened or rather urged to get up and pick up our belongings and prepare to leave. This we did, following the farmer's directions—at times crawling on our hands and knees where the wheat had been harvested. There was an almost full moon that night, and it was covered only at intervals by clouds. After about two hours of wandering through a forest of cornfields we suddenly came upon a newly plowed field. That was the gap. We had to wait while our guide went ahead across a stretch of land on his hands and knees. His signal to us was to be the light of one match, at which time he would be over the border into Hungary. It was a matter of about 300 yards. We crawled the distance. The field had been plowed and harrowed in order to easily trace footsteps and to enable the dogs to easily trace trespassers. After we crawled that stretch of land and met the guide, we had to go another kilometer or two. I lost all sense of time or length of the way. It seemed an eternity. We finally approached a farmhouse, or rather a stable sur-rounded by a mud wall, in which there was a little gate. We were ushered in. The guide went to see the owner, who must have said it was all right for us to sleep in the stable as there were no horses or cattle about. The guide left after shaking hands with us but saying not a word. He departed to make the return trip across the fields and prohibited stretch of land.

It was almost daylight. We settled somehow in the mangers on top of cornstalks of a earlier crop.

The feeling that we had crossed this most incredible abyss—the first border to escape and freedom—was overwhelming! Could it be possible that we were free while still behind the Iron Curtain? We were in Hungary, only a few miles across the border from Rumania and the city of Arad. We had been led through escape. It was not a dream, it was a reality. It was exhilaration to the utmost, and my spirits soared in keeping with it. In my mind and heart there were feelings of praise: *God has shown mercy; we are out of prison; we are free!*

Somehow, we Rumanians had always felt that perhaps the Hungarians would not show cruelty to escapees due to their leanings toward the western world even more evident than in the Rumanian people. The Rumanians and the Hungarians and the German settlers had lived side by side in Transylvania for more than a thousand years and all together had been well administered by the Austrian Empire. Here we three escapees were given shelter in a stable on a farm near the town of Battonya about fifty or so miles from the city of Szeged on the Theis river. I had not been in Hungary before except when crossing it by train from Arad to Vienna with a stop in Budapest, at which time we were not allowed off the train. I was born in Austria-Hungary (1907) when Emperor Franz Josef the First was in power and king of Hungary. Though a Rumanian ethnic, I was an Austro-Hungarian national until December 1, 1918, when the Rumanian ethnics, by popular vote, gathered themselves together in the end of the war upon the disintegration of the Austro-Hungarian Empire.

Now, I was abroad from Rumania and from my home city, which was only forty miles away.

But back to our location in the stable. It was cold and uncomfortable. I peeked out the small window to see a sunny day and soon went outside to try to get warm. There was not a soul in sight, but I could see other houses along the field road at some distance. Vasile and Pete were still asleep. Soon a young man appeared in the pathway and greeted me, saying, *"Jonapot kivának!"* (good day, I wish, in Hungarian).

"Jonapot," I answered.

He inquired if I was related to the household within, as he had not seen me before. I answered him in the affirmative, saying I was on my way to the West where I had relatives. I added that I was a Baptist and had Baptist friends in Paris, France. He told of his travels in Rumania as far as Constantza, the Black Sea port of Rumania. Without much ado, we were soon talking to one another in the Hungarian language like two old buddies. He spoke the Rumanian language, but spoke Hungarian much more freely. I managed the Hungarian easily.

The conversation soon reached a crucial question: where was I going next? I mentioned my plans of going to Budapest and said that from there I would try to get a train to Sopron (a border city in Hungary near Austria). He then offered the information that he was planning a trip to Budapest and would be glad to guide us the next morning to Bottonya Station and the train going to Budapest.

I explained that there were three of us fellows and that we had no identification cards or tickets. He assured me that he would get the tickets and would come to pick us up at 4:00 A.M. to hike to the station, which would take about an hour by foot. So Jeno (Eugene in English) made good his word to help us, and I felt within that he was a godsend in our need to try to make our way to freedom.

Toward evening the man from the farmhouse came to offer us some bread and bacon, which we thankfully ate, and to draw water from the nearby well. We explained to him that we would leave early the next morning to catch the train to Budapest. He made no comment and we gave no other explanation. I felt sure that he had been paid by the man from Rumania who had received the head-money from the brown bag.

The evening drew on early in late September, and we were tired and were hoping for a night of rest. But it was not to be. Soon we heard soft knocking outside and approaching footsteps in the light of a lantern. Then there was repeated knocking on the door with a demand to open up and come out with upraised hands. We were accused of being spies amid curses and with the announcement, "We are the people's police."

I shook Pete and Vasile awake, and when I opened the door there were a sergeant and a soldier standing there with Jeno right behind, explaining that we were honest people.

The sergeant screamed at us as they came into the stable, "Raise your hands! Drop your weapons! We've got you—you SOB's! Rumania pigs! Traitors—spies."

I started to walk toward the sergeant, but he ordered me to stop where I was. I knelt with my arms upraised. He searched my pockets. I embraced his knees, saying, "Sir, I, too, am an officer, and as you know an officer would not degrade himself by lying. I and my friends are not spies, we are on our way to the West where we have relatives. We have little in the way of money, but I have a little Hungarian money and two wrist watches. This is all I have. Take what I have and give to your poor in your town. We are not returning to Rumania, where we would be shot on sight." (The amount of money I had would amount to about thirty or forty dollars.)

The officer accepted the offer, took the money, and gave us permission to leave. He advised us to hurry in order to get the six o'clock train to Budapest. I reminded him that he had all the money we had with which to purchase tickets. He agreed to give money to Jeno with which to purchase our tickets. Jeno bought our tickets when we reached the station, and when we boarded the train it was Jeno who presented our tickets to the conductor, and we were on our way.

We hardly dared to speak to one another, even in Rumanian, but we realized that Jeno had betrayed us and had called the police and might have also been in agreement with our landlord of one day. But at least we felt free again. Now the question of getting away from Jeno was uppermost in our minds. We arrived in Budapest in about five hours. The big station was crowded with passengers going and coming, laden with their luggage. We went out in the street, looking for a street car stop. There was Jeno ready to buy tickets for us and asking our destination. What could we do? We must get away from Jeno, but he seemed to be in charge of things. Pete suggested a plan to us. "Let's move toward the exit of the street car and at the first stop, get off and go in different directions for a little way. Then we'll get together and decide what to do."

We did as Pete suggested. At the first stop we got off the car, leaving Jeno behind. When the car disappeared we got together. Pete said he had some acquaintances in Budapest, but he did not know whether any of them would be willing to take us in. It might be the same situation as in Rumania—no one was allowed to shelter strangers for more than a couple of hours without reporting to the manager of the house or, if it was a family home, to the street housing supervisor.

I recalled the name of a former client, George Dobra, whose inheritance case I had successfully handled in the court of Arad and then in the Appellate Court in Timisoara. Dobra was a cousin of Mrs. Sabo, mother-in-law of my closest friend, Aaron Crisan. Aaron was a lawyer and had not wanted to take the case, which was quite involved. The estate was quite substantial, including a vineyard and villa on the beautiful slopes of the town of Cuvin.

I had met Dobra only once in Arad when he came to look after the estate left to him. He was an orthodox Rumanian, born and raised in Budapest. He was employed in a big factory of sorts. His wife was Hungarian and spoke no Rumanian. Could I call to mind his correct street number? Was it 5 Hollo Utza? I had no papers of any kind except my reserve officer pocketbook, which I might need for identification purposes.

Here in this big city, I felt free again. Here nobody noticed you or followed you and nobody knew who you were and where you were going. There were street maps posted at the streetcar stations which enabled one to find his way without asking the direction.

Pete went on his way. To this day, I could not understand his actions. Did he really intend to guide us to safety across the border into Hungary? Did he intend to then leave us without further direction? There were rumors that many posed as guides, taking fortunes from those who sought escape. And I still wonder whether my meeting Jeno was a mere coincidence. Had he been apprised by the owner of the stable where we spent the day and night in our journey?

The next thing was to locate Dobra. We found that he still lived at the same address. We went to 5 Hollo Utza (5 Crow Street) and found Mr. Dobra in his third-floor, one-bedroom apartment. His wife was away at work at the time. Dobra invited us to stay until we could go on our way.

I do not remember how Pete went about locating Dobra, but he informed him that he would not be able to guide us farther on our journey and that we must try to get out of Austria the best way we could. He maintained that it would be easy since the Austrian police would not question us in any way. He also suggested that the quickest way would be by train to Sopron and then by foot of the railroad station in Austria near the border. We could not question Pete. He was a former Iron Guardist; he had been in the West, coming back to Rumania, and was now with us in Budapest! Perhaps, he did all he could to help us without endangering himself.

I mused, *Vasile has no money or anything of value to help in our escape*. And now I had nothing left after the Battonya incident. I only had my small briefcase, in which there was nothing but some bacon wrapped in a linen towel and some onions and garlic. I remembered my grandmother using garlic in her cooking and of reading about this purest of herbs in the Bible stories about the children of Israel and the use of it in their food. Somehow, it seemed a sort of stimulus or a link with the past.

How could we proceed without a guide? I even wondered if Pete had disapproved of my bringing Vasile with us since he had contributed no money to our escape plans.

It was Dobra who boosted our spirits and made arrangements for us. We were to go to Sopron by train and from there to a certain home not far from the railroad station and remain there until dark, after which we were to go to the streetcar crossing in the middle of the city, look for a young officer in military uniform, and go past him along the streetcar tracks to the end of them at the limit of the town.

With these instructions in mind, we stayed at the Dobra home five days. We played chess mostly, which was about the only recreation available. There might have been danger to us if we ventured about the town. But I did go out on the street in Dobra's neighborhood. I discovered a Rumanian Orthodox church. I recalled that the brother-in-law of one my classmates, Ilie Ardelean, was the parish priest there. I could not recall his name, but Dobra knew him, as he attended the high holy days' mass at that church.

I dared to call him by phone. His wife answered. I explained that I was a friend of Ilie, her brother who was now a medical doctor in Cluj, Rumania. She referred me to her husband, who stated he was the priest of the Rumanian Orthodox church in Budapest, but that he was not closely acquainted with his brother-in-law. I drew the conclusion that we would not be warmly welcomed at his place or even his church.

We stayed at the Dobra home until Saturday morning, when we boarded the train with tickets purchased by George Dobra. He told us he had arranged everything for us and that we were not to be afraid of any trap or hindrance. He gave us sixteen dollars—a ten dollar bill, a five dollar bill, and a one dollar bill—and said it was all the foreign money he had. He also gave me several forints to drink a lemonade in the station at Sopron, to give us the appearance of being at home there, he said.

We had been at ease and happy at Dobra's home and hated to leave. But we must continue our flight to freedom into the unknown.

Dobra went ahead of us to the railroad station to purchase our tickets. I then left first on the way to the station and Vasile followed in sight. Dobra was waiting on the station platform with the tickets. He shook our hands with a "Good Luck," and we boarded the train.

In about five hours we arrived at Sopron, which was the end of the line. The train did not cross the border into Austria. There had formerly been a transit system between Hungary and Austria, but this was no longer in use since the Russian occupation army was stationed at this point.

Austria, like Germany, was divided between four conquering powers, each holding under occupation a portion of Austria. The part of Austria bordering Hungary was the Russian Occupation Zone of Austria. At the station in Sopron we drank a lemonade as planned and then walked along the street and to the proper house to stay until dusk. The path to the house led to the kitchen in the manner of most houses in Hungary and Transylvanian Rumania.

Soon a young woman appeared on the path leading from the kitchen. She said her husband, who was at work, knew of our coming. She asked us to leave the premises, as she was afraid she would be in trouble with the police. She said, "As you know, this town is close to the Austrian border and one can get in big trouble sheltering strangers or foreigners."

So we left, but what to do next was the big question. We could sit for a while in the station, but not for long, as we would be suspected of being strangers there.

THE NEXT BORDER—INTO THE RUSSIAN ZONE OF AUSTRIA

What a long afternoon—it seemed unending! We did not know what to expect. When darkness fell, about seven o'clock, we went to the main street of the city, where the street car rails crossed one another. There was a young officer in uniform, and he recognized me. He smiled at me and said, "I am your man! I am your friend, so do not feel afraid here. Everything will turn out all right! Follow my directions. Walk ahead of me along the rail tracks and I will catch up with you." The sky was dark and the streetlights flickered like little stars on the pathway. After a mile or so the tracks ended. In no time the officer was behind us and said he would go a ways with us. It was a field road or a large path in the fields, leading somewhere!

After about an hour or so of stumbling along over holes and crossing ditches, we came to a whitewashed stone post. The officer stopped and said, "This is the border stone; from here on is Austria. Keep walking in this direction for some miles and you will come to the railroad station at Eisenstadt. There you may take the train to Vienna. But be very careful you do not miss the direction of the tracks, because here at the borderline there are many signs that may be confusing and you might find yourself back in Hungary. I wish I could go with you, but my father and mother and younger brother are here and there would be great trouble for them if I should leave. Goodbye!"

I replied in Hungarian, *"Isten ágya meg!"* and *"Köszönem szépen!"* (God bless you, and Thank you.)

Now we were no longer in Hungary. I thought we would soon reach the railroad tracks and the city, but not yet. We started walking onward but we were hindered in our progress by the little ravines and ditches in the cultivated fields; ditches separating one field from another; little creeks deep enough to get wet to the knees after the recent heavy rains. We seemed to be walking in a sticky, clay-mud sort of way. Once I fell into a creek. Eventually, we saw a whitewashed border stone. We realized we were heading back into Hungary. God forbid!

I knew we were supposed to follow North. I was confused. Were we completely disoriented at this point? Nonetheless, we plodded on. The tracks embankment was quite high because the fields were so uneven. I knew we must travel close to the embankment no matter how difficult it might become. And Vasile could hardly keep up with me, even though he had been a notable athlete.

It was almost full daylight when we arrived at the station, which appeared to be entirely deserted. There were no lights on anywhere. There were no freight cars on the spurs. But there was the usual well with wheel and bucket which worked. I thought it would be a good idea to wash the mud off our shoes and clothes. When I started turning the wheel to take water, there was a blinding flash-light from the second story window with the command, "Don't move or you'll be shot. Drop your guns and raise your hands."

We followed orders quickly. Two Austrian uniformed police officers and a man in railroad uniform came out. They were the chief of the railroad station and his security, the border police.

We were escorted into the station and questioned at length. Now it was Vasile's turn to answer in a perfect German to the questions. He was also the interpreter between the police, and station master, and me.

"Who are you?"

I produced my reserve officer's identification. Vasile had no identification other than his good German speech and his word. They opened my briefcase and there was the bread with a Hungarian stamp on it. It was a requirement that bread be stamped to show that it was manufactured by the government and not by a private bakery. This was true in Rumania as well.

Vasile tried to ask me if we should say we were returning to Hungary, but I knew this would not work; in addition to the stamp on the bread there was a small tube of toothpaste I had bought in Budapest. So we stated that we were indeed Rumanians who had crossed into Hungary illegally and had entered Austria illegally, trying to find our way toward Western Europe to reach either the American Zone of Germany or France.

The police officer said he would have to turn us in to the local police. The town of Eisenstadt was about four kilometers east of the station toward the Hungarian border. After about an hour we arrived at the local police head quarters. We were covered in mud and completely exhausted. We were given a can of water and a brush and shown the well. We did the best we could to rid ourselves of the mud on our clothing and shoes. We even shaved. The young police officer offered us hot tea, which we gratefully drank in the waiting room. We felt almost good! Almost free! We marveled at the kindness of the Austrian police.

We were ushered into the captain's office to await his arrival. The questioning began all over again. We told our story; we were trying to reach Western Europe because we had relatives in France and the United States.

"Do you know anybody in Austria?"

"Yes," answered Vasile, "I have a good friend in Austria, Dr. Johan Strauss, Jr."

The captain laughed. "This name is the best known here in Austria. Do you have any other acquaintances here?"

Then Vasile answered, "But I am very, very serious. I have been a personal friend of Dr. Strauss for many years."

"Do you know his address?"

"No, but I do believe he must be at his summer resort at this time, which is at Bad-Aus-See in the American Zone of Austria."

The captain gave the order to contact Dr. Johan Strauss. The operator came back with the answer that indeed Bad-Aus-See had Dr. Strauss listed, but there was no answer when his phone was called. The captain had no further questions but asked whether we had any Austrian currency. We had nothing but the sixteen dollars in American currency. He then said we should have to change it into Austrian currency or we would be considered smugglers. It being Sunday, the captain said he would have one of his staff go to the post office and have the American currency changed into Austrian. We agreed gladly.

The young officer who had so kindly given us hot tea came and said he would show us the way. We went through a small gate in the walled courtyard that led out into the street. We could see where we were, in the small town of Eisenstadt, in the foothills of the Austrian Alps.

We followed the officer to the end of the street. He stopped and said, "It is the law that I have to direct you to leave Austria and return to Hungary, the country you have come from. Do you see that wooded hill? That is in Hungary. You may wish to return by that point."

We were stunned and did not know what to say. Our hearts failed; so this was what was happening after the kind treatment of the police!

Then the officer turned the other way and said, "Do you see that road wandering through the fields? That is the road by which you were brought in this morning from the railroad station when you were apprehended. Did you notice a big plant structure? That's the sugar plant. It is kept under the control of the Russian Occupation Army."

He paused and looked us full in the face, "The train to Vienna leaves at 4:00 P.M. Good luck to you both."

What could he mean? The train leaves at four o'clock and there was the Russian Occupation Army on the other hand with patrols along the road.

Vasile spoke up, "Let's cross the fields and reach the other side of the factory, where the Russians are."

"That is not a good idea," I said. "This is Sunday and there's no one in the fields and we will create suspicion by our appearance there."

"Then's let's go to the road and go around the town and follow the road to the station."

We set out to go around the town border on a narrow road, made up of footpaths for the most part, and arrived at the main road, which was graveled. We were walking along the edge of the road when we heard the ringing of a bicycle bell behind us. He caught up with us and I noted with horror he was the officer who had directed us to return to Hungary. I thought, *May the Lord have mercy on us and give us strength in still another trial in our escape journey.* He called out to us that he was on his way to see his girl friend in the neighboring town and would go along with us until we passed the factory where the Russians were stationed. He took my small suitcase onto his bicycle to relieve me.

We passed the factory and probably went one more kilometer. The young officer said he turned on the next road and handed me the suitcase and said, "I turn on this road. Good luck." Then he was gone.

I thought to myself that this incident must be of the Lord's doing. And in fact, our experience in Eisenstadt, including our kind treatment at the hands of the station master and the kindness of the police officers, must be God's grace. Are we actually in a civilized country—Austria? Is it actually true that Austria is the cradle of civilization of the largest part of Europe? I concluded with thankfulness to God for their kind and helpful care to us and I wished for their continued good will toward others who would need their aid.

At the station, where we previously had been trying to draw water in the early morning, we found crowds of people going and coming involved in the usual daily bustle and activity. We enjoyed a bowl of soup, for a few kreutzars—less than a shilling. People were sitting around the tables playing chess and enjoying the mild sun of late September on the station cafe terrace and drinking real coffee. It seemed a foretaste of heaven just to be drinking real coffee and playing chess all in the Russian Occupation Zone of Austria. It seemed a miracle!

The train arrived on time at 4:00 P.M. It was crowded and the freight cars were open to passengers, if needed. Vasile and I chose the freight car, where we would be less conspicuous. The train had its own police force, but we saw no Russian soldiers.

It was dusk when we arrived in Vienna. We came out into the *Hauptbanhoff!* (main station), which was in the Russian sector of the city of Vienna. The city of Vienna was divided into four sectors: Russian, American, French, and English.

Vasile said the first thing to do would be to call a friend—a business friend from the days when he was the commercial attaché of Rumania in Berlin. He could not recall her first name but said her family name was Schwartz. After searching through pages of Schwartzes he came to the name Heddy and was sure this was the correct name. He found a public phone and called. Professor Schwartz answered the phone saying that Mrs. Schwartz was in and would come to the phone. She recognized her Rumanian friend Vasile, asking "Where are you—take a cab and come out at once! We will pay for the cab."

She added her street number and we found a cab and went to the address given, a two- or three-story building with a private entrance. Professor and Mrs. Schwartz anxiously awaited our arrival. They were amazed and almost unbelieving as they listened to Vasile's incredible account of our escape and of the many incidents attendant to it.

It was late in the evening, but their hospitality was welcome and heartwarming. We were offered cold dinner and a room in which to spend the night. And a bathroom with running water! It was my first experience with automatic hot and cold running water!

We learned that Professor Schwartz was a law school docent (assistant professor or aggregate) at the University of Vienna. He had not met Vasile previously, since he was continuously in the military as captain in the Austrian army.

The Schwartz home was in the French sector of Vienna. During the next few days they attempted to obtain identification cards for us to travel through the Russian Zone of Austria and to go into the American Zone. They found one for Vasile that had a picture on it that more or less resembled him, but failed to find one that would match my appearance. Their imagination came to the surface and took over. They knew well the intricacies of the Austrian mountains and the roads and railroads and knew where travelers would have to submit to identification and inspection. It was a ruling of the Russians that no one would be allowed to leave their zone without a permit bearing their seal.

We stayed at the Schwartzes about ten days, which was too long, I thought. Vasile was completely at home, talking incessantly—and was in no hurry to leave. I began to feel uncomfortable at our long visit and felt that we should be on our way.

Professor Schwartz came up with an itinerary to get us out of the country. We were first to take the local train to the mountains where the Austrian emperors spent the summer hunting and skiing in the Rax Alpen (the Rax Alps), Semmering. So we set out. At the end of the local railroad, deep in the Alps, there was a funicular railway. To me here was another marvel in Austria. A young man, hired by Professor Schwartz, came along as our guide to see that we crossed the Russian Zone safely into the English Zone of Austria.

We slept in the large cabin that could have accommodated as many as twenty people. The next morning dawned cold and sunny. We were out early and proceeded toward the path that would lead us to the English Zone. The guide came with us to the end of the path at the brink of a fantastic and formidable precipice; the entire slope of the mountain was a sheer rock wall. But the guide assured us that many travelers dared to go that way. There were spikes well fastened in the rock on which the hiker set his foot. Then about five feet up there was a steel rope well fixed in the rock wall, which the Alps climbers hold with their hands ascending or descending, from spike to spike, until the precipice is crossed. We were cautioned to not look down as we might become dizzy or frightened. After we crossed the precipice, the dividing line between the Russian and English zones, there was a mountain path that led to the other side of the Mur Valley (Mur River Valley). The mission of the young guide ended here and he left us.

ALPINE CLIMBING

I had never seen such an abrupt slope of mountain except in the movies or in photographs. Now, it was up to us to cross the best way we could. We approached the cable and the spikes with as much courage and confidence as we could possibly summon. Vasile followed behind me. My small briefcase, which was fastened on my back like a knapsack, now contained only my razor, toothbrush, and toothpaste. Several times Vasile complained of dizziness, but I continually encouraged him to stay close behind me. It was a slow process, taking about one and a half hours to get across. We followed a footpath and passed several houses and cattle farms. By evening time we came to the town of Murzuschlag on the Mur river. We had a few shillings given us by the Schwartzes and took a room in a hotel. What a feeling of freedom! We were indeed free at last and could sleep without fear of any disturbance or harm.

We awakened to a glorious morning in a land of the free, in the English Zone of Austria, in the beautiful surroundings that only the Austrian Tirol Alps can offer (but perhaps could be matched in Switzerland, which bordered the area across the towering Alps).

Soon Vasile phoned his friends the Strausses at the Bad-Aus-See in the American Zone. He was instructed that a local bus connected the railroad station with the Bad-Aus-See, where the Strauss summer home was located. How fantastic it all seemed—to have a business in Vienna and a retreat home in the Alps! And the idea of freedom to travel in Austria, Germany, Switzerland, France, and throughout Europe without restriction was overwhelming. Suddenly, I thought of my long trip abroad in 1936 attending the Baptist Youth Conference in Zurich. I remember I took some side trips by bus into Switzerland. Could it actually be that here in Western Europe—Austria included—the war did not change men from free to slaves? Or could it be that, because the Iron Curtain was so thick and tight, we in Rumania could not imagine that in the west people appeared to be even happier and freer than before the War? It seemed that Rumania remained always under one or another oppressive regime. Was this Rumania's fate? I could only ponder the thought. Even if one knew the land and the history of it, one could never know for sure where his forbears lived and died and were buried, or if any minuscule traces were left behind, such as an oakbeamed little church at Tisa in Transylvania.

I mused on. My father's saying came to mind—"I don't know why we Rumanians must always be behind other nations." He referred to the Germans and Hungarians who lived amongst us. I concluded perhaps it could be that each nation or tribe (like the tribe of Israel) carried its own destiny. Or perhaps the book of Ecclesiastes stated it all in perspective: "Everything in due time!" And now, what an incredible, personal feeling of freedom came over me: freedom from the fear of what the night might bring. We took a local train to Bruck am Der Mur. From here we took the express train coming from Graz toward Salzburg. No permit was required in order to buy tickets. We boarded the train and were on our way to Bad-Aus-See, which was on the way to Salzburg. The train was fairly well-filled with passengers, and we found seats in the second-class car. There were no third-class cars on an express train. I remember that it was a beautiful, clean train and that the passengers were well-dressed and polite. The conductor took our tickets without question, punched them, and returned them to us.

When we approached the American Zone, the train stopped at a small station and the controller of passports, or passes, as they were called, came into the train. The uniformed Austrian police officers asked for passes. We did not have passes. I offered my identification as a reserve officer. He looked at my booklet with interest and said that it would not be sufficient. Vasile had nothing except for his excellent German speech. It was the rule that a special pass issued by the Austrian authorities was necessary to enter the American Zone. We were politely requested to get off the train and we were escorted to the English military control. We were not the only ones without a pass. There were twenty to thirty people of all ages, and probably of as many nationalities, awaiting interrogation of the English Military Control.

The young lieutenant in charge came out and asked who among us spoke English or French. Since I spoke French well and could also speak English, we were allowed to come forward for questioning. I poured out the entire story of our escape from Rumania and of our wanting to go into the American Zone, where we may be able to contact relatives and friends in France and in the United States of America. He seemed impressed by my history of Baptist friends in Rumania; that I was a Baptist fellow with the assurance that Baptists anywhere would give me a hand in my exile. "No trouble," he said, "you may take the evening train and cross into the American Zone."

I thought the word *Baptist* had impressed him deeply. I looked at this young, British armed forces officer again. He was about twenty-two, of reddish-blond complexion, with a scattering of freckles across his nose. I remembered how I had hated my own many years ago, but on him they seemed a mark of distinction! I silently thanked God for this young man who had so kindly treated us in the interrogation session and allowed us to go.

GUESTS OF DR. AND MRS. JOHAN STRAUSS

The next train, which we were allowed to board, came in the late evening, and after about an hour and a half we arrived at Bad-Aus-See Station. We found Dr. and Mrs. Strauss waiting for us. Since we were not on the earlier train they surmised that there had been some difficulty in our crossing over into the American Zone and had been anxious for our safety. And, too, there was no bus at that particular time. My head was in a whirl. Here was the great-grandson of the famous composer waiting in the railroad station in the middle of the night to meet two Rumanian escapees and give them aid. Incredible! How can one ever forget such a gesture of human kindness and Christian civility?

I had always been in love with the German culture because I so admired their skill and utility in managing their farms or business so efficiently. I had always favored a Hungarian girl or a German girl above a Rumanian girl. I was even described as a lover of Jewish or foreign people as a slant on my identity. My becoming a Baptist might have had something to do with this. I was not the type of Rumania fellow who disdained anything not of Rumanian origin. And we were the "grandsons of Emperor Trajan": that connotation left me cold and with something of an inferiority complex. Austrians had been our master for a thousand years or so, at times jointly with the Hungarians. Now one of the most famous names in Austria, Dr. Johan Strauss, Jr., was taking us in to be his guests at his summer lodge in the beautiful spa, Bad-Aus-See.

Bad-Aus-See is only a few train stops from Bad Ischl. Here the Austrian emperors took the hot baths for their ailments, spending the summer there. Dr. Strauss took us there to see it while we were his guests for over a week. He said there probably were some healing minerals in the hot waters to relieve the pains of sciatica, arthritis, and other bone ailments.

Vasile, as usual, was loathe to move on, but I knew we must be on our way again. We must get ready to leave, and we told the Strausses we must get in to Salzburg to the refugee camps. We had been informed about them by Dr. Schwartz in Vienna and also by Dr. Strauss. I had never enjoyed remaining long as a house guest, no matter how welcome I might have been. The old saying, "What is too much is not healthy" recurred to me at the moment as being characteristic of my nature. I said to Vasile, "Let's go." The Strausses had been more than generous to us.

Dr. Strauss, a textile businessman, was about forty-five or fifty. He was tall and well built, with receding, light brown hair. His wife was a woman of a warm, beautiful personality. She was very gracious to us. Their one son was a student in Vienna and in addition attended to some of the family business. Dr. Strauss, as I understood from Vasile, received considerable revenue from his musical ancestors' royalties. I thought, *The musical genius can even produce economical wealth for posterity!* I had never known of such things in my own country.

SALZBURG AT LAST!

We arrived in Salzburg early in the afternoon by the same express train we took from Bruck am der Mur to Bad-Aus-See. I knew little of the history of Salzburg except that it was the city of Mozart. From word of mouth passed on to me by Pete Moraru, whom we left in Budapest, we learned my cousin Miron Butariu was there, probably in a refugee camp. Walking along the street leading from the station to the center of the city (laid out in the usual pattern of cities in Europe) we ran into my cousin Miron. I could hardly believe my eyes! What incredible things were happening again and again in my life. We learned he was living in a room near the station and at the time was taking a stroll about the neighborhood. I noticed he still had his limp, which had affected him since infancy.

Miron had a board and room arrangement in a house belonging to a former bank president, now retired. Miron's room was on the second floor, in which there was a sofa suitable for sleeping purposes. We met Frau Clauss, the housewife, who agreed that I may stay with my cousin in the same room, where a cot would be placed. It was a beautifully furnished room, and the room and board plan appealed to me. Miron received a small subsidy from the Rumanian National Committee in Exile. His close friend, Emil Ghilezan, who had been the deputy minister of Treasury before the Communist takeover in Rumania, had helped him become situated. Miron had previously worked for several years in the office of Ghilezan's father in Cluj. It was a question of a friend's helping a friend in need, which brought a warm feeling of its reality.

I barely knew Ghilezan myself and certainly expected no assistance of any kind from him or anyone else. I felt certain it was up to me to find my destiny for the future in unknown lands.

Vasile had found a place of safety somewhere. He planned to go to Constantz on the Constantz Lake in Germany, where he had stored some of his household goods with a female friend. He wanted to return there, and I agreed that this would be his best bet.

CONTACTS IN AMERICA

I recalled three friends who had left Rumania in 1939 and were in the United States. There were Drs. Luke Sezonor, John Cocutz, and Peter Trutza. And I remembered Rev. Danila Pascu was also in the group. I had heard nothing from any of them after they left Rumania. I had expected a postcard, at least, but had heard nothing of their life in America.

Now for the Catana episode of my life. This period had great meaning for me in many ways, with many surprises. I had corresponded with a client, Stanley Catana, a notary public in Highland Park, Michigan. Our correspondence continued until the Communist takeover and, to my knowledge, he was still in my debt for a small fee. I had written in 1947 or earlier to withhold the fee for the time being. He now sent me one hundred dollars by wire. It was like bread from heaven! A letter followed. He assured me of his concern for my welfare and that I must not worry about the future in my life. He would stand by me in any need, he said. He further revealed that according to his accounts he still owed me something like nine hundred dollars in fees. I was astounded and dizzy-headed at his letter. That was a fortune to Crisan the escapee—refugee—who had no monetary stake at all but who had only his life intact and his faith and undying hope for a good life in a land yet unknown to him. What lay ahead? Whatever it might be, there was no fear or terror of the secret police, which had been a daily horror in days gone by. But now I was in a real world, a free world, and somehow I was filled with an assurance that I would be able to make my way to a new and exciting adventure of living beyond its beginning. By God's grace I had been sustained. I had been encouraged and boosted by a Baptist fellow, Stanley Catana, who had proved to be a providential relation. I did not know where he owed me any fees, but if he did it was a very small amount and of no consequence. Rather this good fortune seemed to have simply dropped from the blue skies to me.

I was trying to get to Paris, France, at the first opportunity. Why did the thought of getting to Paris seem uppermost in my mind? I know that I often thought of the Rumanian Baptist church in Paris. I had stopped there for a few days in 1936 on my way to London from Zurich, Switzerland, after attending the Baptist Youth World Conference. It was akin to instinct to be in touch with Baptist fellows, or brothers, I called them, wherever I happened to be.

Salzburg, in a 99 percent Catholic country, had no indigenous Baptists. However, at the refugee camp, there was a small group of Rumanian-Ukrainian Baptists. These Rumanians were refugees from Bukovina, the province of Rumania that had been taken by the Russians after the war. The Russians maintained that Rumania had kept Bessarabia under her rule from 1917 to 1940; thus, Rumania owed a lot to Russia, so Russia took Bukovina as compensation for its loss, since it now couldn't govern or exploit Bessarabia.

I did not feel at ease or at home among these people. It was true they were Christians in the Baptist tradition, but somehow there seemed to be little rapport between us. They were almost illiterate, but I noted they read only the Holy Bible. And then, too, I was constantly thinking of how to get to Paris. I thought of Paris as the City of Light—indeed as the capital of the free world, a city where all literati were recognized and every talent could bloom. Oh, to be in free Paris! I did not stop to consider that Paris is a great city in size and that millions of talents died daily under the *pontes* of the Seine; that in dingy mansards the great and not-so-great artist might find a cheap room to pursue his studies. I did not think of this side of Paris at the moment. I was in love with the idea of getting there, no matter what might be awaiting me. I did not remember any specific names, but I recalled that back in Rumania I had heard that one Mr. Schiopu, a former student at the Business Academy, went to Paris and the Baptist brothers there had made him their minister. All these things, however, had happened before the war.

I inquired of Miron as to the feasibility of entering France. He told me to apply for a visa at the French Consular Office in Salzburg. He added that two girls of Rumanian parentage worked as secretaries in that office and would be of assistance to me. When I obtained the application form, they warned me not to expect an early reply as there were thousands and thousands of applications on file.

I began visiting historic and artistic sites in Salzburg on foot. Distance did not matter. I visited the house of Mozart—the house on the slope where it was supposed he composed most of his music. I visited the Bishopric Castle on the mountain. I attended a few of the concerts in the music hall called Mozarteum. Salzburg is a beautiful city to visit and enjoy, but, I mused—to stay? Miron foretold that Americans would in time bring many of the refugees to the States after the United States Congress passed a new law to that effect.

One Sunday afternoon we had a most wonderful concert in our own living room. The grown-up children of the house owner performed for us. The lady accompanied them on the piano as they sang arias from operas I knew quite well. I thoroughly enjoyed the fine singing of these three young people, thinking all the while that only the Germans produced such music and were able to enjoy it first-hand in their own home. My thoughts went back to the home of my childhood where we had often gathered to sing songs we knew from memory or from the Baptist song book, but had no piano to accompany our untrained voices. We just sang spontaneously from our hearts and for the joy of singing together.

In Salzburg I met all kinds of people—people of varied political, religious, and life philosophies. Myron spoke to me of one Mr.

Mailat, which is a Rumanian name, who spoke Rumanian and wanted to meet me. He appeared to be a well educated man. Miron said this man wanted to talk to me and, from what I might tell him of my experiences, he might be able to help Rumanians at home to attempt to liberate themselves from their Communist-imposed rulers. This man lives in a small town near Salzburg. He came for me in his car, and I spent the night in his home. We slept in a room with two beds. It was the first and last secret interview I ever gave to anybody. Mr. Mailat gave the impression that he had good connections with the Americans and with the English and French Occupation Forces as well as the political administration. I had my doubts about all this information given so freely. But I definitely believed he was paid by some outfit to find out all the data he could as to what was happening at the time behind the Iron Curtain. Certainly from there only a few arrived in the West, and they were either ignorant as to the state of politics or were stooges sent by the communists to attempt to learn what the West might be plotting against their regimes. One must constantly keep in mind that a goodly number of Rumanians in Rumania, and probably all who succeeded in escaping, were of the persuasion that the Allies would force Russia's or that of her new allies to have free elections and then the entire communistic buildup would fall apart. The elections held in 1946 were not only a mockery but an open forgery. Others, like myself, knew many things like that, but did not know for sure where and how the political prisoners of my National Peasant party were imprisoned or how they were treated or even if they were alive.

Miron told me he, too, had spent a night in Mr. Mailat's home and discussed many things. Miron told me that Mailat was a former legionnaire, or Iron Guards of a milder faction, and that he had escaped from Rumania when the German armies withdrew from Rumania.

I also learned from Miron that there were thousands of former Iron Guard members in Austria and Germany. He maintained that they were "good Rumanians" who could be trusted, and that they would in no way try to jeopardize my freedom or my getting to the West.

Mr. Mailat spent an entire night in questioning and waiting

patiently for my answers or asking about some variances in my observations. Much later, here in America, I wondered if the questioning in the bedroom had been recorded. Might it have been?!

As a Baptist fellow I might have appeared in the sight of former Iron Guardists as a Communist or whatever, but by all means "no genuine Rumanian." Mind you, it was the Iron Guard and the government of Antonescu that closed all the Baptist churches in Rumania, saying something like, "whatever is not Rumanian orthodoxy is either Jewish, Communist, or Mason, thus an enemy of Rumanian nationalism."

When I think back to that time, November 1948, I do not remember whether I stayed there for two nights or only one.

Mr. Mailat was helpful in that he gave me several names and even the addresses of several of his friends in Saarbrucken in, or rather near, that city. This industrial city was all but destroyed by the war and was now under French occupation.

I became, somehow, an important person to meet; I had a friend in the USA who had sent me one hundred dollars. This was really a great thing, for many, if not all, these people were waiting for some miracle to happen, either that Rumania, Hungary, Czechoslovakia, Yugoslavia, and Bulgaria would be liberated or that they may be taken to the United States or somewhere else and given something to do. These people were highly educated people, of a younger vintage than myself. Whether they were former Hitlerites, who can tell? There was no doubt in my mind that they were all of the right or extreme right in their zeal to liberate their nations.

Many people I met and talked with were still of the belief that Hitler wanted to save Europe from Stalin; that the Allies recognized that and would go to war sooner or later against Stalin and destroy and eradicate Communism in its cradle. I had some interesting conversations with quite intelligent people there. They were well educated, well read, and were in the professions such as law, medicine, academics, and engineering. All in all, however, I thought it was a fatality that these people fell into the web of Nazism; their views of a nation, of a freedom, of religion, were completely walled in by the authoritarian philosophy—they were people who would follow the leader thinking everything would be all right. The thought was prevalent among them that the democracy of the French, English, and Swiss tradition was "really the work of the Masonic people—mostly Jews—because they have their money in international banks and have no allegiance to any land and can take their money and move on whenever they chose." These views were Hitler's slogans and dogma: they, like Hitler, divorced completely the teachings of the Old Testament and of the New Testament and thought Jesus Christ had nothing to do with the teachings of the Old Testament or with the establishment of a Christian church. I pitied them. I thought of an old Rumanian proverb; "Good cheese in dog skin—only the dogs eat it." These were good minds, but the skin, the philosophy they acquired was good only for the dogs, that is, for those who cherished such principles.

Mr. Mailat continued to inquire about what was happening to the Iron Guardists. I only knew that quite a few of them had joined the Communist party; others had disappeared into the forests and still others disappeared in the night, taken by the Security Police. He was trying to find out whether the "partisans" in the mountains were having any success gathering momentum in their effort to overthrow communism. I had heard of some partisans being captured, but I did not know of any serious insurrections in Rumania having been caused by such partisans.

It was indeed a pity to see such a great number of students wrapped up in such ideologies. I believed it was a fatality. Rumania was isolated from the mainstream of Western democrats and was a neighbor of Russia, which, since the fall of Byzantium, was considered by herself the "Mother Church," "Second Byzantium." The Church of Rome was considered "an anathema in the sight of the Rumanian Orthodox church." The Rumanian Orthodox church taught the same kind of theology and history of the church. There is no other true Christian church but the Orthodox church. Any innovation was a heresy. Were the Rumanian Nazis saying the Catholic church in the West has too many sectarians; it was in the West that there arose a Luther and a Calvin and so on, but never in the Orthodox church? Of course not, but the Rumanians and the Russians were entirely uneducated in comparison with the Western nations of Europe.

The most highly educated man in a small village was the priest, trained in the slavonic institution of the Byzantine tradition. In fact, many times these priests barely knew how to read and write. The First World War brought some emancipation, but the priests did not like it. It was a natural aversion to see a lad from a small town going to school and being able to read books, like the Bible, printed in the west and believed to be subversive. All these ideas and reminiscences came thronging back to my mind while I was being interviewed by Mr. Mailat in a suburb of Salzburg.

ANOTHER CROSSING—WITH NO PERMIT

I was becoming restless in Salzburg. I went to the French Consular Office several times, only to be told that there was no answer to my application for a permit to enter France. I decided I must try to go without an entry permit, but it would be necessary to cross the Austrian-Western Germany border near Salzburg. Then I would have to travel by train to Munich and from there by another train to Karlsruhe, across the Rhine. From there, with God's help, I would cross the Saar Valley occupied by the French. And from there I'd cross into France, still on foot, and eventually take the train from Metz to Paris.

It was Mailat who helped me with his knowledge of how to cross into Germany. I obtained a permit from the local police to cross the border into Germany because I had a *friend* with whom I was to stay. On November 15, 1948, I left Salzburg with a new wristwatch with a second hand, purchased at the great price of twenty dollars (probably smuggled from Switzerland). This watch gave me excellent service for over twenty years and I have it to this day, but so far have not found a jeweler who will undertake its repair. So I started out, the little suitcase still in my possession. It had been manufactured from my father's pig skins and made to order at some time before the war. It had come to be a sentimental companion to me. In Salzburg I had purchased a New Testament in English (or it may have been given to me—these pocket-size copies were handed out here and there). It was of small print and difficult to read. My eyes became reddened from reading in poor light, and I consulted an eye doctor, who recommended reading glasses. The doctor assured me my eyes were good but it would help my eyes to have reading glasses.

None of my few new friends in Salzburg were particularly concerned at my leaving for the unknown. They advised me to accept the requests to work in the mines or textile industry. Only in this way will one be given a permit to remain in France. It was in Austria and West Germany that the refugees were helped by the UN organization. A Rumanian lady from one of the UN organizations, who processed my papers as a refugee, told me the same thing. I was told the best thing would be to wait for the Americans to give us help or take us to United States. But for the time being, the USA quota was filled, unless a new quota might be passed by the Congress.

The identification paper I got from the ONU (French UN) auxiliary organization, with humanitarian purposes, helped me to cross the border into West Germany. I arrived in Munich in the evening and went to the hotel indicated by Mr. Mailat. There were no rooms but with another fellow, a Rumanian Jew. I accepted, and a cot was placed for me. This man was waiting to go to Palestine (Israel) to fight for a new Israeli homeland. I could not see why, but he was sure I was Jewish—"one of those renegade Jews" who did not want to fight for his country. Perhaps my long, brown wavy hair—not the usual Rumanian characteristic—threw him off. I was not able to convince him that I was a Baptist fellow, looking for some Baptist brotherhood in France.

Within the next few days I was able to get in touch with the person Mr. Mailate directed me to, who would help me cross into France. This man was evasive and vague and did not seem to trust me. He said I was to call someone in Saarbrücken; that someone else would call a certain number and that eventually someone would come and talk to me and help me with directions.

I waited a couple of days in Munich. Then I boarded the train for Karlsruhe, a city on the West Bank of the Rhine.

My connection either forgot or did not know that a passenger for Saarbrücken (bridge over the river Saar) cannot cross by train in the French Zone of Germany. Approaching Karlsruhe, the passengers were advised by the train attendants that this was the last stop and that unless they had a pass to cross the Saar, they could not board the train; that the French military authority would detain them for investigation or even put them in prison.

I got out of the train at a desolate station that had been badly damaged by bombs. Next to it was a log cabin, serving as a waiting room. At one end of the room drinks and some rolls were sold. The room was almost filled by the time I made my way in. Then, one by one, people left until there were very few waiting there. One young man, sitting across the table from me, said he had relatives in Saarbrücken and wanted to go there, had no pass, but would try to walk the distance across the ravaged Siegfried Line, Hitler's fortification against France.

I thought to myself, *Here is a man who can give me the needed directions!* I got into conversation with him and said that I, too, was going to Saarbrücken where I had friends; but it would be my first trip to this area and I had no knowledge that the French Occupation Armed Services would refuse to allow one to cross without an entry permit. Hans (German for John), as he said his name was, said he would welcome my going with him, provided I help him carry his load, a very heavy knapsack, as I experienced later. *"Gemacht"* agreed of course! What else!

Let's go! He was an eager beaver, an efficient German lad, I thought. He wanted to help but for the bargain to carry his load. He was carrying my load, which weighed less than two pounds. His knapsack was quite heavy, at least thirty to forty pounds. I only guessed he had flour in his bag, which he either was taking to relatives or planning to make a profit by selling it on the black market. Whatever it was, I felt how heavy it was to start with.

He led the way through some fields, then through a brush area, then through a sparse growth of forest. He easily knew his way. We arrived on that tortuous pathway in an open field and then approached fantastic rows of giant, tooth-like fences all turned toward the west, toward France. Hans stretched out his hand, announcing, "This is the Siegfried Line!"

This was the most formidable modern defense line built by Hitler against any possible French invasion or attack. It looked so incredible in its dimensions and length on both sides that faded out of sight. I had read of this fortification to match the French counterpart, the Maginot Line.

We crossed this monstrosity of a mouth easily, because the Americans had bombed it almost meter after meter in some places to make space for the tanks and infantry to get through to pursue the German armies. The moon was a little help to us. When it shone on the ruins of Hitler's fortifications it easily appeared somewhat like the vision from *Dante's Inferno,* except here there was no longer anybody being tormented, twisted, and torn as result of bombs and tanks fighting. It was long ago when I crossed the Siegfried Line—about 34 years. I had never seen anything either in nature or in pictures more horrifying—it was mute evidence of man trying to surpass any imagination, looking for security against his fellow man. There came to my mind the story of the tower of Babel. Man persists in his perennial search for security and grandeur and power, yet his finality is well known: he is not immortal, he cannot save himself. He must be saved by a higher power, even God in Jesus Christ. These thoughts kept recurring through my mind, and even seemed to make my load seem a little lighter. I was perspiring even though it was mid-November and quite cool.

Hans and I did not talk much. Of course, he was ahead, which made my burden seem heavier, but I trudged along as fast as I was able. At about four or five o'clock in the morning, Hans stopped and pointed in the distance at several lights. He said to me, "There is the station in Saarbrücken. I must hurry. Give me the knapsack. I have to leave you. I must run." And run he did. I saw him like a dark shadow in the dark of night moving fast—to outdistance me, it seemed, as fast as possible. Wasn't that strange? I had carried his knapsack all night, during which time he had not offered to relieve me for awhile, and he did not thank me for carrying it or even wait for me to say something to him in my thanks to him for showing me the way to Saarbrücken.

It was a long way in the night toward the city, but I kept in my sight the lights in the distance as a guide and made it. I felt much better with the lifting of the heavy weight from my back. I had never carried such a heavy burden before. But I was determined, knowing that through the Siegfried Line and on in the distance was a ghost city, Saarbrücken.

Whenever that night comes to mind, that dreadful night of journeying through the concrete teeth of Hitler's "mighty fortifications" and trying to figure out just who Hans was, I rest with the idea that he must have been a smuggler of food goods, like flour, grain, or rice; such things were scarce in Europe at that time.

It must have been about seven o'clock in the morning when the

199

ghost city began to come into sight before me; there was not a single roof to be seen. There were only parts of brick or stone walls, chopped into hideous forms. The railroad station was not entirely demolished; the ground floor had been repaired a little with boards and there was a ticket office.

I asked the man behind the little enclosure whether there was a hotel in the city. "Right in front of the station," he said. "They operate it." At one time it might have been an imposing building. Now only the ground floor and the next were in use, in part. The ground floor was good enough, I thought, probably it had resisted the bombings well because it was rather below the ground level on the one side.

There was a hall in the hotel and there was a little vending stand with fruit on it. I noticed oranges for the first time since before the war. I asked the price of an orange and, as it was not expensive, I had an orange for my early breakfast for my hunger and thirst. I realized that as this was in the French occupation, oranges were available from the French Mediterranean coast or from the French colonies like Algiers or others. France had many colonies at that time.

The street car was running. The main street was cleared of rubble, but there was not a single building untouched by the war devastation. Yet people continued going about the streets in their daily chores. Where were they living? Probably among the rubble, where they had managed to save or repair a room in the basement on the ground floor of their home.

The city appeared ash gray in color. Some of the towering walls had been burned by incendiary bombs. Before the war, this city had been a large industrial center, one of the most important steel industries in Germany. There were coal and iron ores in practically the same place.

The Saar Valley area had been contested by the French and Germans since the Napoleonic times. The population was a mixture of German and French. France had wanted to keep it after the First World War, but after a time had to turn it back to Germany. To be sure, it was the German industrial talent that had developed the entire region into a formidable "steel city and citadel"!

SEVENTH CROSSING

I walked about a bit after leaving the street car until I found the little hamlet or village and the person I was looking for, the one Mr. Mailat had directed me to who would help me to cross the seventh border to illegally enter France. The man was living with several others—Rumanians and Germans. He asked me to stay to supper and he would afterward give the directions to cross into France and the pathway to the main road (or the foot trail to the road).

While I felt somewhat at ease in Saar, nevertheless I was told that the French would put you in jail if you crossed the border without an entry permit; at which time they would ask you to go back or undertake work in the coal mines where labor was needed—no white-collar refugees. So the word got around.

At dusk, after supper, this man, whose name I never learned, took me out through the orchards and pastures and then, from a slope, showed me in the distance the railroad tracks and the road for vehicles parallel to it. "You go down there," he said, "and then when you reach the railroad tracks cross without fear (for there will be nobody around) and then go on down the road for two or three hours and you will reach the railroad station at Metz." He then asked me, "You've heard of Metz?—That is the largest city in France on the east side of France toward Germany." Then he related that early in the morning there was an express for Paris. "Take it and you will be in Paris early in the morning."

I left him, saying, "Thank you very much for your help, and may God bless you."

So I set out with my small case in hand to reach the railroad and the road leading to Metz. As I walked I indulged in meditation and thinking over my problems and difficulties. I pictured myself in the City of Light. It was the dream of any dreamer in Rumania to make even a short trip to Paris. Will the dream of freedom bring also the reality of reaching the City of Light? Will a Rumanian Baptist there help me to find a place under the sun in freedom? Such were my thoughts as I trudged along toward Metz.

I could not see the road markers or any signs. I did not know whether I was still in the Saar Valley or in France. I could not risk any pitfall now or being caught by the border police. Snatches of song went through my mind as a sort of comfort: "Do not be afraid though storm clouds gather about you, do not be afraid but call upon the Lord who will steer your boat safely to a quiet shore." Such were my thoughts and my prayer of the moment was that I not fall into a ditch but stay safely on the road and above all not fall into the hands of the border police!

How long had I been on the road to Metz? What if Metz is heavily patrolled? What if the city is dark? What would I do then? Had my informer been correct in stating the express would leave shortly after midnight for Paris? It was November 20, 1948. It was a Saturday night. There were glimmers of hope in my heart, but no glimmer of lights in the city. Even in the dark I must locate that railroad station no matter what.

After another curve in the road and the railroad I could see a flickering of lights about four kilometers ahead. It must be Metz! I was fast approaching lights along the highway and I soon saw it was the railroad station of a little town. It was the first station stop inside France after my crossing the Saar Valley territory.

It was a small station, with a bar serving wine or coffee. A lone policeman leaned on the bar stand chatting with the bartender. I ordered a cafe au lait. I was surprised that the policeman took no notice of me. Could it be that I had arrived in the land of the free—even though I was an illegal alien entering France at this particular point? Could this be real? A feeling of encouragement and joy welled up within me. Immediately I bought a ticket to Paris and learned that I was to change trains at Metz—the largest city in eastern France. Nobody paid any attention to me and nobody mentioned a permit to buy a ticket. I could hardly believe it! This freedom of control was overwhelming to me. Could I believe there was no necessity to constantly glance behind me? It was a feeling that cannot be described to one who has not known life under a dictatorship either of the left or of the right. It had been ten years since I had enjoyed a feeling of personal freedom; it had ended about 1938, when the rumors of war pervaded Europe and Rumania. In the train I found a seat in a corner by myself in order to avoid any conversation. Although I spoke French with ease, I felt it well to be cautious and careful in the circumstances. The conductor came along with the customary, "Le tickete, s'il vous plais?" He punched my ticket and returned it to me without further conversation.

The express made good time and by 6:00 A.M. or shortly thereafter arrived in Paris at the Gare de l'Ouest (the East Station). Crowds of people swarmed back and forth from one train to another.

VIII

PARIS, FRANCE

WHAT now? Where do I go from here? Naturally, I thought first of the Rumanian Baptist church in Paris. I must locate it at once, and I looked about for a telephone book and found that many telephone books were lined up along the wall in the station. The railroad station itself was the largest I had ever seen and covered over with a glass roof. But I must have seen it before when I was in Paris in 1936. But possibly not, as I realized again that there were many railroad stations in Paris!

Diligent searching failed to reveal the address of a Rumanian Baptist or any other Rumanian church listing in the telephone book. But I found a listing, *Eglise Batiste*, 48 rue de Lille, and I determined to go there. I studied the city map at the subway entrance and found how easy it was to get about the city. One had only to push a button at the point of his destination and the light would tell him the correct route and exit. I found my exit was at "Rue du Bac."

The subway was crowded with people, which surprised me, as it was early in the morning. But of course this or any other large city would be teeming with crowds of workers, employees, and travelers from all over the world.

So I pursued my search for the address rue du Bac and then for the street rue de Lille. It was still dark when I began looking for the number I wanted. I shivered suddenly and the thought occurred to me that I might be taken for a burglar. I finally located the number 48 on the wall next to a huge gate, in which a small gate was carved. On the larger gate were printed the words *Eglise Batiste*. But the little gate was closed, and I did not dare to see whether it was locked.

Having located the address I needed, I went back to the Metro station where there was a coffee shop open. I went in and ordered, *"Café au lait, s'il vous plaît!"*

"How about a croissant, too?" asked the waitress.

Of course, I would have that too. It was a delicious repast, and I remembered how much I had enjoyed it back there in 1936 on my first trip to Paris. I lingered long at my table, waiting for daylight as well as enjoying my breakfast. When I left with a wave of the hand and *"au revoir,"* receiving an answering, *"au revoir, monsieur,"* it was a pleasant feeling.

I returned to the huge gate and saw at once that the small gate was open. Beyond this small gate was a dark, tunnel-like passageway leading into a courtyard. In the courtyard there was a small house with a door and window facing the pathway. Should I knock or wait a little later in the day? In these tense moments my mind went back to the ill treatment I'd received at the hands of the Hungarian police in the stable. But this was Paris, and so I summoned an added courage and knocked gently on the door. The curtain over the window was pulled aside, and I saw a pretty young girl who shouted, *"C'est Mr. Crisan!"* (This is Mr. Crisan!) For a moment I actually felt faint. Was this a hallucination? Was someone still after me even in Paris? Who in this city even knew my identity?

The door opened, and a lady of about forty years appeared in the doorway. I tried in French: "I am sorry to disturb you so early in the morning, but I am looking for the Rumanian Baptist church." The lady cut me short asking whether I was Brother Crisan and whether I could speak Rumanian. I learned she was Mrs. Helen Balazs and the young girl, of about eighteen years of age, was Lenuta Balazs, her daughter.

I was invited inside and it was soon explained why Lenuta thought it was Mr. Crisan who was knocking at the door. In August 1948, an American-Rumanian preacher, Rev. Danila Pascu, was in Paris and Europe. He had come from the Baptist World Alliance Executive Committee meeting in London and had impressed upon the Baptist leadership that something definite and sure should be done for the Rumanians and other refugees in Austria or France, indeed, in all of Western Europe. He had visited with the Balazs family, the janitors of the building, where the French Baptist congregation had been holding their services in the morning and the small Rumanian Baptist group held their services in the afternoon.

Reverend Pascu, among other things, had told the Balazses that "he had a friend in Romania, a lawyer by profession, George Crisan, who, he felt, would try to escape from Romania at the first opportunity—within a year or so." The young girl had listened to the conversations between Moise and Helen Balazs and Reverend Pascu, and that morning she had a spontaneous intuition that the man Reverend Pascu had been talking about was indeed knocking at the door!

On Sunday, November 21, there was a sort of mist in the air with overcast skies—a usual day in Paris. In the afternoon I attended the small church service of the Rumanian Baptist community of Paris. I was asked to tell something of my experiences to the gathering. I related some details of my escape, of my actual crawling on my hands and knees through fields and marshes, across forbidden borders. It was an emotional story to me, and I remember I was moved to tears at times. Many in the audience were touched and, too, shed tears of sympathy. At the end of the service a youngish looking man, tall and slim, came up to me saying, "Brother Crisan, do you remember me?"

"I think so," I said, "let me look at you a moment."

He answered, "I am Roy Starmer, the American Baptist missionary in Rumania, director of the seminary there."

I was deeply touched emotionally, though I didn't know whether it was because of meeting someone who had known me before or whether some element of self-pity crept in. I suddenly had a feeling of being resurrected from a dead life to a new life! He had met me before the war—the only Baptist practicing lawyer in Rumania at that time and who was now an outcast—I felt—here in Paris!

Everyone crowded about me, shaking my hand and embracing me in friendliness and good will. I met several young people of the congregation, some from Baptist families and some who had just come to the meeting at the Baptist church in the Rumanian language at 48 rue de Lille. I remember two young people I met that night: George Bejenaru, aged 19 years, of Bucharest, and Petrica Fulea, aged twenty years, of Bucharest. They immediately offered to put me up and I happily accepted. I felt I had met brothers in Jesus Christ in Paris, France!

Roy Starmer came to speak to me and said that he would like to see me next day and talk with me.

The next day, a Monday, I met Brother Roy Starmer in his office. He told me that he was the director of the Baptist Seminary in Tivoli, near Rome, Italy; he was asked to handle the relief for refugees in Eastern Europe in Paris. The Baptist World Alliance had asked the Southern and Northern Baptist conventions to establish a relief for refugees in Paris and Dr. Roy Starmer, who knew the Rumanian language, was to be the director or administrator of the relief.

Dr. Starmer, being of an unassuming and humble personality,

had hesitated about taking on this tremendous project. He talked to me about it and asked if I would consider helping him, as I knew several languages—French, German, Hungarian and some Russian—and would be able to communicate well with the refugees from these countries, Rumania, Hungary, Yugoslavia, and the German refugees from Rumania. He also informed me that he would give me a letter to the effect that I was his assistant, and in these circumstances the French authorities would grant me residence in Paris.

Dr. Starmer had his family, wife and three children, in the Tivoli Baptist Seminary. He would be in Paris for some weeks and then return to his responsibilities as director of the seminary.

IN PRISON AGAIN?

With the letter in hand that I had a job with an American relief office, I proceeded to the Prefecture du Police, located in one of the most imposing buildings in the Île de la Cité in the middle of the river Seine. There were thousands of people of all languages and races waiting to get in and file papers or waiting to be investigated to become eligible for residence in Paris, like me.

However, I was ahead with my piece of paper in hand from an American and was quickly and courteously ushered in and given forms to fill out. Such questions were contained in the forms as to why I had come to France, why I had left my homeland, whom did I know in Paris and so on. For the first time I was introduced to the modern civil way of investigation. The person was allowed to fill out his paper the best he could and then questioned to ascertain why the person wanted to remain in Paris and any other information he wished to furnish. One of the most frightening questions was to state whether I had entered France illegally. Another question which appealed to me was to state when I had been in France previously and this was the occasion of my attending the International Congress of Baptist Youth in Zurich and returning by the way of London and Paris.

When my papers were delivered to a clerk for review, he asked still further questions as to why and with whose help I had arrived in Paris. He did not ask me to pronounce my name for him but called me Monsieur Crisan and I kept his French pronunciation while in Paris. I did not put a comma under the s in my name. The original name, Kroesus or Chroesus, did not have a comma under the *s*, and I was delighted to leave out the comma.

I was sent to still another official. He asked very few questions but did ask whether my name was French. I explained that it was possible, since the Rumanian nation and language were akin to the French. I probably added that the Rumanian culture and literature came from France; that my French teacher was a Parisian sent to Rumania to teach the French language in my college as a French cultural extension of Rumania. He was apparently pleased with my explanations and my knowledge of French history and civilization, imitated by the Rumanian intelligentsia.

This official then called a police officer, gave him my completed forms, and asked that he accompany me to the fifth floor. I was shocked at this procedure, for I knew that the fifth floor contained the Paris police headquarters and was the prison for political matters. I reasoned within myself that I was in France with an American employer and surely my detention would not last long. On reaching the fifth floor we were met by a police guard at the door. The police officer showed him my papers and we were ushered into another office where there was a clerk behind a desk. He looked at my file, came around the desk, unhooked a chain from another room, and invited me into it. He then put the chain back in the hook after me. So now I was in a political prison! Or so I thought. From the window I could see the Notre Dame Cathedral nearby and the river Seine flowing lazily along.

I began to try to reason things out the best I could. I had come from a communistic country (and an enemy country during the war), and it was natural that every person coming into France would be investigated on the suspicion of spying. Take my situation: A lawyer of forty-one years leaving his country, arriving in Paris with only his testimony to vouch for his integrity. What could be done but to seek help from humanitarian organizations? But on the other hand, I reasoned, I was not such a political clog to cause any disturbance. It seemed that my detention on the fifth floor had made me one.

I did not finish my reflections as I was called by the man at the door, "*Monsieur Crisan, s'il vous plais, venez dehors*" (Mr. Crisan, come out please).

I came out of the room and he asked me to sign a book in front of him. He gave me a file and asked me to go to the third floor. This I did and presented my file. I was assured that everything was in order, that I might remain in Paris and continue my work at the American office and in three days return to pick up my permit of residency in Paris.

A few days later I understood the entire process of events I had gone through. I had entered France illegally and for this reason there must be an administrative penalty—either a jail sentence or a fine or both. Hence, I was detained in jail for a few minutes and in this way the law was satisfied.

WORKING WITH THE REFUGEES

Now I was ready to do whatever Dr. Starmer required of me. We had an office, and I placed a desk next to the window leading to the courtyard where I was recognized my first day in Paris. I was able to secure a typewriter to place on my desk. Starmer assured me that my help would be of tremendous assistance to him, as he was new to his job, too. We both realized that my legal experience would come in handy. I kept a card index on the people who came asking for help from the Baptist Relief, as our office was soon called.

There was a room downstairs containing some clothing from America, and more was expected. There was also a sack or two of flour, which was dispensed in small amounts to those who needed it. Roy had tickets for meals at the Blue Danube Restaurant. We gave, selectively, tickets for meals, and Mr. Costica, the owner, manager, and cook (a Rumanian) long established on the left bank of the Seine in Paris, honored the tickets, giving a full-course dinner. It developed that the place became the cafe of the Rumanian refugees in Paris. It came to mean the place to meet other stranded Rumanians. Starmer took me there where we had a good dinner and met other people, many of whom looked to us in time of need.

Dr. Edwin Bell, the representative for American Baptist churches in Europe, had an office on the third floor of our building. He was some years older than Dr. Starmer and seemed somewhat firmer in whatever he said or did. He spoke some French. He had a say in the relief, as his convention was contributing toward the funds, foodstuff, and clothing. I understood from Starmer that it was the

Southern Baptist Convention that carried the greatest share in this relief.

There were days when I stayed at my desk from eight in the morning till six in the evening with a short pause for luncheon at noon, as there were so many people who came to our door. I made out a card on each person, and at times there were as many as forty people in line. Most of them were young people. Many, I discovered later, were living from hand to mouth, going from one relief office to another.

It was my responsibility also to attend meetings with other relief organizations. I was impressed that many were of American initiative or sponsored by America.

On Sunday I attended the Rumanian Baptist Congregation church services on the second floor of our building. I tried to organize a Sunday school class for the refugees, many of whom had never heard of the Baptist religion in Rumania. There were also a few young people who were Baptists in Rumania, like Petrica and Georges, and a few more. Some had not heard of Baptists, yet came to church in order that I might recognize them and be more ready to give them help in securing clothing and food tickets.

Since the Baptists are eager and ever interested in singing, we succeeded in forming a sort of choir to sing as Christmas was approaching. I, with the help of several of the refugees, organized a Christmas program and party. It was my first Christmas in Paris and the second away from the home of my parents and brothers and sister. The first Christmas away from my home was when I was in Russia in the war (1941).

A young lady by the name of Lya Constantinescu, a former radio singer in Bucharest and of a beautiful voice, was present. When I asked if she would sing for us "A Homeland My Eyes See" (Gurdon Robins, arr. D. B. Towner), we all wept. There were about fifty people there, including my cousin Miron, who had just arrived in Paris from Salzburg, Austria, where I had left him in early November 1948.

Only in the evening did I have any free time to meet with friends to talk over our situation, to have a good look at our exile, or just to sit in the Café de la Paix (the Peace Cafe) and to listen to fine orchestra and singers playing there.

It seemed that the most frequent thought in my mind in those days was that God indeed works in mysterious ways. The highest dream, so I thought, for a Rumanian intellectual was to visit Paris, the Notre Dame Cathedral, the most famous church building in the world to my best knowledge and according to my readings, to attend the Paris Opera, to walk along the Left Bank and stop at some cafe where Sartre philosophized on the meaninglessness of life, to see the Montmatre Cathedral, the Louvre, Place de la Concorde, L'arc de Triomphe, Bois de Boulogne, nearby Versailles, and so on and on—all those places I had read of in school and in my favorite literature, the French novelists, encyclopedists, and philosophers. All these lived in Paris. Great composers and painters had lived there—had made their *chef d'oeuvre* (masterpiece) in Paris.

In the past, I could only read of all these marvels of civilization of Western Europe to be found in Paris, but now I could hardly realize that I was here within reach of it all. The place where I worked, 48 rue de Lille, was only a block from the Seine and across the bridge was the Tuileries, the most famous museum in the world, where the kings of France had accumulated treasures of art and where Napoleon had brought all the best of the treasures from the places he had conquered. I enjoyed tremendously all these wonders and more.

I gained certain notoriety among the refugees and the French because of my involvement with the Baptist church and the Baptist Relief and my having a room a few blocks from my office in the Rue des Saint Peres, where the owner and manager of the hotel cooperated fully with me. Many refugees came early trying to catch me before I departed for my office, where people were crowded and waiting for me at eight o'clock.

I met the president of the French Baptist Churches Federation of France, Belgium, and Switzerland, Dr. Henry Vincent, who was located in the same building as my office. I also met the pastor of the other church where I once interpreted from Rumanian to French for Dr. Starmer.

A few days after my arrival in Paris, I discovered that one of my Baptist friends, Emanul Sezonov, and his wife and two daughters lived in the same building. They invited me to dinner and Emanul took the first picture of me in Paris.

When Roy Starmer came from Rome he took me to dinner one night on the Champs Elysées, where he introduced me to French fries (*pommes frit* in French), which you pick up with your fingers, not with the fork, which I thought was correct.

I wanted to speak in French as much as possible, so after office hours when taking a walk I asked one or two students to accompany me to keep up a conversation in French. My French improved to the point that the lady manager of the hotel thought I spoke it perfectly, with a provincial accent or intonation.

The Baptist brothers of Paris were plain workers who had come to France in their youth looking for work, bringing their wives with them or going back to Rumania, marrying, and bringing their wives to Paris. They all wanted me to meet their families and at least have dinner with them.

The Rumanian Baptist preacher resigned to take his sick wife to the South of France. There was speculation, even rumors that I might become the pastor of the Rumanian Baptist church in Paris (and in France). I thought at times I might like it, but at other times did not consider it. Here I was, a newcomer to the city of Paris, and I felt it might be well for Rumanians to join a French Baptist church rather than banding themselves together and remaining apart because they spoke Rumanian when they could really speak good French, too. I was surprised that for so many years they continued to retain a Rumanian Baptist church, even through World War II. I thought it might have been better for them to merge themselves in the French nation to their advantage and growth both in their faith and in their social life. Their children spoke Rumanian at home.

Some refugees asked me whether we would ever return home? At first, I remarked that most of the refugees would return home when the conditions were right but many made their home where they were located, just like the Jews, I added, who made their homeland where they could live in freedom.

Of course, I wondered on many occasions just what was going to happen to my family in Rumania because of my escape from behind the Iron Curtain. But again, one must think of his own skin first of all. This is the law of nature, so I thought at the time.

It might have been in March when Starmer came from Rome to supervise my work and see what was being done. He had received a letter from Rev. Danila Pascu of Cleveland, Ohio, in which he asked that he talk to me to learn whether I would be interested in studying theology at a seminary in America. Starmer said, "I don't understand Dr. Pascu. Why would he think of such an idea? Mr. Crisan, you are a lawyer and were for many years in Rumania. I don't think you can study theology in America—there is the language barrier and, besides, theology is a most difficult subject."

Before I could even further think of such a suggestion, Dr. Pascu again wrote to Starmer saying that in case I accepted the idea, the chairman of the Board of Trustees of the Colgate Rochester Seminary would secure a scholarship for me. He stated he had talked to Dr. Doris Sharp, the chairman, who thought it might be feasible.

Somehow, I was embarrassed to say no and reluctant to say yes, because, after all, I never felt I had a vocation for the ministry. I told Starmer that I would think and pray about it and let him and Dr. Pascu in America know my decision.

The load of my work was large: interviewing people daily, attending meetings of the relief organizations, planning what topic to use for my Sunday sermon when I was asked to preach, traveling by bic to Rouen and Le Havre with Dr. George (Zeno) Paclisanu (whom I had met and befriended in Paris), making arrangements for him to see sick refugees in their little rooms or attics (like the painter Sutianu), or visiting the hospitals. All these things left little time to consider tossing all my past life with its experiences out the window and to come up with some light at the end of this tunnel, even if the tunnel was Paris.

When I think back to this period of my life, I now see it as a leavening, with the idea coming from Dr. Pascu. I was of the disposition of not coming to a conclusion at all quickly. It took a little time for me to make a decision. That little time amounted to a night's sleep, and on awakening the next day, I was determined to go!

The spring comes early in Paris. In fact, it seemed that we had no winter except some drizzling rain and a temperature near freezing, but there were no frozen ponds or rivers. I thoroughly enjoyed sightseeing in Paris and its environs. France itself is a museum of architecture, of human habitation; since the dawn of history it had been a large country in Europe, with the greatest traditions in Europe in literature, philosophy, painting, and luxuries of all kinds. It is a blessed location with mountains on the west, rolling hills in the middle, the Mediterranean Sea on the South, and the Atlantic Sea on the west. It has rich lands for an infinite variety of produce, and the grapes of France have an envied reputation throughout the old and new worlds. Added to this were the tropical or semitropical produce which came from the French colonies in Africa or Asia. It is a country in which to enjoy life, a country of plenty ever since Caesar conquered it for the Roman Empire.

Now, here I am, so to speak, settled in this land with a job with the American Baptists, no matter how illusory or temporary it might have been. One does not question one's circumstances when former kings, ministers, and people who had accumulated great fortunes in their own countries before the war were now in Paris virtually begging for a piece of bread and a place to sleep, where the highest French officials in the government possibly had less pay than I had from the Baptist World Alliance. I believe anyone can allow himself to be lulled into complacency, at least for a while, in such circumstances. I and many others like me had not awakened from the tormenting nightmare we were in in our countries, now all behind the Iron Curtain.

There was, again, among these myriads of refugees in Europe the idea that the Allies would not allow things to stay that way, since Stalin had not kept his word, since the peoples' will was blatantly falsified, or just without an election. A government of a handful of Communists terrorized an entire nation.

But there is always another alternative—the one I had thought of in Rumania—that the Allies would not start a new war with Russia. Some little nations like Rumania, Hungary, Czechoslovakia, Poland, and the Baltic countries came to mind. Then I thought of the God of Israel who promised Abraham a country flowing with milk and honey but did not promise it as to an infant—"just sit down and eat and drink"—but Moses spoke to the Israelites and Joshua that they would receive the promised land but they must first stand fast on their feet, fight for the land against those occupying it, that Jehovah himself would help them to conquer it. "Be ye not afraid, I will be with you in the midst of strife and give you victory over your enemies."

To be sure, I thought, the nations that want to live under a democratic regime must find themselves the way in which to throw off the yoke of slavery, of dictatorship either of the left or the right. The Russians were there for sure, but they would not stay forever, and if the people want a thing deeply enough they have to strive for it and even die for their ideals. The Christians, they stood fast

214

for their faith during their history and were ready to give up their lives for "a life beyond the grave," their ideal.

ITALIAN HOLIDAY

Easter was approaching. Dr. Starmer told me that someone had sent one hundred dollars for a refugee and he was going to give that amount to me, that I might spend a holiday in Italy. I happily accepted it. He also told me that he would see to it that I could visit several Baptist churches in Rome and vicinity and that I meet one of the pioneers in the mission work in Italy, Dr. John Moore. How loving, thoughtful, and generous all this was to me. It would be such a needed respite to me to get away for a little while from the strenuous work I had been involved in so long.

A few days before Easter I left by train for Italy. After arriving in Rome, I had no difficulty finding a room in a private home that rented rooms to tourists. It was near downtown Rome. I enjoyed these wonderful days—an opportunity for some time to be alone, to meditate, to appreciate at close hand the marvelous arts created by man. Viewing the ruined walls of the colosseum sent shivers up my spine, bringing to my mind the tragic history of humanity that occurred there, those who died for their beliefs.

Dr. Moore invited me to dinner and later took me to the largest Baptist Church in suburban Rome, where I heard the entire congregation joining in singing together a swelling chorus, the most magnificent I had ever heard. I was able to follow the tune and here and there some few of the Italian words. I could read Italian with understanding, but spoke it with some difficulty.

I spent hours looking at the Emperor Trajan's columns, where the conquest of Dacia was carved in bronze (A.D. 106), when Rumania, at that time Dacia, became a province of the Roman Empire under the name of Dacia-Felix (the Happy Dacia).

On Easter Eve the service is held on Saint Peter's Plaza, with hundreds of thousands of worshippers and tourists jammed into the square. I was there. For the first time in my life I saw a pope on the balcony, greeting and blessing the crowds with the sign of the cross over them.

I happened to think of a young lady, Novella Zamppetti, a

215

professor of Italian culture, who had taught at the Girls' College in Arad, Rumania, whose home was in Rome. I had met her at a Baptist meeting house. I was surprised to learn that although she was born and reared in Rome, she was of a Protestant family. They were members of The Waldesians, a sect which preached the baptism of adults only. They had been severely persecuted by the Catholic church in the tenth and eleventh centuries; some were drowned and some escaped into France living in the most inaccessible of the mountains. I located Novella by attending a service at Waldesian Church, a large structure near the Vatican. I found her address, where she lived with her elderly father, who himself had been a professor of literature but was retired. It was like finding someone who was resurrected from the dead here in Rome. It brought to mind afresh my own miraculous escape from behind the Iron Curtain.

I visited Naples and went to the Island of Capri. I read the books of Axel Munthe, the Swedish physician who fought against the plague in Naples, who collected so many archaeological finds and who built a villa on the Island of Capri (the Goat Island), the most beautiful island imaginable in the gulf of Naples.

I always found great enjoyment in walking, and so it was in Naples I was filled with zest and enthusiasm in exploring the galleries of art and history and seeing something of its social side. Naples is situated on one of the most favorable gulfs on the Mediterranean Sea, or perhaps on any sea. It is a very wide gulf with a towering mountain in the background. That is Vesuvius, which in A.D. 79 buried alive two great and prosperous cities, Pompeii and Herculaneum.

Long after the burial of these cities under the lava, some poets and writers were still writing of regret at the sad fate of these two cities. But there were others, like Virgil (I believe he was the one) who said, "It is useless to cry over the ruins of Pompeii." It occurred to me at that time that doubtless God had given me the power to forget—forgetting the loss of my wealth or fortune at the hands of the Communists—and helped me to look forward to other joys of life, other paths, and other encounters.

There they were, the encounters in Naples. Walking back to my hotel, I had only to look from side to side to see sharp contrasts. I saw through the open windows of houses in the basements level with the street ten or more people lying on the floor to sleep. Then on practically every corner there were others begging for a coin to buy something to eat, or asking me something I did not understand, and still others who had something to sell. They all seemed to be following me! They made me think of the gypsies of the old days in Hungary or Transylvania.

Here were two worlds side by side; one of majesty and splendor, of beautiful renaissance palaces rising from the blue-green bay of the Gulf of Naples, beautiful as the Goddess Aphrodite, born of the sea foam, but next to it the drudgery of humanity in search of shelter or food or fun. All these are discerned under the watching column of Vesuvius' steam and threats.

One must be insensitive in visiting such places. Only several miles across the bay is the Island of Capri with the Axel Munthe villa, with its panaroma and serenity, then, here in Naples, there is splendor and squalor. Somehow, seeing both of these conditions or states causes a man to be aware again that he is human and that he indeed may be compared to grass of the fields, "Beautiful and strong in the morning but beginning to wither at noon and ready to be put into the fire for the evening meal."

But I knew I could not stay on the Island of Capri or in the city of Naples. My American job had the say as to my time, and Father Crisan, or Brother Crisan, or just Mr. Crisan of the Refugees of Paris must return to his "flock."

The events of the past days crowded into my mind: The Easter services at Saint Peter's Plaza, meeting my Waldesian friends in the midst of Catholic Rome, participating in the services of two Italian Baptist churches as a Rumanian brother in faith, seeing the colosseum where so many of the early Christians met death because of their beliefs and even the hilarious laughing of the plebes all caused me to reflect again on the suggestion of Rev. Pascu that I go to America to study divinity to learn more about my own belief and of others sharing the same faith as mine.

Upon my return to my Paris friends or refugees, whom I was to assess and give some help from our Baptist Relief, I learned there had been some criticism of my spending Easter in Rome. They were not certain that Father Crisan was well established in the eyes of his American Baptist friends, the Baptists of America, of whom they had not heard before. How can a refugee who had nothing but the clothes on his back indulge in a trip to Rome, Naples, Capri, Torino, et cetera? The refugees became a little skeptical of me, not understanding the details behind my time off for a rest.

PREPARING TO LEAVE AGAIN

The next time Dr. Starmer came to Paris, I spoke to him about my decision to go to America as a student of divinity. He gave the news to Dr. Bell, upstairs.

Dr. Starmer inquired at the American Embassy about my obtaining a visa. The answer was that it would be most difficult if not altogether impossible for the reason I was 41 years of age, formerly an attorney at law for many years in Rumania, and, too, I might not be a *bona fide* student, but rather seeking a means of getting to America.

Pascu quickly answered Starmer, sending him a letter from the Colgate Rochester Divinity School (CRDS), which was on file at the American Consular Office in Paris.

I was not sure whether Starmer had asked Dr. Bell to see about obtaining the visa or whether Dr. Bell, as a representative in Europe of the American Baptist churches, wanted to help with the processing of my case at the Embassy. Dr. Bell asked me to luncheon at the King Georges Hotel, reputed to be the best place for Americans to stay as well as eat. He explored my thinking and my decision. We were able to communicate with ease because he spoke French fluently—almost in keeping with mine. He agreed that he considered I had made a good decision and stated he was ready to help me at the American Embassy.

A few days later he called, asking me to go with him to the American consul. He had already arranged for the required physical examination by the American doctors there. The doctor who examined me informed me that he found me in excellent physical health for a man of my age, in spite of my arduous life through many untoward experiences.

Dr. Henry Vincent, the president of the French Baptist Churches Federation, kindly offered his assistance to me in any way needed. He gave me a certificate to the effect that should I return from the United States there would be a place for me within the church organization in Paris and France. I was deeply impressed at the kindness of Henry Vincent. Later, in America I learned that he had graduated from CRDS many years before the war.

I had to obtain a passport to enter the United States of America. I was stateless, without classification of any kind. I was advised by Vincent and Bell to go to the French police and ask for a passport issued to the stateless. As a lawyer, I had never heard of such a thing. But this was true, I was issued a passport for stateless George Crisan, which also guaranteed that I would be accepted in France as a legal resident should I return to France.

The summer of 1949 was the most eventful of my life. The Rumanians, mostly of Orthodox faith or Catholics, were discreetly inquiring whether I was going to America to study for the priesthood. I tried to explain to some that the Baptists and protestants believed that each believer is a priest in his own way. Further comment said we were left here without a *father*, meaning priest, who gave help to the homeless, the stateless, the refugee without skill and work and without even a permit to reside in Paris.

The Baptist Relief or the American Relief under Starmer's management (and in fact mine too) and under Bell's supervision in Starmer's absence, helped many refugees to resettle in Brazil—some in Venezuela and some in Chile. Some went to Canada. As I understood later, many of the Rumanians remained in France. In 1950 or 1951 a new law in regard to the number of refugees to be accepted into the United States was passed, and under that enactment many of my Rumanian and Hungarian refugee friends found a new home in America.

In the summer of 1949, many American students went to France and Europe. Some of the Baptist faith worked in the project to restore some of the churches and other buildings destroyed by the ravages of war and then remained to see the many wonders of Paris—the Eiffel Tower, the Louvre, the Arc of Triumph, the Champs Elysées, and many, many others. Some even came to see the French Baptist church at 48 rue de Lille and to see the relief office for the refugees.

In one of the groups there was a young girl who spoke a little French and I was able to converse with her. Her name (Eleanor Buzzell) sounded French to me, and I remember she said she had heard from Dr. Bell that I was to enroll at CRDS and that she herself had already registered to begin classes in September, 1949.

The most interesting thing of this acquaintance with Eleanor is that we became friends for life. She married Robert Pope (now deceased), and there were three children, now married and with families of their own. What a beautiful and faithful family! She was one of the very earliest friends I made and later showed the same close friendship to my wife and children. We keep in touch through correspondence and telephone calls and visits.

Time was flying by for me, and at times I wondered if I had made the best decision to leave Paris. Here I had a good job and was well situated in every way. Then there was the problem of the English language. After the war I had bought a book titled *How to Learn English by Yourself*, by Professor Candrea. The author had published similar books on learning French and German.

I had carried that book with me in Rumania up to the time of my imprisonment. By that time my study had been paying off. I knew more than a thousand words and was able to communicate my thoughts and ask questions. But that was a while ago, before March and May of 1948, when I lost everything.

Dr. Starmer stressed to me that English was not like Rumanian, French, German, or Italian, a phoenetic language, but it was a spoken language. You spell a word in one way and who can tell how to pronounce it except by hearing it spoken? Dr. Bell was more encouraging. He said, "George, you know French, German and other languages. You will learn English too."

I hired a young Hungarian refugee who spoke English well, and we took walks in the evening, speaking only English.

The summer was flying by and the time of my departure for America was near. I hastened to cram in all the sightseeing I could possibly do. I even hired a bike in order to get about quickly. 1 saw the cathedral of Chartes, the one in Rouen, Boise de Boulogne, the castle of Versailles, Le Havre, Calais, Dunkirk, Lille, Lyon, and so on and on. Through it all I thought what a most amazing country France was, rich in culture and civilized people!

The American Embassy delayed issuing my visa until Dr. Bell accompanied me to the ambassador. I understood much of their conversation. They discussed my intention to study and whether it was not simply a pretense to enter the United States; that Dr. Bell was vouching for me as well as the French Baptist Church Federation through Dr. Henry Vincent, president and pastor of the largest church in Paris.

G.C. with a group of refugees in Paris, September 1949.

On September 18, 1949, I was to board a plane at Orly for New York to cross the Atlantic by plane—a poor refugee with no money. Dr. Bell and Dr. Starmer took care of that emergency through the Baptist World Alliance. In addition to my small briefcase I had a larger luggage purchased in Paris, in which I packed all my belongings, including my American-sent clothes, several French books, many pictures, a painting with dedication to me, a special certificate of recognition signed by a dozen or more prominent refugees including the poet John Velicu, who wrote a poem on my departure.

Dr. Starmer reminded me again that I might have great difficulty with the English language and also in my studies in theology, as it was a most difficult subject. He stressed that I must study hard. I knew what I was facing—I had been a lawyer all my professional life. Dr. Bell encouraged me by saying, "Just learn English as you have learned French and German."

221

IX

Coming to America

My closest friends were crying; some just saying, "Please do not forget us"; others in a more skeptical vein said, "We are parting forever!" or "You will never come back!" And it was a rather joyous drama. "Father Crisan, the 'big brother' of the Rumanian refugees in Paris is now leaving for the New World. But not like the others in the past—he is flying over the Atlantic."

The good-byes were going on at 48 rue de Lille. These friends had no money to accompany me to the airport at Orly.

I remember well, there was no excitement, no increased beating of my heart as we passed through the French control and the checking of the papers and luggage, cursory in detail. I had never been in so huge a plane before, but there was no unusual excitement at all. Only once before, I remember, I had taken the plane in Rumania going from Braila to Constantza and I was the only passenger. Now we were getting ready for take-off with the propellers roaring, and I noted that the two rows of double seats were about filled. Soon we were moving and leaving the land!

It must have been a French Airline, as everything was in French. Once we were informed that we were crossing the English Channel. After some hours we came down on Irish soil at Shannon, to refuel the mammoth plane. As I looked down I could see nothing but dark waters and here and there some whitish spots, and above I could see some clouds and from time to time the sky with stars but no moon. I lost all count of time, but I knew we were running with the time or trying to catch up with it. I was never able to sleep while traveling except for a few very short naps. So I was awake for many hours and drifted into meditation on various past encounters with people from whom I might have gathered some deep observations on the meaning of life. And then the melody or hint of a song or hymn would come to mind and finally the words would become clear to me. This sort of meditation could last for hours.

Some hours later the next landing was announced: Gander, Newfoundland. We were invited to breakfast, and I noted that it was included in my fare. It was daylight with sunshine as well as some cloudiness. I could see the ocean down below and the American coastline. I was beginning to feel great excitement at seeing the coast of the new continent—the new world—where I would soon land. We could see some steamboats on the water, and I was amazed to see numerous spots of land along the coastal lines. These were islands and I soon learned that we were landing on an island—Long Island—at the Idlewild Airport (now Kennedy).

There was a great crowd of people in the airport—more than I'd seen at Orly in Paris. My travels did not end here. I had to go to Detroit to meet with my sponsor, Stanley Catana, who had given me an affidavit of support to stay in the United States for as long as I wanted, which had been provided for from his estate as stated in the affidavit. *How interesting*, I thought, and I was profoundly touched to consider his confidence in me and my life—one he had never met except through some business deals by correspondence.

Now I had to change airports to get a flight to Detroit. The people at the French Airlines counter helped me to find my way in the babble of people speaking English or other languages I was not able to follow. Without mishap, I arrived in Detroit that evening and was met by Stanley and Ecaterina Catana. I glanced around the uncrowded airport and I wondered why there was such a flood of lights, as it did not seem to be needed. Their home was located in Highland Park, which is a town itself, encircled by the large city of Detroit. I had never heard of such a thing in Old Europe and concluded it was just another curiosity of the new world!

Of course, my guarantor immediately called Reverend Pascu in Cleveland to tell him I had arrived. Reverend Pascu asked that I come to Cleveland by bus to attend a conference of the Ohio Baptist Preachers at which he wanted to introduce me. Dr. Sharp and many of the ministers from Ohio were graduates of Colgate Rochester Divinity School. I met many of the preachers all at once and they all wanted to exchange views with me but they did not understand me, nor I them, without interpretation by Reverend Pascu.

Next day was a Sunday. Reverend Pascu asked me to stay with him and his family and attend his church. In fact, he introduced me to a newspaper man who tried to talk with me, with Reverend Pascu acting as interpreter. He took pictures of me, which I considered

223

quite unnecessary. Next day, however, Danila showed me the article containing my picture and his.* I read the article and fully understood it, even though I had not yet mastered the language. I liked the article. It was illustrative of my involvement in Rumania in defending my coreligionists.

Next day, at the Rumanian Baptist church of Cleveland, Reverend Pascu asked me to say something. I spoke of my experiences in Rumania and then in Paris; and that I was here in America due to Reverend Pascu's help; that I had come to study for the ministry. People gathered around me giving me paper money, dollars, for my personal needs, and I left for Detroit with a couple hundred dollars in my pocket. I considered it a fortune indeed, certainly unexpected and completely overwhelming!

I learned I was running behind the school schedules; the classes had started at the Colgate Rochester Divinity School. So I was to take another plane for Rochester, New York. Stanley Catana showed me the location of Rochester on the map. I pictured Rochester as being in New York City before I realized that New York was also a state and Rochester was hundreds of miles away from New York City. I was discovering more and more that America was much larger than I had ever imagined.

AT COLGATE ROCHESTER DIVINITY SCHOOL

I arrived at Rochester on a Saturday afternoon. I took a taxi to the school and the driver let me out in front of a big gothic structure on top of a hill. The doors were closed. No one was in sight, and I hesitated to try the door. Just at that moment a young man came from the building and came forward to meet me, saying, "You must be George."

I understood my name in English. I later learned how he knew who I was. The school bulletin had published my picture and some personal data on the new student coming from Rumania via Paris, France, to study for the ministry at the Colgate Rochester Divinity School. Another surprise—the American way of life and dispersing information on students or faculties or activities.

*"Minister Cancels 20-Year-Old Debt to Refugee," *Cleveland News*, October 1, 1949.

A young student, Bob (Robert Fletcher Smith) was himself first year, spoke some words in French. What little French he knew helped me to understand. He took me in to meet Dr. Froyd, director of research. Bob was able to tell me a little that Dr. Froyd knew me from my own description as filed with the questionnaire I had prepared in Paris, as requested by the school for admission purposes. Still Dr. Froyd called the dean of the school, Dr. Oren Baker.

In about fifteen minutes another professor appeared. It was the dean. I understood from Bob's interpretation that he had been working in the garden and apologized for being late. I was completely taken by surprise by the unexpected consideration given me by the dean. And it was a Saturday afternoon! But the dean paused in his gardening, changing his clothes, and came to meet a foreign and new student, me. He called upon another student, Alfred Neushaffer, to guide me to my room. I was assigned a room with Alfred (Al), with a large joint living room on the second floor, looking over the city of Rochester.

Next day, Dean Baker came to take me to attend his church; he had been pastor there before being called to teach and later becoming the dean. After the service, he invited me to his home to dinner with him and Mrs. Baker. After dinner he took me for a ride around the Rochester area.

The following day he assigned me to read from the New Testament in English, to see how much I understood, explaining as best he could in French; he knew little French. Much later, he explained to me that he had been much concerned about admitting me to school, as I knew so little English. But once admitted, he had no intention of sending me back to Paris but spoke his own philosophy, "Let's try, George"!

I believe that the friendship and constant assistance Al gave me was the encouragement that I needed to face each day. I remember how he even patiently helped me to hold my mouth properly to say water (not vater)! He helped me to learn the states of the United States from memory. He placed a map of the U.S.A. on the wall in front of my desk. And soon afterwards he was bragging to other students on our second floor corridor that I knew by heart all the forty-eight states (at that time, 1949), with their capital cities. I believe (and I smile at the comparison) that he was saying I knew the states, rivers and capital cities better than most of the students. That proved

Student of divinity at Colgate-Rochester
Divinity School, Rochester, New York.
School tower in the background.

a tremendous uplift for George Crisan, a first year student, but
twenty-two years senior of most of the first year students.

At the end of the first week of classes I was invited to dinner
by Bob Withers and his wife. They had a little baby. It was difficult
for both sides to communicate little pleasantries. But Bob and his
wife let me talk and they tried hard to understand what I was saying.
Then came another surprise! After dinner, Bob said, "Now, George,
we have to do the dishes. . . . That is the American way: the wife
prepares the dinner and the husband does the dishes."

A good lesson, which I have faithfully followed all my life!
While washing the dishes we used short sentences, to learn the
name of the dishes. We had fun.

In class, I was many times embarrassed within myself. There
were about 40 students in the first year. The professors came to
lecture and ask questions of the students. The professor talked, the
students took notes, laughed, or raised a hand to ask a question.
I understood very little of what was going on. But I was determined
to keep up my courage. I met my friend from Paris, Eleanore Buzzell,
who tried to converse with me in French and continued to encourage

me. She encouraged me by just saying, "George." It seemed so friendly and warm and loving to speak on a first-name basis. I liked to be called by my first name by the professors and the dean and my classmates. But it was hard for me to reciprocate because of my pronunciation. I tried to see the name in writing and pronounce it accordingly. I soon found out this did not work in English. Why say Bob instead of Robert or Mike instead of Michael?

In class, after about two or three weeks, many students asked me what I was writing in my notebook. It was in Rumanian, notes from the lectures I was following. Many asked how I translated into Rumanian so quickly. It was easy for me if I really understood the words in English. Gradually, I was able to hear distinct words in English, not only to guess, like "and," "that," "he or she," "class." After about two months, I was surprised at my own improvement, since in my notes there were many words in English. Step by step, by the end of the first semester, my notes were taken entirely in English, all in all.

The subjects we were taking were fascinating for me, e.g., the history of the Old or New Testament; the Christian philosophy as written by the earliest fathers of the church. I was not able to turn in my required papers in the first semester, but was allowed by the Dean and the professors to do that over the summer. During the second semester I was able to write my term papers. I enjoyed the readings as required by the courses and suggested by my professors. My papers started coming back marked, "Very good," "Excellent," or "A."

All of the students had places of church affiliation where they served as either assistants to the pastor or as student pastor. I was invited to speak to various groups of my experiences behind the Iron Curtain or of education behind the Iron Curtain. I do not remember how or who introduced me to a radio station, where I was interviewed. Then schools and university students called on me to talk about my escape and what life was like behind the Iron Curtain. Organizations like the Lions, Rotary Club, University Women, and others invited me to speak something of my life experiences. The largest newspaper in Rochester, the *Democrat and Chronicle*, asked me to write or describe in my own words the life in a communistic country and tell of my escape from it. I did this and there was a series of five installments. Almost overnight I achieved notoriety in the County of Monroe, New York!

Speaking to church groups and civic organizations gave me the feeling that I was wanted and accepted into American society and even looked upon with a special interest.

The subjects studied in classes became more and more interesting. I was ready, I felt, to express my own views, and the instructors as well as the students on many occasions expressed their surprise at my insights in the subject of faith, church of Christ, virgin birth, and Deity. My dean was ready to say with the others, "George, you have a wonderful personal philosophy of life," for which I was truly appreciative.

I believe that those years at Colgate Rochester Divinity School helped me to understand life in general and my own life in particular much better. I realized that life calls for assertion, for giving what you have—experience—and sharing it with others; feeling that you are looked upon as somebody with a special experience that the listener was eager to hear and to understand.

I was told repeatedly that I had made a most amazing adjustment to my life in the U.S.A. or as a student at Colgate Rochester Divinity School, where I had enrolled at age forty-two.

I met a student named Leon Pacala whose parents were born in Rumania and who could speak the language well. But really, he could speak only some words. We became quite good friends. I was often invited to dinner in his home. His wife, Janet, showed a loving understanding of my awkward use of English. Leon and Janet took me to visit their parents in Indiana and there I was considered an adopted member of the Pacala family. And what a fine family!

Leon, after studying at Louvain, Belgium, under a Rotary International Schlorship, graduated from Yale with a Ph.D. in Christian philosophy, and was probably the youngest dean ever appointed by the Bucknell University, Pennsylvania, and no doubt the youngest president Colgate Rochester Divinity School ever had. (Now, in 1983, he is the executive director of the Association of Theological Schools of the United States and Canada.)

ALIEN STUDENT

In the summer of 1950 I had to extend my student visa, which was expiring. The French Consul wanted me to go to Paris and only there could it be extended for another year, because I entered the

United States with a French reentry permit, or a passport for an alien residing in France. How could I go back to France for that visa only? Dean Baker said that the school would give me a certificate to the effect that I had accomplished all that was necessary to be ordained in the Christian Ministry. I told Dean Baker I wanted to finish my studies and have a degree! He was concerned at that point that I was a sort of perennial student. At forty-two years of age, I was not eager to leave the school!

The dean said that now they knew me well and would try to have me granted a further scholarship by the American Baptist Convention. How about my staying in the United States with a French traveling paper, as my visa to stay in the U.S.A. as a student would expire in September? Dean Baker put me in contact with the Chamber of Commerce, where I met the officer in charge of community affairs, Mr. James Tipping. Surprises again. The man, with graying hair behind a mahogany desk, rose from his chair and came about half way across the room to receive me and shake hands with me. What a courtesy shown me! In a few weeks Mr. Tipping called me and wanted to see me, telling me that Congressman Keating was filing a bill in the Congress of the United States of America that I may become a permanent resident of the U.S.A.; that meanwhile, as a matter of courtesy, the Immigration Services would not order my deportation to France.

In my heart and mind I cried my recognition to God for all these people at the school and in the city who had put so much interest in my behalf and in my cause of becoming an American resident. Then a letter from Congressman Keating came directly to me saying he considered "it a real honor to act through the Congress in your behalf; it will be a gain for America to have you here."

I was called a modest man. Some of my political friends mentioned the fact that I was intelligent, hard working, and reliable, but I was too modest and too humble in outlook. Here the Americans spoke differently, saying I was a worthy person to become an American citizen. One said, "George, this is America, it is not Europe. There is no social hierarchy here. These Americans take you in stride, tell you, looking you straight in the eye, just what they think of you and also what they would like to do for you."

I thought back to my childhood days in my homeland and my school days there. My father sent me to boarding school when I was ten years old. I remember how my mother and grandmother cried when I left saying I was too young to be sent away from home. They felt I should not be sent away from the ancestral home where the family had plenty for the well-to-do life in the village of Tisa and where the family had always lived well and who had been made gentries from time immemorial. My father's only argument for such a move was, "I don't want my child to tread the same muddy paths both winter and summer that we have always had to do—for him I want better things." And now I remember the impression of America by a few peasants who had made some money there and returned home to buy their own acres of land. The same impression was expressed by all, "It *is* a new world! It's different from anything we have seen before. The people are different. They are all so kind."

Now, I agree that it is all true. Those people are different! They made me feel at home and took me to their hearts with every kindness and consideration. All these kindnesses were demonstrated to me before I went to a theological school, but back when I was a stranger to them.

I was elated by Keating's letter and I wrote him a lengthy letter in reply, telling of my escape, my work in Paris, my desire to study at the Colgate Rochester Divinity School, and how privileged I felt that a United States Congressman took my case to his heart and wanted to help me stay in the United States. I stated at the end that if I had his consent I wanted to publish the letter in the *Democrat* and *Chronicle* of Rochester, New York. Of course, I was authorized and the letter was published. That brought in many calls and invitations to speak at various churches, school gatherings, and such throughout the state of New York. Once I traveled to Binghamton, New York, to address the university women and to give an interview on radio. The local papers were making comments at the same time concerning the Rumanian student who escaped from behind the Iron Curtain. In short, I had become a sort of speaker in demand.

On occasion Dean Baker expressed his concern that my publicity in speaking out against the Communist-dominated regimes in Rumania might result in endangering the safety of my folks in Rumania—my parents and my four brothers and their families. I tried to assure Dean Baker that because of their faith they would face suffering, imprisonment, or worse, and my speaking out against communism would make little difference in their lives one way or the other. I felt I had to tell what I knew from first-hand experience of the treatment of the Communists toward those in their power. I felt a moral duty to do so, and he accepted that view.

One by one our instructors invited small groups of students into their homes for dinner and group discussions. This amazed me. Here the dean or the president of the Theological School and the professors were opening their homes to the students they were teaching. It was unheard of in Rumania or in Paris.

On such occasions, the hosts treated the students as equals and were ready to hear the view of any student on no matter what subject—theologic, political, social, or foreign affairs.

In the spring of 1950 the school chorus took a lengthy trip, stopping in many places; singing in the local church where a graduate of CRDS was the preacher. We traveled through Southern New York, Pennsylvania, Maryland, and down to Washington, D.C., the nation's capital city. Dr. Lehman, professor of public speaking and music, was our choir director. It was most interesting and revealing to learn of the activities of the school. We were housed by the local people. I got to see an American family, its home, its open door to students, and usually after each performance there was a reception. I thought that all this attention might have been too elaborate for an itinerant chorus.

In Washington, D.C., we sang at the First Baptist church, which is located downtown. I learned that the assistant pastor was a graduate of CRDS. We sang in many other places. We sang in many black churches, too. There were quite a few black students at CRDS. I was invited by some of them to speak in their churches. Such churches or the attendants there were happy to give me money for any appearance.

In Washington, it was Reverend Dowdy who guided us to see the city. What a city! We went to the capitol. We saw the Supreme Court, about which we had read all our lives. We saw the White House. We had a visit to the Library of Congress. On our way home, Dr. Gustav Lehman, our beloved professor of music, asked me how I liked the capital city and what impressed me most. I replied that I was deeply impressed with the Library of Congress and its reading hall. I added to Dr. Lehman, "Dr. Lehman, I am a sort of book collector and I've been called a bookworm of sorts. I've never seen so many books in one place."

The mysterious happenstance comes to everyone at one time at another, so it has been said. Who can explain it? It happened to me in this way: After my graduation and after having a job with my denominatioon, I received a telegram from the Law Librarian of the Library of Congress to the effect that my name had been indicated to him as one who would be interested in working in the Law Library. (I will refer to this later as I spent four years working in the Law Library of Congress as a legal analyst.)

Many of the students were married. Some had their own churches and invited me to speak or even preach (in later years) in their churches. I was amazed to see that every student had his own car. I knew nothing of the cost of a car then or of its upkeep. I felt even reluctant to accept a ride to or from school and some of my colleagues accused me of being bashful in accepting rides, or that I was not yet Americanized as to allotting my time, and they could not understand why I would prefer to walk an hour or two when a ten-minute ride would cover the distance.

Some of the married students became my lifelong friends. One couple I especially remember, Ken and Genevieve Peterson. First they invited me into their home, and, as time went on we became close friends and this friendship has endured for thirty-four years. Even now, I receive cards from them on my birthday and our wedding anniversary. I was their guest many times in places where Ken was pastor.

Bob Withers invited me one time to speak to the Baptist Youth Union in Spencer, where his father, Dr. Gordon Withers, was pastor. Every invitation extended to me was heartwarming all over again for the kindnesses of the American students to a stranger who could not fully express himself in the English language.

Once I was invited to speak to a group of senior high school graduating students. Of course, I learned from the time of my first speaking engagement that there would be questions from the audience. It really thrilled me to answer some quite simple questions put to me by the boys or girls and to see them satisfied with my answers. Once at such a group and after the question and answer session had ended, people gathered around me, both young and old, with such comments as, "I wish I could hear you talk to us for a longer period," or "I would enjoy hearing your views for a much longer period." Such expressions were my highest gratifications—a personal satisfaction of the greatest depth.

AMERICAN STUDENT

My scholarship from the American Baptist Convention covered my tuition and room. I faced the problem of food and the sundry necessities, but Dean Baker also considered this problem with me. He, I assumed, asked the student pastors or whoever had invited me to speak to pay me a modest honorary fee, say five or ten dollars. This was a modest amount for even 1950–52, but to me it meant a great deal.

For example, when I was invited to speak at a certain place—like Charleston, West Virginia—that church paid the airfare, gave me transportation, housing, and some pocket money. It was given with no obligation on my part. It was difficult for me to take in the American way of doing things—direct, unassuming, kind to the other—and every day brought me ways to see the way of life in America!

Dean Baker and his wife, Margaret, never forgot to show a special interest in my behalf during my student days at CRDS. It seems I was considered their adopted child and I considered him as my father here in America. Any inquiry of a personal nature about me should be addressed to him. By the middle of my three-year term as a divinity student he informed the faculty that I had made an amazing adjustment as a student in America. Such recognition from my dean lifted my spirits beyond telling!

The dean, knowing my financial needs, made it possible for me to work in the school library. CRDS has a unique Baptist library in that it has books that cannot be found anywhere else. I painstakingly wiped each and every book of the dust and remember one day the elderly lady who had charge of the Baptist collection saying to me, "George, don't work so hard, take it easy, some of these books haven't been moved or dusted since the establishment of the Library in 1912!" But to examine the books was intriguing, and it was exciting to look at the first page of some printings long out of use. I felt more and more that God's hand had led me to this place.

Reverend Pascu and his pastor friends continued to invite me to speak in their churches and at their conventions. It was a considerable distance to travel to Detroit for the annual conventions, but the ministers found a way to pay my air fare. I met many old Rumanian folks at these meetings, many of whom had left Rumania or Austria-Hungary long before the First World War. I noted they spoke a very odd Rumanian. The Rumanian language had changed a lot in 50 years, and these wonderful folks had never attended a Rumanian school, or any school for that matter. Many wanted me to visit in their homes and wanted to know more and more about the old country. I had met some of their relatives to whom they might have sent money through the offices of Stanley Catana, my client or correspondent in America. The world was shrinking in size to me—I was meeting Rumanian-Americans whose relatives I had known before.

I heard stories of life in the old country and of events that had happened before I was born. And there were stories of how they made the trip to New Canaan, as they called America. I heard stories of how they built churches here. Their stories included their various activities: schooling for those who wanted to enter the ministry (some of whom became leaders among the Rumanian-speaking people); establishment of a publication in 1913 organizing the First Rumanian-American Baptist Association. Since this establishment, an annual convention is held. They learned from the American Baptists that while the Baptist churches are independent they all share and have fellowship with one other and are united in the work of Christ in the field of missions among Rumanians in America who had never heard of Baptists.

Reverend Pascu and his fellow preachers pointed at me with interest in my life history—I was an attorney in Rumania (the only one in the Baptist faith); had escaped from communistic Iron Curtain life; had enrolled in school to train for the ministry of Jesus Christ. The editor of the paper, *Luminator*, asked me to write some articles for their publication about my life. I did this, and the articles were well received and I have since continued to write for them. Later, I became the editor of the *Luminator* and continued in this position for many years while at the same time I was the counsel of the association.

SUMMER WORK IN NEW YORK

I never learned by what coincidence the former vice prime minister of Rumania, Dr. Sabin Manuila, found out that I was studying at CRDS. He invited me to work for Free Europe in New York over the summer. I was one of the last men to have knowledge of the Rumanian situation in 1948, after the communistic takeover in December 1947. He had learned about me and my whereabouts in Paris and of my involvement with the Baptist Relief, as our office was called in Europe. He arranged that I come to New York and prepare a questionnaire for the Department of State (or CIA) with questions to be put to Jewish immigrants from Rumania to Israel, or refugees themselves. It was a well-paid job for me. Dr. Manuila hinted that at my age and with my experience I should not continue my studies at the present but join the people at Free Europe and become involved in the work of the Rumanian Committee in Exile. I told him that while I appreciated the suggestion, I had committed myself to finish my training at the divinity school. He respected my position but did not understand me, since he was surrounded by other people in exile who had held important places in the Rumanian government before the communistic coup. I just could not see it like they did; namely, that the Americans will force the hand of Russia and free Rumania, or at least let the people express freely their will in Western Allies-supervised elections.

All this is a sort of puzzle to me now as I look back at my attitude at that time. It's true, I am an optimist by nature. I wanted to see my parents, brothers, sister, and the Rumanian nation all freed from the communistic terror. I wanted to be able to communicate with my people in writing at least; yet I did not embrace the idea to become a "politico in exile," sponsored or supported by the American State Department. I understood later that it was my cousin Miron who had told Dr. Manuila about me. He had also spoken to Emil Ghilezan, former Deputy Finance Minister in the last democratic government in Rumania.

While in New York over the summer I was a guest of Dr. and Mrs. Manuila and of Mr. and Mrs. Emil Ghilezan. Later, when Miron arrived in America in 1951, he mentioned that Ghilezan had commented that I was "quite intelligent but too humble."

GEORGE, THE BACHELOR

The best and lasting friendships I made were with the students who were married or about to be married. They invited me for dinner when possible and often the question was asked of me, "George, why don't you marry? You seem to be a fine housekeeper, of acceptable manners, with no apparent vices!" Such questions held no embarrassment. I was forty-five years of age and at about the end of my theological studies. An old bachelor! Some of the students might have asked me whether I believed in celibacy! The answer to this question is No! In fact, I never thought of myself at the age of forty-one or forty-five as a bachelor. I was a lawyer in the depth of the depression years, 1930. To take the responsibility of a family was serious thinking at that time, and besides, there was no income in sight. So the years flew by. When I began to have an income, I turned to helping my brothers finish their educations. Certainly I had friends among the girls whom I enjoyed in the social circles of our community.

The rattles of war came upon Europe on September 29, 1939. I was called into service, and there I remained almost constantly until 1945. I probably was a sort of "thoughtful" fellow, whatever that means. To me, now looking back, it probably meant that I really did not want to marry just for the sake of having a spouse along with me. Well, anyway, it seemed to me at that time that there was nothing exciting going on; the life in general was rather subdued and somewhat uneventful. It might have been that I took my responsibility in life too seriously. Anyway, when I was able to take on responsibility, the war broke off.

Then, I remember telling my friends that I did not feel old, being "an old bachelor." I cited other examples: Apostle Paul did not marry; Jesus Christ did not marry; St. Thomas D'Aquinas did not marry nor Saint Francis d'Assissi, et cetera. Someone came back with the comment, "George, you have the right answer to such personal questions!"

A classmate introduced me to his sister-in-law, who was a child psychology student. We developed a friendship. She helped me by typing some of my papers and correcting some of my expression in my writing. The girls in my classes were quite young, and I hesitated to make them feel embarrassed with any attempt to befriend them. Several friends attempted to match me with some of the older girls who were either divorced or widowed. But as it happened, I did not develop any great personal interest in any of them.

ORDAINED

The students in the third-year class were either long since ordained into the ministry by their churches or were to be ordained before leaving the divinity school. My main thought at this time was to finish what I had started—to start doing some work as a minister or else be ordained into the ministry. Leon Pacala approached me on the subject of ordination. "George, are you going to ask for ordination?"

"I don't think so," I replied.

"And why not?" was his next question.

I commented, "I don't have a church to serve in."

His reasoning came then, "The school prepared us to become ministers, but that does not mean we have to take a church—in fact, we may never be called by a church. We may switch to other fields like teaching. As for myself, I want to teach after I take a Ph.D."

At this point, I had not thought a great deal about what I would attempt after graduation. But this questioning was opening up new vistas in my mind. I was not living in the past, but had not become too much concerned about the future, either. It set me to thinking about the future at this time. My inner thought was, *God's will be done!* That's what I was reaching for regarding what would happen in my life!

So I asked for ordination in the First Baptist church of Rochester. Dr. Deems, my pastor, assured me that he would be happy to arrange the procedures of my ordination. Of course, I was called to appear before the county committee of the Baptist churches. I related to them my feelings about being a Christian, and about being called to proclaim the gospel of Jesus Christ and to give a living example of following in the footsteps of Christ. I may have impressed the council with my life experience in Rumania behind the Iron Curtain or administering the Baptist Relief in Paris, France, before coming to Colgate Rochester Divinity School.

I was ordained in the same service with Ed Ribnicheck, a classmate from Minnesota (I believe) whose parents came from Czechoslovakia.

The ordination service was most meaningful to me. My closest friends of the faculty participated in the services. First, there was Dean Baker, my adopted father in America, and there were Dr. Lehman, Dr. Hudson, and Rev. Nick Titus, whose parents had come from Rumania long ago. At the time of my ordination, Nick was minister in a church in East Syracuse.

At the moment when Dean Baker gave me the charge, among other things he said it had been a privilege "to have George among the students at the school and that possibly he was the most illustrious student to have passed through Colgate Rochester Divinity School."

Once again, such remarks only served to buttress my confidence, reassuring me that I was not a lost being but was well thought of by Americans who knew me and who recognized some abilities in me.

It was hard to realize that I had come to the end of my theological studies just when I was enjoying it the most; just when my power of expression was proving itself to be good; just when I was feeling close to all this family at CRDS. I felt almost as close to these friends as to my brothers back in Rumania. These friends had been real brothers to me, caring for me and feeling a profound interest in my welfare and future. We all looked forward to keeping in touch for life—which has been true to this day.

X

WORKING AGAIN

ABOUT one year before my graduation from the Colgate Rochester Divinity School, Rev. Joseph Ardelean, pastor of the Rumanian Baptist church of Akron, Ohio, asked me whether I would accept a call from his church. He explained that he had retired from his job with the Goodyear Rubber Company and was ready to relinquish his pastorate to me. I very gingerly declined to make any definite commitment at the time. About this same time, while attending the Rumanian-American Baptist Convention of the U.S.A. and Canada in Detroit, Rev. Truta of Gary, Indiana, asked me whether I would consider a call from the Rumanian church in Gary. To him I was more direct. I learned the church was dying and there were only three or four families attending the church. The surrounding neighborhood had become a slum area. The young generation of Rumanians had moved away and those remaining of the older generation were less than a dozen.

During my third year at CRDS, officials from the Baptist denomination began recruiting upcoming graduates to fill jobs in the denomination. Dr. Baker knew I had decided not to return to France, and he set about making an appointment for me to be interviewed by an official of the American Baptist Convention. It proved to be an interesting interview for me, and not long before graduation I was informed that I had been "hired" by the American Foreign Mission Society of New York City. I was to work with them starting June 1. I did not ask any details of the job or the amount of money I would receive.

Dean Baker made further inquiry about my housing and I found out I could stay in the Biblical Seminary (49th Street East) in a student room while the students were in summer vacation and I was learning my way around the city of New York.

I packed my big locker and my suitcase and, with the help of some students, managed to get it all shipped through to the post office.

I faced the parting with a fairly serene mind. The school's in-

Dean Dr. Oren Baker and G.C. at G.C.'s ordination in the Christian ministry, May 1952.

fluence and its trainings in many directions now stood me in good stead in my adjustment to this new land. I could look forward with full confidence that many good things were in store for me even though I had not accepted calls to become a preacher or minister in a Rumanian-American church.

I had learned from Leon Pacala and others that it was not a "must" to take a church pastorate following graduation and ordination in the ministry of the gospel of Jesus Christ. Some of the most brilliant students, like Leon, were pursuing their studies toward a Ph.D., aiming to become educators. So I began thinking along these lines and talked to Leon about it. I learned that some schools furnished scholarships for graduate students; that is, one might as an assistant instructor obtain a scholarship.

I began to consider seriously studying toward a Ph.D. and possibly a teaching career in a college. I inquired as to such possibility at Northwestern in Chicago and others.

Before leaving, I set about getting some pictures of my beloved

Dean Baker (my American adoptive father). And in the melancholy of farewell I realized that all good things must come to an end—my studenthood and these associations. Soon afterward, I left by train for New York City.

NEW YORK CITY

I arrived at the Biblical Seminary on 49th Street East and found it empty except for the attendant in the lobby. He knew about my coming to stay there for two months or so and showed me to my room and gave me a key. I looked around and there I was on the second floor of this building—alone and dependent upon my own resources here in this big city. Because of two previous summer vacations spent in New York City working for Free Europe and for the Rumanian Welfare Society I thought I knew something of Manhattan.

On Monday morning I started toward my office at Madison and 33rd Street. I wanted to judge whether I would be able to walk the distance rather than taking a bus or the subway. It took me about forty-five minutes, which I considered not bad for a seasoned walker like myself.

I went to the offices of the American Baptist Foreign Mission Society (ABFMS) located on the seventeenth floor, to learn my next step. There I was met by three young women in the front office, and one of them introduced me to Dr. Dana Albaugh, executive secretary of the ABFMS. He was cordial and friendly to me and assured me he had been informed of my background and whereabouts by my school. He related to me something of his own background—that he had been a missionary in the Congo (now Zaire) in Africa for a time but had to return home because of ill health. He had since written a book about the mission field in Africa.

A new profession in a new job faced me. My position was research assistant: to do research, collect, and digest the policies of the society regarding the missionaries in various mission fields throughout the world. I was supervised by a young woman.

One of my co-workers, a young woman, had been a teacher for the mission in Japan and Thailand. We easily became friends and talked about our previous work. She invited me to lunch on a dutch-treat basis, saying, "It's always dutch-treat."

I declined, not knowing what a dutch-treat was. When she explained, we laughed and had a pleasant luncheon at the luncheonette, Chock-Full-of-Nuts, on Madison Avenue.

Two weeks or so later, my supervisor expressed agreement that I was doing a fine job of researching as well as typing the digested policies that I had collected from the files. It was a simple job and in fact I became quite tired of reading here and there and making some notes of it. If I remember well, I was paid about sixty dollars a week in 1952.

On returning home one evening I found a letter that had been forwarded from CRDS to the Biblical Seminary from my old friend and former pastor, Dr. John Cocutz. He was writing from New York City and asked me to call him at the enclosed number at my earliest convenience, which I did at once.

He related his story in detail. He lived in Manhattan not very far from my address. He had come to America in May 1939, with Pascu and Sezonov. Because of the war he did not return to Rumania. He had been married to Anna Marian of Arad. He was called to be pastor of the Rumanian Baptist church in Akron, Ohio, where he became involved with the wife of one of his parishioners. He left the ministry and his wife divorced him. He married the woman he ran away with and later went to live in Atlanta, Georgia. There he was helped by the Southern Baptist Board to finish his education here in America and he graduated with a Ph.D. in Philosophy. He, or someone for him, wrote President Truman seeking a place he could work. And there he was at the desk of the Voice of America (I believe the office was on 59th Street in New York City).

How did he find me at CRDS? Probably from Reverend Pascu of Cleveland; I was not sure. But he had learned that I was studying for the ministry at CRDS. He wanted me to write for him and broadcast messages to the Rumanian people concerning the treatment given them by the Communist government—how they were jailed and so on. He paid for each "script" and for its delivery. Suddenly, I realized that it was possible for me to work in another field and thereby increase my earnings, which at that time were meager. The whole thing was like a "shot in the arm" and a boost to my life.

Cocutz urged me to try to secure a scholarship or fellowship; that it would not be difficult for me to take a Ph.D. and obtain a position in teaching. He spoke from his quite expanded experience in America!

242

I spoke to Dr. Dana Albaugh of my encounter with an old friend, and he was quite impressed by the story. He told me that "he was sure I could do a good work for the Voice of America" in view of my experience behind the Iron Curtain and in Paris and now in America for three years.

While I had a faculty for taking things in stride and was a more or less happy-go-lucky man, the words of Jesus on one occasion came to mind, "Look at the birds of the air, they do not sow or reap and their Heavenly Father provides for them in due time." So at the time I thought, *Why worry?* I thought back over some of my experiences—how I had escaped the terrors of the past, and now I need not worry about tomorrow but look to today with its opportunities and requirements.

I attended several churches on Sundays trying to learn where I might find a fellowship close to my heart. I attended services at the Calvary Baptist, the Collegiate church, and the Riverside Baptist church. I attended several services at the Riverside church and was especially impressed by the type of service and the preaching of Dr. MacCracken. Somehow, it seemed too large for me. Also, I attended services at the Mount Olivet Baptist Church, a black church. The preacher, Dr. Maxwell, probably prompted by his son, Lowell, recognized me in the congregation of a thousand or so, and greeted me from the platform.

Early in July, I found a telegram in my mail box that had been forwarded from Rochester to the Biblical Seminary. It was the first telegram I had received in America, and I was excited and intrigued as to its meaning. The message was from the Law Library of the Library of Congress, Washington, D.C., telling me, in substance, "Your name was referred as one potentially interested in a job with the Law Library of the Library of Congress. If so, please call or wire availability after which will send the necessary money for traveling expenses to Washington for an interview. Signed, Keath."

I was completely mystified. I had not heard about the Law Library. I thought to myself, could this be just a prank from some Communist-inspired people trying to entrap me? I was unhappy with the wire. Here I was, just starting work for my denomination which had kept me in school for three years. Receiving this message was an upsetting surprise, to say the least. Who had given my name, when, and why?

I told John Cocutz about the wire. He was excited. I was not!

243

I hesitated to speak to Dr. Albaugh about it. Eventually, he sensed my uneasiness or an extrasensorial aspect in my manner, and one day asked me how I was doing with VOA and whether I had found a church to join in fellowship in this big city of New York. Then I told him about the wire I had received from Washington and showed it to him.

Without much ado, Dr. Albaugh said, "I know what is bothering you, George. You think you have an obligation to work for our denomination, which sponsored you for three years in the school. You are not obligated to do anything, George. You can serve the Lord wherever you may be."

How could I ever forget such words and such meaningful advice! He continued, "You go to Washington to see what sort of job they have for you"; and he added, "The government pays much better than we can. According to your salary, you are classified as a beginner. We may not be able to increase your salary in six months or more. However, by far, we cannot pay you and our other employees a salary equal to what the government pays its employees. Of course, you are not a beginner in the work. You know all that we know here. But go and see what they offer."

This was an eye-opening speech to me.

I went to Washington in early August 1952. I met with the law librarian, Mr. Keath. He was impressive in appearance—tall, lanky, a Texan, and a "hardcore Baptist," as he expressed it. I did not know just what he meant, but pretended that I knew.

He passed me on to his deputy for an interview. It was rather short and went somewhat like this: "Have you practiced law in Rumania? Have you argued cases in court? Have you prepared memoranda for court, briefs, et cetera?" My answers were equally brief. "Yes, I practiced law in Rumania for eighteen years as an attorney at law. Sometimes, I argued several cases a day in our local court. I had many appearances before the courts of appeal and even before the Supreme Court of Rumania, where I had been accredited after five years of practice of law."

He said, "We need you and your experience. When can you come? We start your pay at the grade seven level ($260 a week), but after six months we will raise your salary to the level of Grade GS9."

I was not greatly excited at the big difference by this salary and my previous pay. (It was about four times higher.) I was not looking to make money as my first incentive in my new homeland. But I was, indeed, looking for work that I would enjoy. That was the work of analyzing the laws of Rumania for the Congress of the United States. At that time there were no diplomatic relations between the U.S.A. and Rumania. The Iron Curtain was quite tight. The Congress wished to be informed of the happenings behind the Iron Curtain and what sort of laws or order or rules the communistic regime imposed by Russia govern the Rumanian people. And I knew, from experience.

"When can you come?"

"I have to talk this over with my employer in New York, but I believe he would release me shortly."

I went back to Dana Albaugh. I told him of my interview and he quickly advised me, "Take it, George. You are an accomplished man. You are a lawyer here in America, too. You help the country by working with the government. And also you are at the age when you should look to your personal life; to look forward to a home and family of your own here in America. You are a young man, George, regardless of your age."

I wired Washington that I could be ready to start my work with the Law Library of the Library of Congress on September 8, 1952.

Of course, I had enjoyed writing and sending the speeches to the Voice of America. Cocutz said he would expect to continue to receive the speeches. He said, "George, just write it, lay it aside overnight, read it over in the morning, and mail it to me!"

How kind and encouraging his encouragement was to me!

WASHINGTON, D.C.

I took the train to Washington and went at once to the Library of Congress. I noted a number of tourist houses on East Capitol and found a room I could rent. It was about a block from the Library building. I discovered that the lady of the house was a Baptist believer. She said I might have the room until the following March because the tourist season was over.

So I settled into my large room on the second floor with a bathroom on the corridor. The landlady and her husband were friendly and helpful in every way possible. I learned that they had been married by Rev. Kent Kiser's brother-in-law. Ken's wife's sister was married to a preacher in Maryland. That made our tenant-and-

G.C. at the Library of Congress September 1952. The Capitol is in the background, facing the Library of Congress.

landlady relations quite friendly, and after a short time I felt like a member of the family.

In the Law Library of Congress there was already established an East-European Law division. Former judges or attorneys, who had succeeded in getting out from behind the Iron Curtain, were hired to do research and analyses for the benefit of the Congress or other lawyers and people interested in the development of law behind the Iron Curtain. Representatives included those from Soviet Russia, Poland,Czechoslovakia, Hungary, Bulgaria, Yugoslavia, Rumania, and the Baltic countries—Estonia, Livonia, and Lithuania.

In the Rumanian section there were three young lawyers who had not yet at that time practiced law in Rumania. This also was an added incentive to me to join the researchers here and the analysts of law under the supervision of Vladimir Gsovski (a Russian who had escaped from Russia before the Second World War—a scholar in the true sense of the word, who had a Ph.D. in law and who did law studies in the U.S.A.). His deputy was a former Polish judge and law school professor.

In a short time I was befriended by many in this group, especially by the Hungarian "scholars in residence," as the law librarian called us. I soon realized that some of these people had never worked in a day-to-day workload routine. Some of them were former diplomats in their respective countries; some were sons of well-to-do industrialists; and one of them was the son of a former chief justice of his country (even his grandfather had been a chief justice). They enjoyed talking of the good old days and of the positions they had lost. Some of the young had hopes of returning to their country as heroes. Among them there was a former ambassador of his country (Czechoslovakia). There was one of his counsellors and a former vice prime minister of Czechoslovakia and several former university professors.

Some became interested in me because I had a "double profession," as they called it—I was a "priest" and yet a "lawyer." Most of them could not understand this "mixture" in one person—George Crisan—that is, reverend and esquire!

While it was fascinating to work within such a scholarly and dignified circle of "learned brothers," to me it was even more fascinating to be surrounded by these millions of books, to work in the largest and richest library in the world—the Library of Congress of the United States, across the plaza from the Capitol of the country and across the street from the Supreme Court of the United States! *Where in the world was there a more interesting place to work? The real center of the Free World,* I thought.

The Hungarian "learned brethren" were the first ones to invited me to have a coffee break or luncheon with them. I soon realized that as "scholars in residence" we were sort of privileged people. The Congress and the American international lawyers and politicos, in one way or the other, were calling on the Law Library of the Library of Congress for some insight into what was happening behind the Iron Curtain.

The Department of State asked for opinions on laws, on confiscation of property including that of foreign citizens; the American citizens, through their lawyers or Congressmen, or both, inquired as to what was happening to their investments in foreign countries, like those taken by Russia, as her sphere of influence under the so-called Yalta Protocol (1945).

Some in the group were too serious in the position "of trust," not showing much sense of humor; others took the situation with a grain of salt. They were looking forward to the day of liberation of their respective countries; and in the meantime were doing something in the Library of Congress for a living.

George Torzsay-Biber, one of the Hungarian fellows, cynical in

247

his humor, caught my attention. He made fun of his ancestry as a descendant of a count family going back to Louis XIV of France, who sent one Torzsay to the king as counsel for the administration of justice and ever since that time in the seventeenth century his family have held the position of greatest rank in the Administration of Justice in Hungary.

The Hungarian fellows called me Gyury, Hungarian for George. We often spoke to one another in Hungarian. I was told that my speaking Hungarian language improved tremendously during the time and was about perfect. I had not had an opportunity to speak Hungarian since before the Second World War.

The Hungarian fellow who worked side by side with me was Hugo Kalnoky. A newspaperman by training, he was the son of a former Foreign Minister of Hungary. He was a very knowledgeable and versatile man but inclined to be a little excitable at times. Almost every day he would remind me that I was a Hungarian and not a gypsy as the Rumanians are! He said, "George, you were born and lived in Transylvania, which was under the Hungarian king's Scepter for a thousand years. How can you, Gyury, say you are Rumanian? Nonsense!"

We were writing a study on church and state behind the Iron Curtain, I the Rumanian part, he the part on Hungary. I remember the count became excited and quite angry with me when he saw my introduction on my part of the paper in which I quoted Herodotus and several other ancient sources which told of the Gothic Dacian people as being Christians between the third and fourth centuries A.D. and that they had an organized Christian church and sent a bishop to the Nicaean Council of Nicaea in 325. The count was outraged on my assertion and he said, "George made the Rumanians as Christian even before the coming of Christ."

The matter was quite serious, but our boss was persuaded by my showing him the sources where I found such a historical fact.

The count was a Catholic. He became ill, and it was discovered that he had cancer. Biber asked that I visit him in the hospital. When we entered the ward, he said, "Away, George, you are a heretic [Protestant]. I would not take communion from you on my last day here on earth."

He never lost his good humor to the end of his life. At the funeral services I was asked to be and was one of the pallbearers.

The other Hungarians, Leszly LeNard and Alexander Bedo,

claimed to be of Hungarian nobility. They attempted to persuade me that my forefathers had been ennobled by one of the Hungarian kings; I thought the nobility had been granted by the Austrian empress, Maria Theresa. Be that as it may, I was of "equal rank," at least in the eyes of my Hungarian friends.

Mr. Koczvara, the former vice prime minister of Czechoslovakia before the Communist coup, was a very quiet man and appeared to be somewhat subdued. I learned the reason. While in Prague, as vice prime minister of the government, Masaryk (the son of the first president of Czechoslovakia), the foreign minister of the time, was thrown from his third-floor office to his death on the street. The Communists, who overthrew the government, claimed that he had committed suicide. Mr. Koczvara was a protestant and attended the Lutheran church about a block from the library. He asked me whether I would speak to an evening gathering in his church if invited by the minister. I accepted the invitation and because of my fluent English (with accent) I was well received and was able to answer many questions put to me. I felt that now I had something to say even in Washington, D.C. I heard such remarks as, "George is a priest and should be treated with due deference."

Kiril Jazsenko, the fellow scholar in the Yugoslav section, was born in Saint Petrograd, now Leningrad. When the Bolshevik revolution flared up in 1917, his parents took their infant and managed to escape and settle in a Baltic country for a short while then made their way down to Belgrade, Yugoslavia, where Kiril grew up and became a lawyer. Then came the Second World War, and Kiril and his wife and two children escaped from Hitler's occupation in 1945 or 1946 and came to America. So many of us had followed this same path.

Once Kiril came to me and asked whether I would talk to him about a private matter. Of course, I agreed. We took a walk around the library grounds and he poured out his story. "George, you are a priest in another denomination. I am Russian Orthodox, but I believe we are all Christians. Since my childhood and later, my family and I attended the church liturgy and holy communion. I tried to live a righteous life. I will tell you what happened to me last week. While traveling toward New York before crossing the Delaware Bridge, my wife, who was driving, was involved in an accident in which a police officer was killed. A widow and three children were left. My wife collapsed and is quite ill in a hospital. I am not sure that she will recover. Why has my family been so punished in this terrible way? Can you give me some solace?"

"Kiril, I am an ordained minister of the Baptist faith. I have never had a church of my own; neither do I serve as a minister or as a priest as in your church. However, I have something to say. No priest in any denomination would be able to tell you why this tragedy has happened to you. Neither can I except to say that in my life pilgrimage I have met with many terrible dilemmas. I shall refer to the story of Job of the Old Testament who lost everything: family, fortune, and health. He questioned God as to why he was so punished.

"We always ask why these things happen to us. There is no answer and I can give you none. But I would say to you only as Job confessed that we are indeed too small, too limited in our humanity to understand tragedies that happen to us. But we must believe if God in the past granted us good things, which has also included a good land of refuge in the United States, then He must have in his love and mercy more good days in store for you, Kiril, and others like us. I cannot say more than 'Keep the faith,' and in our life pilgrimage we will all find new joys and rewards in the keeping of the faith!"

This conversation made me aware that some of my fellow workers were looking at me in some special way. Kiril and his family became my friends for life, and we continue to keep in touch to this day even though he lives in Florida and I in Maryland.

One day the law librarian called me into his office to show me a letter from the Department of State praising my work. There was also a special article I wrote, "A Rumanian Minister of Justice Decapitated by His Party." It was Patrascanu's story. I was familiar with the gruesome story of what happened to Patrascanu. I could only conclude with the sad refrain, "Whoever digs another's grave may fall into it himself." The minister had been a Socialist and had accepted the position of the minister of justice in a communistic government. Because of his civilized approach to the dispersing of justice in a communistic regime, he was accused of being a traitor to the West, jailed, sentenced to death, and executed.

Another piece of writing that received praise was my study, "The Early Workers' Union in Rumania and Its Development Till the Communists Took Over and Its Strangulation." It was the only work of the kind. Nobody had made a study or did any writing on the workers' labor unions in Rumania.

When our study, *Church and State Behind the Iron Curtain* (New York: Praeger Publishing Company), was published the European churchmen and others wrote reviews of the study. Reviews also came out of West Germany, Denmark, Holland, and other Scandinavian countries. Dr. Vladimir Gsovski, under whose editorship the book was published, pointed specifically to the part of the Rumanian study that pertained to the protestant denominations and their development during centuries past up to the present time. It was my part of the study and naturally I was pleased, as were my supervisors. The reviewers said that the history of the Catholic churches and/or the Orthodox churches was well known. Such history had been much written about, but no one historian had written in detail about the protestant or sectarian churches in countries where the official church was Catholic or Orthodox. "But now George Crisan has undertaken the task and did it well," stated some of the reviewers.

One day, the deputy law librarian asked me to come to his office. He showed me a letter from my former dean, Dr. Baker of CRDS. In essence it was an answer to librarian inquiries about me because I was still an alien and it was regarding exemption as to work with the U.S. government. Among other things, Dean Baker gave me a favorable report regarding my honesty as a resident of the United States, waiting to become a lawful resident and eventually a citizen, and in his words stated I was an "almost" brilliant mind.

XI

Work and Study

My pursuit for a Ph.D. program continued. I inquired here and there to learn what was available to me as a graduate in divinity. I had a fine consultation with Dr. Robert G. Jones, who was teaching Christian philosophy at George Washington University, and learned that history would be the closet field to my background. So I enrolled as a graduate student in history. I took American social history, diplomatic history, and a course on Latin America during the colonial period. I took three semesters and was ready to be admitted to the Ph.D. examination and to write my dissertation. The examination fee was quite high.

While pondering and reading and studying the required books on the list, I enrolled again in a graduate course, advanced English writing. I was following my keen interest and attraction toward writing and just how to do it. One semester we composed essays. I was able to draw extensively on my Rumanian life and what I had learned there. I learned one essential truth: in writing one must honestly express his own personal thoughts, never tend to mold his thinking along the lines of another writer. Another semester was devoted to research, which I was doing at the Library of Congress. At that point, the teacher advised me to withdraw as I already knew well what he was teaching.

My Hungarian fellow workers urged me to study law and obtain a degree in law here in the United States.

Alex (Shany) was eager to make a career in the library and law. I knew and occasionally discussed with friends the difficulty of opening a law practice in one's native country. I could not see myself going back to law. There were other friends who were taking classes in law at George Washington University or the Catholic University of America, working toward a degree and hoping eventually to pass the bar.

In my position as an expert on Rumanian law, I met all kinds of lawyers seeking information on Rumanian law, which I gave them.

Meanwhile, I continued my weekly scripts for the Voice of

America. In fact, the office in New York City moved to Washington, D.C., which was closer to me. The new chief of the Rumanian desk, Mr. Valimarescu, was eager to have my contributions. He sometimes asked for them twice a week.

CHANGING JOBS

July 28, 1956, marked a red-letter day in my life. I was married on this day! (I tell more about it in the next chapter.) Of course, it was a big surprise to my friends. They had pegged me as a confirmed bachelor. When I returned from my honeymoon trip I found a telephone message on my desk with the request to call a certain telephone number. When I made the call, a Mr. Rhode answered. A lawyer, he had asked my views on several occasions. I knew nothing of his background except that he might have come to America sometime in the early thirties. It seemed to be of some urgency that I come to his office as soon as possible. We could not seem to get together on any certain date, as he kept insisting that I come even earlier. Finally, my supervisor suggested, "George, they are with another government agency and we should try to cooperate with them as best we can."

I went to his office on the third day. I discovered that Mr. Rhode was one of the lawyers working with the Foreign Claims Settlement Commission. I had never heard of this office. Mr. Rhode introduced me to the general counsel, Mr. Andrew Maguire. The interview did not last long; Mr. Rhode had briefed Mr. Maguire thoroughly on my background. Maguire rather abruptly asked me when I could join their team of lawyers, who had the task to propose decisions on the American nationals' claims against the Russian, Rumanian, Bulgarian, and Hungarian governments for having taken their property or interests in such countries without the indemnity.

The job was to work as expert counsel on Rumanian law and to prepare proposed decisions for the approval of the commission. I thought it might prove to be an interesting, even exciting, type of work. I learned that the commission had funding for only three years. I was offered a higher grade than I was receiving at the time and would even make a higher salary if the Congress extended the function of the commission beyond the three years. I informed Mr. Maguire that I had recently married and would need to talk with my wife before deciding about the position.

We discussed the offer and my wife made the comment that changing jobs at the time might be a strain on me, but I assured her that I did not think so and she said to me, "Take the job if you think you would like and enjoy it."

I decided to take the job offer and in October 1956, moved to the FCSC, an independent agency established by the Act of Congress to handle and dispose of the foreign claims.

I discovered that my Hungarian friend, Alex, had been there for some months. A sort of self-styled adviser, he asked me over again, "Why don't you go back to law school and take a degree and be admitted to the bar in America?"

I thought about this and realized that I knew as much as any of the lawyers I had worked with and now to be admitted to the American bar began to appeal to me. I talked it over with Eunice, my sweetheart wife, and she only admonished me not to take on too big a load. I assured her that it would not be too much of a study load for me.

LAW STUDENT AGAIN

The dean looked over my records from a couple of affidavits to the effect that I had graduated from a law school in Rumania (King Ferdinand University Law School of Cluj, Rumania) in 1930. He suggested that I study toward a master's degree in comparative law, American practice, which would require twenty-eight credit hours in order to graduate.

I started classes in February 1957, with classes three or four evenings a week. There were about one hundred and fifty or two hundred in class, and there was little time to make friends. Most of the time was taken up with study and research in the law library as well as outside reading at home. It was usually midnight before I was ready for bed except Saturday and Sunday. The work was amazingly easy for me. My wife waited up for me with some snack ready and when the weather was bad she met me at the bus stop in the car. She used our car during the day to get to her work at the Department of Health of the District of Columbia. We were then expecting our first child.

By taking cramped summer courses, I completed the requirements and graduated in February 1959, with a master's degree in law. By that time we had two children: George Stewart, born in June 1957; and Patricia Ann, born in June 1958.

Shortly after graduation, I attended the bar-reviewing courses and took the D.C. bar examination, but failed.

In the summer of 1959 most of the lawyers at the commission were put on notice to look for other jobs because Congress did not extend the budget for the commission. I was one of the twenty-five lawyers to go. The chairman, Mrs. Pace, a Baptist friend, the first woman to be sheriff and then commissioner and chairman of a government commission, told me that she would not be able to do anything for me other than keeping me one month longer. I was out of a job July 25, 1959. I was not an American lawyer. Several times I had felt I made a mistake moving from the law library, but as the old saying goes (it was a part of my philosophy), "Do not cry upon the ruins of Pompeii" (do not feel remorse over what you have done which cannot be undone).

GENERAL SERVICES ADMINISTRATION

I was out of work from July 25 to August 30. Eunice worked one or two days a week while I took care of our babies, and now she was expecting our third child. And Dad had no job, but we did not give up hope.

At the advice of my pastor, Dr. Pruden, I approached Harold Kennedy, a member of our church, who was a lobbyist for the Ohio-Texas Oil Company. He had lavish offices. He was gracious and cordial to me.

Several days later, he called me to let me know he had talked to one of his Texas friends, the administrator of general services, Mr. Floete, who promised to see whether I could fit in his agency. The General Services Administration (GSA) was having international problems with suppliers of some strategic materials. I was considered an expert in the international rule of law. I was appointed legal assistant with the Defense Materials Division. Mr. Edwin Kurzius was the assistant general counsel of the division. Mr. Kurzius apologetically explained to me the GSA personnel office could not give me a higher grade than a seven, but as soon as I passed the bar, I would receive a promotion.

The administrator wanted to see me, and I was told by the

general counsel that I was the only employee or lawyer he had asked to meet personally. I met him in his office. He was an impressive man in appearance and very friendly in manner. He related he had traveled in Europe with the task of accomplishing the job of doing relief work for European people or countries after the war. He said he went only as far as Vienna and was not in Rumania. He said he hoped I would like my work with GSA, and I really did.

Mr. Kurzius told me he had been a lawyer in New York before coming to Washington. His father came from Vienna and his mother, from Hungary. He said it was very difficult to be in private practice in New York, as it was quite difficult to collect fees owed from the clients. For this reason, he decided to join the federal government.

Allen Robinson was my immediate supervisor. His voice was so soft it was almost inaudible. I was told he had heart trouble and had a pacer in his heart. Only rarely did he ask me to do something. Instead, his clients, the contracting officers, came to me for assistance and conference.

The assistant general counsel for the Defense Materials Division, Edwin Kurzius, gave me a special task. There was a six-foot-tall file cabinet full of files all in one contract. A corporation from Brazil and the Brazilian government jointly had furnished "rare earth" to the GSA. GSA had paid for the materials, but Brazil and the corporation had raised all kinds of claims for other compensations. The claim or claims were for the amount of 1,5 million dollars. It was the first time that I had heard the term "rare earth," a substance furnished from the sands found in water beds of Brazil.

My task was to read the material, the contracts, the deliveries, and to see how much, if anything, the contractors were entitled to. Ed Kurzius asked me to ask Art about this, as he had worked on the case. He added that when I had a question, go to Art. Art was a Harvard graduate, I learned, and had a long experience in government contract matters. He had worked on the claims but had not reached a conclusion.

I talked with Art and he said the case was quite complex; that there was a possibility to make the wrong conclusion, which could result in a bad precedent for GSA which might be raised by other foreign suppliers of strategic materials. I concluded that he did not take things in stride. I took the position that no matter the eventuality of a problem, it must be solved in one way or another.

The current contracts or correspondence I was to clear for legal sufficiency were for agricultural produce, e.g., jute, long staple cotton, or down (from China). All these were esoteric to me, but before long I got acquainted with the strategic materials and the statutes under which we were operating.

I had dedicated much of my time to the Brazilian claims. In about six months I reached a conclusion. Art asked again whether I had taken into consideration all the clauses, and the statutes including the tariff clauses. "That is my final finding, Art," I answered him.

"Well, give it to Ed Kurzius," he instructed.

Ed went with my opinion to the general counsel, Macomber, and his deputy, Henry Pike. We established a date for a conference, all four of us, with open U.S. code volumes and contracts and tariff schedules. In a few weeks, my opinion was accepted and, after polishing here and there, was enacted as the opinion of the general counsel and printed for distribution to all GSA general counsel offices.

Ed Kurzius, without telling me at that time, had proposed me for the highest award, the "Sustained Superior Performance award," for the work on the Brazilian claims. I was also awarded a monetary award.

Now, other lawyers and friends said I was Ed Kursius's brain trust. So be it! He asked me to lecture to the lawyers of his division on the common law as applicable in federal cases. I did this, and all the lawyers (about 10) had a fine discussion on the subject.

Ed gave me a promotion after about nine months of working for him. Then I took the bar examination in July and was admitted to the bar of Maryland in October 1960. Ed granted me another promotion and I was no longer legal assistant, but an attorney adviser general with the Defense Material Division. I liked that!

Ed, by assigning me "the nasty job on Brazil claims," recognizing my work, and proposing the award for me, made me feel like worthwhile American lawyer. He influenced my life and career to a very great degree. We became lifelong friends. It was he who sent me to take special courses on government contracts at the University of Virginia, where the army set up special courses once a year or so for the lawyers in the Defense Department to get to know the latest development on government contract law. As a

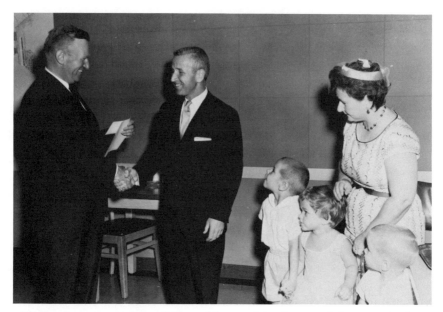
Ed Kurzius congratulates G.C. on his award for Sustained Superior Performance, 1962.

lawyer with the defense materials of GSA, I was qualified to attend such courses.

At Charlottesville, Virginia, I met many Defense Department procurement lawyers. I felt I was one of them without any strings attached regarding my foreign accent. How satisfying it was to me to feel part and parcel of the American dream—to each according to his abilities. God grants us great awards in due time, I felt. I had to come from Rumania, to have crossed many deadly hurdles to appreciate all these opportunities.

"George, you've made an amazing progress in America," Ed would say, "But look forward for more challenges and rewards." The picture taken of Ed handing me the award and my wife and children looking on is a cherished momento, framed and hanging on my studio wall. Ed and his wife, Veronica, are our most wonderful friends.

In our working world, Ed moved to another position, that of chairman of a contract board, and another boss took his place. Byron Harding did not seem to take the personal interest in his attorneys displayed by Ed, so I felt. He seemed to be the usual bureaucrat, and an efficient one for that matter.

It was a special satisfaction to me to see that quite a few of my opinions were adopted by the general counsel as "General Counsel Opinion" and published as such. I developed a straight style of direct facts, law, and conclusion. I felt it was my native ability to see the issue involved and to take a definite stand, therefore a legal conclusion. Some lawyers might hesitate and ponder whether this is the right decision or opinion, or is this the only one? No, it is not the only one, but to my view and as I see it, this is my best decision. Neither man nor God ask more than our best. I had been trained also to give my professional opinion as soon as possible. I thought then, and now, that a lawyer should act as a judge—not halt in indecision, but deliver his own opinion.

In November, 1963, while I was attending a bid opening session, a woman burst into our conference room, shouting that the president had been shot at, and the radio did not say how bad it was. That was the day Pres. John F. Kennedy was shot to death in Dallas. We were horrified. Later on, reviewing my life philosophy, I remembered a quotation from Ecclesiastes to the effect that "We do not know when and how our days end." Why or how or with what the assassin did it becomes irrelevant—dead is dead forever! The psalmist tells us that our days are like grass, which sprouts in the morning, blooms by noon, withers by evening and is ready to be thrown into the fire.

We talked of the event again and again. Is it a Communist plot against the president of the United States? Was the assassin sent back to America for that purpose? The investigation of the commission did not find a plot. Writers of thrillers are still speculating in their writings that the commission has not looked that way or in that bit of evidence! It is only human to speculate. But for how long? That is God-given wisdom—to do your task diligently and put down a final conclusion.

In talking to some of my fellow lawyers I remarked that since my law school days in Rumania where I studied criminology, I adhered to the idea that a criminal is both physically and psychically abnormal. To what degree? Only the jury can answer. But this does not mean that society must not defend itself according to its own rules.

Administrations changed, and so changed the administrators of the GSA and their general counsels. The lawyers were not career employees; they were subject to change. I held the title of expert counsel at the Foreign Claims Settlement Commission, but the tenure was temporary. This meant that it would end if Congress did not approve further funding. Ms. Mary Jean Downing, a lawyer there, a fine lady from Iowa, became close friends with me and my family. Her birthday was the same day as that of my oldest son, George. We celebrated the occasion a couple of times at her place in Georgetown. She had been state attorney in Iowa before coming to Washington when a new administration came into power. She said there is nothing complicated about keeping a job with the government and staying in your job to accumulate the necessary number of years to reach retirement. This philosophy had not occurred to me, and I had no thought of looking forward only to retirement.

At GSA my enthusiasm for a higher grade increased, but I soon learned there were very few promotions granted unless a lawyer found a desirable opening in another agency or department, his abilities were attractive, and the time was opportune.

In order to get more experience or to make room for a younger lawyer, I was transferred to the Regional Office, where contracts for federal buildings and supplies were handled. I had the opportunity to sit in day-long sessions to discuss the awarding of contracts for federal buildings in Washington, Baltimore, and other cities in the region.

Some of the contracting people came to me for personal counsel. I remember one young man came seeking my help concerning his difficulties in family matters. One day, the lawyer in the next office came in and told me "my client" had died. He left two small children.

My chief counsel was a very good lawyer and always pleasant in his association with others. He would come in the office early to distribute the mail and to have a conference with the other lawyers in the office. When he failed to appear for several days, I was told he was in a hospital to receive detoxification from the use of alcohol. I was saddened at this news and wondered how could such a fine and distinguished and able lawyer become so addicted to excessive drinking that treatment to quit became a necessary action. Again, I reminded myself and remarked to close friends that man is subject to many temptations in life and can act in inhuman ways toward others. But when he comes to God through Jesus Christ, his life is changed and he becomes God's child and abides in his love. He then is able to walk with a newness in all areas of living.

At GSA, region 3, the lawyers had an occasional luncheon together in the building cafeteria. We discussed various subjects and many questions were directed to me regarding my experiences in Europe and work as an ordained minister, a theologian, and a historian. Joe Calvin once said to me, "George, you see something good in everything. What possible good did you or do you see in Hitler's actions in massacring the Jews and others?"

For a moment, I was dumbfounded, then I replied, "It seems to me that from Hitler's life we can draw the conclusion of what not to be—those who act like Hitler must ultimately end like Hitler."

My solution of the question seemed to be appreciated and there was no dissension.

While at the GSA, region 3, I would often have luncheon in the various cafeterias in the neighborhood, in the NASA (National Aeronautics & Space Administration) and in the other agencies nearby. One day, returning to the office I met my former coworker at the Library of Congress, John Riismandel. He was an Estonian by birth. I had not heard from him for quite a while.

"Hi, George," he greeted me. "How are you? I'm just back from the Philippines, where I was working under contract for several years. Now I am with the navy at the main building on the mall."

Then he wanted to know how I was getting along. I told him of my work, which I enjoyed, but that I had been expecting a promotion, which had not materialized. He asked me if I had thought of changing jobs, to which I answered in the affirmative, but I had seen no opportunities.

"George," Riismandel said, "I am going to talk with one of the lawyers who is in charge of hiring lawyers to see whether they need a good lawyer at this time!"

I assured him I would be glad to hear from him. That same afternoon, John called me to say that Bill Brown would be glad to see me the next day. When I saw him the next day, we spoke. I filled out a form and he concluded our conference with the request that I meet two of the bureau's counsels. I also met the deputy general counsel in charge of hiring lawyers for the Office of General Counsel of the Navy.

My resume of my professional working background in other government agencies brought a favorable impression all around. Mr. Stein wanted me to meet the general counsel, but we learned that he was not available that day. Then I went to the navy department to meet with Mr. Steger. He had been briefed on my background. He asked, "George, I note your age. Now, are you willing to be supervised by younger lawyers? All of them here are younger than you, except me."

I replied that I had been working for a boss, my wife, who was much younger. He enjoyed my remark!

"When can you come on board?" he asked.

"Let me see my people at GSA. I can wind up my work there within a month." In early March 1966, I moved to the Navy Department.

IN THE DEPARTMENT OF THE NAVY

I joined the Navship Command Counsel's Office. Paul Snow was my immediate supervisor, and our counsel was Mr. Sam Pinn. My assignment was to draft contracts for the construction of naval vessels, which, though long and detailed, proved quite interesting to me. I also wrote General Provisions of the Contracts. In the same command was John Riismandel, who had influenced me to look at the Navy Department for a new challenge in my profession.

Later on, John became the chairman of the Armed Services Board of Contract Appeals. He was (and is, I suppose) a very hardworking lawyer, much younger than I, and ambitious enough to climb to the top of the ladder.

After some months I was moved to the Electronic Devices Contracts Department. It was a busy office. At times, I had ten contracting people coming in for me to see their contracts for legal sufficiency. It was very pleasant work, having a variety of clients and matters to tend to.

About this time, I figured I was familiar with many angles of work. Also, I had tried several cases before the Contract Board of Appeals. I applied to be qualified for the examining officer position. I had to file a lot of material on my experience in every field of law where I had worked. I had to have twenty-five lawyers as reference. I did all the required paperwork. After some months I received notification that I was qualified for the position of examining officer, but I was a GS12 at the time and I would get such a position when I became a GS13. I was happy with the qualification even though I could not be promoted for that purpose.

One day, I found in my mailbox an announcement that the Office of Counsel of Naval Research (ONR) was looking for a replacement for a lawyer who left. I was not familiar with the location or the details of the work of that office, but soon learned it was located in the adjacent building on the second floor. I discussed the announcement with Richard M., a lawyer in the office next door. Richard was a retired colonel (attorney) from the army, and was now a lawyer with the navy. He advised me to make inquiry regarding the position to decide whether I would be interested in accepting it or not.

I went to see the counsel of ONR. Mr. Pace, a youngish man, about my height, received me with a very friendly manner and informed me he was looking for a lawyer to fill a vacancy in his office. He asked what I had done in previous positions. When I told him I was a trial lawyer at GSA and in the navy too, he said, "You may be the man. I never went to court or prepared a trial and neither did my deputy, Art. When can you come? I will give you a higher grade."

In a month or so, I moved to ONR. Mr. Pace became a good friend to me, as he was to all the people who worked for him. He was a fine man, a Baptist Christian, from Fort Worth, Texas.

Some time in 1970, our main navy and munitions buildings were condemned to be demolished. These buildings had been erected in 1917 during the First World War as temporary buildings for housing the navy offices. ONR moved to Arlington in a rented space. Shortly after the move, Allen, at fifty-five, retired. He had worked for the government for almost forty years. He had been a page boy when he came to Washington and slowly but steadily advanced. He went to college, law school, and climbed the ladder to become counsel of the Office of Naval Research.

After Allen left, Art became acting counsel and I his deputy. We worked that way for quite awhile. Art hoped he would be made counsel. I was hoping that, too. But it was not to be so! The position appeared to be a political plum, and someone from nowhere came aboard as counsel, James Macmillan. He was a few years younger than Art and very new in the navy as a lawyer. Altogether, we did not know much about him or his background. We heard he was from Ohio.

For the first time in my career with the United States government, I met a man whom I could not understand. I did not understand what he was aiming at other than a higher position or grade. He had had a short stint as a lawyer in the government contracts

263

business and several times told Art and me he did that and that and he was all by himself at the navy. Whenever he talked with Art and me he would close the door, or even when he called me in for some directions or observation, he would ask me to please close that door. He would talk very slowly and never looked straight at you, but rather turned and looked out the window.

Our secretary in the office was a young girl, cheerful and efficient. Not long after Macmillan came on board he fired her, saying to Art and me, "Cherry was too mouthy."

For the first time, I realized that James Macmillan was after changes. He called me into his office and pointed to certain phrases in some of the contracts, saying, "You, George, are a senior attorney and should not pass on such a contract."

I responded, "Jim, you are now the counsel. If you want me to do some of the contracts differently, I certainly will do so. You are the counsel!"

He then said, "Well, George, these things should come from you."

I answered, "We operated, two lawyers only, this way and did well. It is up to you to make changes if you think there should be changes in clearing the contracts for legal sufficiency."

One day he called me into his office, closed the door, and turned to the window and said softly, "You should have observed. You should have done this that way. You should be more aggressive, George, with the contracting people."

Several months after his coming to ONR, he would pass my open door and I would say, "Good morning, Jim"

Almost imperceptibly he would answer, "Good morning."

Art Neuses stayed close to his desk. Once in a while I remarked to Art that I wished I understood what Jim wanted me, us, to do. "I wish I knew, too, George," Art would say.

Jim wanted me to review all the contracts, about twenty actions a day, to take care of the cases to appear before the Armed Services Board of Contract Appeals, since I was the only trial lawyer. It did not appear to be too much for me, but I wondered why I had to handle everything coming to the office.

The strange conduct became open when in October, 1974, only after three months of his duty as counsel of ONR, he called me into his office, closed the door, and announced that he could no longer operate with me; that he wanted me to leave and find another position so that he could replace me with a younger fellow whom he wanted to train as he wished.

"Jim, I want to stay here for several reasons. Because of my age, it would be difficult, if not impossible, to find another postion or appointment. I have three young children to raise; I had been rated as a first-rate lawyer wherever I have worked; I was awarded the superior performance award; and none of my supervisors were dissatisfied with my work."

He listened to me and then in a cold, steely voice stated: "If you do not leave by the end of the year, I will do something drastic with you. I want you to leave. Don't you understand me?"

"Jim, I want to say to you only that I am a hard stone to swallow." Then I left.

I filed a complaint with the Committee on Discrimination that Mr. Macmillan threatened to fire me because of my age, sixty-eight years. Admiral Van Orden, chief of ONR, and Captain Featherstone, his deputy, were quite unhappy.

I realized once again, that everyone knew that Macmillan had strong backing—only a tool in the hands of general counsel of the navy, a young lawyer brought in as general counsel under the new Republican administration.

From that day forward he would not talk to me. Each morning when I came in, I said, "Good morning, Jim," and he mumbled something not understandable.

I realized he was mad at me for filing a complaint against him for discrimination because of age. I had not studied the rules of the law and I would have found that after sixty-five years of age, nobody was entitled to file a complaint for age discrimination.

I hired a lawyer, George Fisher (now clerk of the United States Court of Appeals for the District of Columbia), and he planned to have a public hearing with the press attending, of course.

Captain Featherstone, deputy chief of ONR, persuaded me that the admiral was quite upset at the developments in my case, that a hearing would attract undesirable publicity, et cetera. In short, I was persuaded to withdraw my complaint, hoping that Jim Macmillan would present a new start and better relations in the future.

Macmillan gave me a memo in writing requesting that I summarize my last year's work and report to him weekly in regard to my work—as to how many contract actions I cleared; how many contract people I counseled, how many meetings I had attended, and so on. It was not difficult to comply with this program, except it kept me quite busy, having to compile data on my work on a day-to-day basis. I started keeping a large calendar on my desk, marking down people or papers crossing my desk.

At times I thought it was comical; a childish comedy; all people in our division and others were aware of the tension between the counsel and his subalternate lawyer, George. People came to me for advice, such as scientists working with projects in Alaska, asking for legal opinions as well as counsel. I furnished the help they asked for and which was accepted. I furnished copies of all my opinions, brief in content, to Jim Macmillan.

Art and others, including the new secretary, a fine young woman, all kept their distance from me. There was no more joking among us. I related to my wife all these happenings and her comment was, "Can you take it, honey? Are you not depressed by it all? I trust you don't break down under it all."

My reassurance to her was that she must not be worried about me. If I had escaped from the most terrible war in Russia, at Stalingrad, from the communistic jails and from the Iron Curtain, surely this present difficulty would have little ill effect. My answer to her was, "I want to fight this man's conduct against me to the end." I thought to myself, *No doubt he is just a cog of another wheel; he wants to hire another lawyer in my place, but in this I must be strong.* I felt again the surety that God has never let me down!

Shortly after the first of the year, 1975, early in the morning, Macmillan came to me and asked me to move to another office, "Today, George."

I moved all my belongings, that is, my files and books, to an office just vacated by a colonel who had been assigned to ONR for certain research matters. That same day, a younger lawyer was installed in my old office, where I had worked for five years. *The way of politics,* I thought to myself.

Macmillan had expressed the desire to hire a younger lawyer, and I had not resigned against his incredible pressure on me. Now I was just put out without any further ado. Macmillan sent me a memo to develop and write the history of ONR. I started in on this at once and found it quite interesting to study the legislation and the legislative history.

A few days later, a package of twenty or more pages was delivered to me from the office of the chief of naval research. It was a notice of unsatisfactory performance. Macmillan cited about twenty contract actions, as cleared contracts, which had mistakes on them, e.g., the date of beginning or ending or of the amendment might have been erroneously typed. There were several things which were outright distorted. The general counsel and the admiral endorsed Macmillan's proposal of my unsatisfactory performance.

I asked a dear friend from the church, John Shouse, to be my counsel. He had been retired from the Department of Agriculture where he was chairman of the Contract Board of Appeals. He was outraged by the lies set in Macmillan's memorandum of unsatisfactory performance.

John prepared memos on rebuttal. He told me that from the beginning, being a lawyer, I was hired at the will of the general counsel; that I was in an excepted position and the general counsel was at liberty to hire and fire an attorney. Well, I wanted to fight just the same.

I discovered that the admiral was doing whatever the general counsel was asking him to do; that he himself did not want to antagonize the general counsel. He wanted to have his tenure with ONR extended.

It was the admiral who signed the notice of my dismissal, effective April 12, 1975. Jim MacMillan had already left the position of counsel ONR and had joined the General Counsel's Office—"He had done a good job getting rid of George Crisan, and now he was promoted from GS15 to GS16 and moved to the Office of General Counsel."

So my career with the federal government, starting in an incredibly wonderful way, now ended with a bitter taste in my mouth. I have learned long since that there is no sweet taste if there is no bitter also—all we do in life we compare as, good-evil, sweet-sour or bitter, just-unjust.

I wanted to take my case to the Court of Claims. John said that he would not spin the wheel for nothing, meaning the court would not upset the ruling of the general counsel and the admiral. I said, "I will go to the end."

I then filed complaint in the Court of Claims. I had two hearings.

After two years, the complaint was dismissed for the lack of showing moral or other damages caused to me by the government, because of dismissing me from the job, being in an excepted position. That closed the case.

Even before that decision of the Court of Claims, I had filed for retirement, to which I was entitled, and so I was retired under the civil service retirement system.

For two years I worked for a charitable organization, Retired Federal Employees Counseling. One day Eunice read an ad in the local papers that the legal services of Prince George's County, Maryland, was looking for a lawyer with experience to work in the field of family law and related proceedings, for a small indemnity. The organization was established by judges and lawyers in Prince George's County for legal aid to low-income residents. I joined this organization in January 1978 and am still there, enjoying my legal work for women with children, litigating child support, paternities, divorces, adoption, bankruptcies, and the like. The founders are Bill Yoho, an attorney, and Edwin Hutchinson, a retired master on juvenile matters.

XII

THOUGHTS OF ROMANCE

DURING MY years of adjustment in my new homeland, America, I never gave up the thought of marrying and establishing a home of my own. My classmates often commented on the fact that I was still a bachelor and even went so far as to try to find a compatible candidate for my serious consideration! But all to no avail! It was not that I was against the idea, in fact I was all for their plan for me. It seemingly was the circumstances of the time that I failed to meet a woman who created a special interest for me.

About a year after my graduation I went back to divinity school for the spring convocation. I enjoyed reunion with my beloved Dean Baker and the other professors and my friends there. Dean Baker inquired about my work at the Library of Congress and agreed that my salary was quite good. In the course of our conversations, the possibility of home and family of my own came up. I related to him that I had met quite a few women but so far had not met one who held my sustained interest. He mentioned two or three women I had known in school and encouraged me to get in touch with them on my next trip to New York. Later when I went to New York, I called a certain young woman, whose father had been a minister among some Armenian ethnics here in America. We exchanged letters for a time, and I ventured that I would like to know her better and expressed my serious intentions. She told me she was honored at my intentions toward her, but did not feel that she was the right girl for me.

My friends at the Library of Congress and other friends continued trying to "find a girl for George." Even some of my friends jokingly remarked, "You should be better off than we, the married ones. You are scot-free and do whatever you want; we are not."

About this time, Reverend Pascu of Cleveland asked me to meet a girl from Cleveland. She was of Orthodox faith, well educated, working with the internationals in the Cleveland community. We met by appointment in the lobby of the largest hotel in town and had dinner there. Then we went to her home, the house of her mother, who was a native Rumanian. It was a very pleasant evening.

We discussed the plan to become better acquainted and she promised to write. In her letter she stated she was dating another boy, who was sick at that time, and she had no heart to tell him she was writing to me. I appreciated her candor and was relieved to end the acquaintance.

At this point, I questioned myself as to what I was really looking for in a woman. I concluded I was looking for a perfect person: well educated, in the Baptist faith, and so on. I was looking for someone who did not exist.

A preacher from Rochester, who was the minister of the Italian Baptist church, wanted me to meet a woman in Miami. She was a teacher and daughter of a minister and had her home in Miami with her older sister. I met her at her home, at which time she had prepared a dinner party for several friends. After dinner there was dancing. She was of Spanish extraction, a lovely person, but she held no appeal for me. I felt somewhat awkward at the dinner party because too much attention was paid to me.

My cousin Miron was with me that evening. He was impressed by this lady and felt she would be a fine choice for me. After returning to Washington, I wrote her thanking her for the lavish dinner party. Period!

Not long after this time, a Rumanian composer, D., who was teaching at a Baptist college in Texas, called asking me to go to Texas to talk to his classes of my work with the Voice of America; I could choose my own subject and the delivery of it. I was hosted by the president of the college and taken to other locations to tell my story as a political refugee, covering the period of my work with the Voice of America and as a freelance writer.

The professor-composer had two lovely children, eight and ten. His wife, younger than he, was beautiful and possessed a marvelous voice. I fell in love with the children then and there and thought how wonderful it would be to have beautiful children with a pretty mother and a real lady.

My friend introduced me to a German woman who taught the German language in the college. But I must say I had no thought that I might be meeting the future mother of my children! Later, as a matter of politeness, I suggested that we correspond. She wrote me in a forthright manner that she could not consider a continuing correspondence between us.

At the Library of Congress a young widow and several girls planned a party, which I thought was probably for me, and I did not like the idea.

One day, a call came from Washington from Reverend Withers of Charleston, West Virginia, in whose church at Spencer I had spoken while at the divinity school with his son, Bob. He wanted to meet me for lunch.

"George, do you know that John Hoff, the young high school graduate you met in my house, is here in Washington working for the gas company? He has graduated from Alderson Broddus in Philippi, West Virginia, has married, and lives in Washington. Do you remember him?"

I replied that I might when I saw him. That evening, I met John and his wife, Jean. They were living in an apartment on 16th Street and attended Luther Rice Baptist Church, where a graduate of Alderson-Broaddus College of West Virginia (ABC) was the minister.

John was of a lively personality. His wife, a nurse, a graduate of ABC, appeared more reserved—a beautiful personality in appearance, speech, and manners. We renewed our acquaintance of 1950 in the spring of 1955. The Hoffs invited me to dinner. In return, I invited them to dinner in my little apartment and in my small kitchen cooked dinner.

The Hoffs were expecting their first child and moved into a rented house to make ready for the baby. I visited them several times. Usually Jean wound up our discussions by wondering why I was not married and establishing a home of my own. I readily agreed that it was a pleasant contemplation, but so far I had met no woman who captured my interest. I usually ended by saying that if I could meet someone as nice as Jean it would be easy. Jean laughed and said there were many nurses at her alma mater, Alderson Broddus College in West Virginia. I had only to investigate. She invited me to come along with them and meet some of the nurses there. Around Christmas time, one of Jean's classmates visited her. I met the young woman, but the mutual attraction did not last long.

WEST VIRGINIA MOUNTAINS

In early 1956, John and Jean traveled to West Virginia to visit Jean's mother in the hospital. They asked me to come along, and

I was delighted to make the trip and enjoy the fellowship of these two fine people. They were young, forward looking, smart, and hardworking. They discussed with ease politics, science, philosophy, or literature. And they were both of the Baptist faith! I found they were from the country where my beloved Dean Baker was born and raised. Dean Baker was a graduate of ABC, as was Dr. Gordon Withers. They were all mountaineers—reminding me of my own background in the Transylvanian Alps in Rumania. It even occurred to me to consider whether people from the mountains possessed a wider horizon because they always wanted "to climb that peak and see another mountain."

Shortly after our arrival in Philippi, West Virginia, we were invited to a dinner given by three teachers, Louise Callison, Loretta Duffield, and Eunice Stewart, who shared the second floor of a house. It was a very lively dinner with an informal air—old familiar stories as among old friends. These three teachers were instructors at a college. Their sense of humor and general enjoyment of life as shown by their vivaciousness gave a refreshing sparkle to the evening.

Right off I felt Stewart (as everyone called her) was the most attractive of the three. Her beautiful blue eyes and immaculate complexion set her apart as she played her part as hostess at the dinner. If any woman caught my interest, she was the one.

On the way back to Washington I learned a little bit about Stewart. Jean relayed that she had graduated from ABC and obtained a master's degree from Western Reserve in Cleveland. Also she was singing in the local Baptist church choir. I was impressed with her scholarship and felt at the moment I could become more interested in her. Then I thought, *I am older and foreign born.*

I had always enjoyed writing. My chief concern all along was to perfect my English in pronunciation and in writing. I had always expressed my speech in a rather literary manner, even back to my early high school days. The Latin teacher I had then once remarked, "You, Crisan, speak such a literary Rumanian. You were not born in Paris! You were born in Tisa in the Transylvanian Alps. How come?"

I could not explain. "I just speak the way I am," was my reply.

At the divinity school, my papers were marked Excellent or A-plus. At the Library of Congress my supervisor remarked, "George, you know how to write!" Then at the Voice of America, my freelance articles were accepted with no difficulty. Perhaps, these encouraging things were adding strength to my efforts to improving my English, both spoken and written.

Gradually the feeling was developing within me that I wanted to be truly American, in language and all things. I thought that marrying a Rumanian girl would be like an uprooted person marrying another uprooted person—the couple would be an uprooted pair.

Then my thoughts went back to the girl I met in Philippi. Was she too young? There was that reservation still in my mind. Dean Baker and Jean Hoff repeated to me again that I was not old! Of course, I did not feel old at all, but some sobering thoughts came into my consideration of my next step. I could not guess her age—she was young and very pretty! All these feelings and thoughts could not be shared with anybody. But they were whirling around in my heart and mind and I could only pray that God would enlighten my way.

Jean Hoff wondered if I had felt any special interest in the group of women we met in Philippi or in any one girl? "They are all so young!"

Jean summed up the visit. "Don't think that way, George. You are as old as your heart tells you. I believe the girls think the same way. They are not asking for a birth certificate! But rather they look at the man!"

I felt better after having talked to her about it.

NEVER TIRING OF TRYING!

The chance came for another trip to Philippi. The Hoffs were making another trip to visit Jean's ailing mother and invited me along. I drove them and we enjoyed the ride over the countryside, although we met some snow on the top of the mountain on Route 50.

Next day I called on Miss Stewart and asked her to have dinner with me. Her acceptance was a good sign to me, and we agreed to go to the Chinese restaurant on a hilly street. It was not a pretentious place in either location or price. She was quite at ease, talking and laughing and discussing things about us. There was no pretense in anything she said or did.

Back home, I wrote her to the effect that I had been delighted to have dinner with her and would be even more delighted to entertain her in Washington. I suggested the time of the Cherry Blossom Festival as a time to also explore the nation's capital sights. She answered, accepting my invitation.

Miss Stewart drove to Washington and stayed with our mutual friends, the Hoffs. We attended the Cherry Blossom Festival at the Jefferson Memorial and walked around the tidal basin. We went to the Lincoln Memorial and walked along the reflecting pool.

I turned the conversation from the sights and sounds about us to what was uppermost in my thinking. "Eunice, I would like to tell you a little about my life. I was a lawyer in Rumania but I am not here in America. I studied at the Colgate Rochester Divinity School and graduated and was later ordained into the ministry. But I've not accepted a pastorate here. Instead, I am working at the Library of Congress.

"I like you very much—in fact, I admire you so much. I am not a young man in my twenties to fall impetuously head over heels in love. But my feelings are deep and lasting."

Here, Eunice responded softly, "I know all about you, George. You don't need to mention age. It is of no importance."

"Then I think of the distance we are separated. I will not be able to come to Philippi as often as I want to. I want us to know one another better. I want you to marry me!"

She was silent a moment. "I am honored by your proposal of marriage, George, but I'm not ready at this moment to answer you. I must pray about it."

I felt somewhat disheartened and somehow humbled, but tried to not show it. I could not keep from hoping she would say yes to me.

Returning home, I also prayed about my life at this point. Here I am—almost forty-eight, and I've found the girl and she was a little evasive. In thinking it through, she proved to be thoughtful and quite wise in her Christian attitude—"I must pray about this."

I counted the days, eager to receive a letter from her. I was even calling her *my darling* in my thoughts. I was in a state of turmoil at the waiting. I remembered some of my friends in Rumania said I was coldblooded like an Englishman and that I was slow to embrace a new idea or a new friend. But such was not the case now as I waited for a letter.

I suddenly remembered a novel occasion back in 1945 in Rumania when a girl friend had suggested a proposal of marriage to me. I quickly agreed but regretted it next day, and wrote her to disregard my answer of the day before.

Two weeks passed. No letter. Then came the letter with the answer yes. I was thrilled but not exuberant, I remember. I was just thankful to God in my mind. I felt the answer was good and came from her because of God's blessing and answer to our prayers. I considered myself engaged. I rose considerably in my self-estimation!

And then, since I am so-called "cerebral" in nature, I began thinking, *Is she the right one? I hope she is the right one, she is a Christian, I hope she never looks down on alien people,* and so on and on. Then I remembered her saying she must pray and give prayerful thought about what she would do.

ENGAGEMENT ON TOP OF THE MOUNTAIN

I looked for an engagement ring. With the help of the clerk at the jewelry store I finally selected a platinum ring with a small diamond, with date and name inside. I called "my darling" and settled on a date when I could come to West Virginia. I went by train, and she met me at the station. We drove to the highest point on the highway toward Morgantown and pulled in at the lookout place. I put the ring on her finger and kissed her for the first time. We were then really engaged. We could talk about a date for our marriage.

We drove on to Morgantown. My professor of music and public speaking, Dr. Lehman, after retiring from CRDS, was teaching at the West Virginia University in Morgantown. The Lehmans asked us to have dinner with them. We told them of our engagement and they were delighted and wished us well. They had befriended me during my three years of study at the divinity school in Rochester and had always extended to me their love and kindliness.

It was an exciting moment for me and for the Lehmans and, I suppose, for my fiancée, Eunice E. Stewart. The Lehmans were the first to know of my engagement and early marriage. We had a most joyous visit and enjoyable dinner and even received some engagement gifts. That evening I returned home by train from Clarksburg,

West Virginia. I was not able to doze in the train during the long hours spent in the coach, which was practically empty. Next day at the office I casually mentioned to my Hungarian friend, George Torzsay-Biber, that I was engaged to be married. He showed tremendous interest in my future wife and asked a flood of questions: Where was her home, what was her profession, what was her background, where did I find her? I patiently tried to answer him the best I could. Later I related to him as well as to others that Eunice was the girl I found most appropriate for my background of the Baptist faith. She was active in her church and sang in the choir. She had a profession but would probably be forced to give it up, coming to Washington as my wife. She had all the aptitudes a pretentious lawyer may wish for; she projected a distinguished presentation; she presented a beautiful personality whether to me or in company of friends; the most pleasant and yet impressive demeanor a man can expect in a woman he wants to marry. I realized again that I was somewhat if not entirely overtaken both mentally and intellectually by the appearance of this woman in my way and felt completely rewarded in my ego that she accepted my proposal of marriage.

At the coffee hour, Dr. Helen Bush asked me to have coffee with her. She was among my earliest American friends at the Library. She was a member of the First Baptist church, Washington, D.C., where I met her for the first time after Dr. Pruden had invited me to speak one evening of my experiences behind the Iron Curtain. I had been invited to her and her aunt's place, and a couple of times she revised some literary articles I had prepared for publication. Casually, I mentioned to her that I was engaged to be married.

"Why, George, did you tell me this wonderful news in such a casual fashion?" she asked.

"Well, I do not want to make such a big fuss; it is a very personal matter to me."

Soon my friends at the library learned of my engagement, probably through George Torzsay-Biber.

About this time, I received a letter from the woman I had met in Florida in which she inquired when I planned to return to Florida again. I sent her a note that I was engaged to be married shortly. She did not reply to my note.

I got into the habit of writing Eunice every evening and placing the letter in the mailbox at the main post office next to the Union Station. I always enjoyed writing letters, but now I had the most exhilarating motive to write them! And too, we could not discuss our plans together, so I attempted to discuss them in writing.

EUNICE'S FAMILY

Eunice wanted to introduce me to her parents and her brothers and their families—all in Philadelphia. The Hoffs told me her father had been in the navy but other than that, they knew little about her family.

Eunice came to Washington by train and stayed overnight at the Hoffs. Then we drove to Philadelphia in my car. It was an easy encounter for me to meet her family. I felt at ease with them and I felt that "Dad and Mom," as Eunice called them, were pleased to meet me. I met her brother Howard, already an ordained minister in the Baptist faith, and his attractive wife Evelyn and their two young, red-headed boys. Then there was John and his wife and their two daughters. All the children were between six and ten years of age. I readily fell in love with the whole family. I felt within that God had granted me a new family to belong to here in America—proving better than any human wisdom might have planned.

I had heard the saying all my life that when you become serious about marrying it would be well to look at the mother of the girl chosen, because more than likely she will become like the mother. After I met Eunice's mother I felt even more assured that my choice was the best God-given choice. Her mother personified the ideal mother—and mother-in-law for that matter.

Much later, I learned that Eunice's mother's ancestry went back to the Pilgrim fathers who landed at Cape Cod in 1620 and that her father's grandfather came from Aberdeen, Scotland.

In the position of an instructor at Alderson-Broddus College, Eunice wanted to separate from the college when the work for the semester was completed, about the end of June or early July. She set the date for our wedding at July 28, 1956, in Philadelphia, Pennsylvania. Meanwhile, I traveled to Philippi several times and she came to Washington on occasion by train. Together we chose furniture for our apartment, and it was up to me to find an apartment.

I finally located one on Davis Place, at the edge of Georgetown close to the streetcar stop on Wisconsin Avenue. It was also near the Washington National Cathedral, Glover Park, the Avenue of the Embassies (Massachusetts Avenue, Northwest) and the Mount Alto Hospital (at that time).

At the First Baptist church in Washington, D.C., I met a young man, Grover Rogers, who had just returned from his graduate studies in Europe under a Fulbright Scholarship. We became close friends. He lived in a rented room near the Library of Congress. At Christmas time in 1955 he asked me to be part of a team of theologians to take part in the program for religious emphasis at his alma mater, The Virginia Polytechnic Institute at Blacksburg. He went back there to teach after completing some research at the Library of Congress in preparing a navy manual. He was an exceptional young man, a Christian, and a brilliant scholar, and came from a Baptist family in Virginia.

He was more than willing and delighted to be my best man. I even thought perhaps he might meet some women at my wedding and become interested in one of them. On one occasion, I took him and Betty, our youth director, to lunch and harbored the thought that they might become interested in one another. But such was not the case.

While at Colgate Rochester Divinity School I had attended a couple of weddings, but only as a guest, so I did not know all that was involved. I did not realize that a myriad of details would be needed to have a dignified yet simple wedding that would be within our means. Again I turned to my friend, Helen Bush, for advice regarding bands, suit, gifts, and the like. I talked to my beloved fiancée about all these things—she knew so much more than I regarding a marriage ceremony and reception and what is involved. She was beautifully persuasive in suggestion without projecting only her wishes one way or another. Her brother, Howard, was to marry us in the church Eunice attended in Philadelphia.

At the end of June I moved my few belongings from my apartment on Constitution Avenue, Northeast, to Davis Place, Northwest. The furniture company then delivered the furniture we had bought. The one-bedroom apartment appeared well furnished, but in no way cluttered. I thought it looked perfect. I even had a radio console. And my old sofa looked very well in our living room.

I heard remarks from my friends. "George, you are moving along quite fast! You barely meet a girl, then get engaged, and now the wedding is set—all in about a couple of months."

My brief reply was to the effect that at my age in this whirlwind world one could not hesitate!

Needless to say, I was living in a state of euphoria! And the thought kept recurring to me: How I would have liked to share the news of my marriage with my parents and my brothers and sister. I had been receiving an occasional postal card from my father addressed to some old Rumanian folks in Detroit who forwarded the messages to me. My father was not worried about me. He always ended his notes with these words: "May the peace of God which passes all understanding be with you always. That peace only Christ can give, and the world cannot take it away from you."

My thoughts went back to Paris, France, 1948, and Dr. Roy Starmer. His influence was certainly like a God-sent means of helping a refugee from Rumania. I came to know that peace of mind then which endures to this day in a real way in my life and affairs. My studies at CRDS served to increase this peace of mind within. Then the succession of astounding events in my new life in America made me even more confident that God in Jesus Christ was surely guiding my destiny. And now He was leading me in finding this wonderful woman who would be my wife. I felt with assurance that we would be guided by His direction in the future in our life together.

THE WEDDING

The date of our wedding, July 28, was fast approaching! Eunice quietly took care of the various details. Anyhow, I was "in the woods" and certainly of little assistance in the way of wording of the invitations and to whom to send them. I was completely at sea when it came to discussing the bride's gown, the groom's suit, or the time of day the wedding was to be or the reception or even the sequences in the service.

I remember that July 28 was a hot day—about in the nineties with high humidity—but nothing bothered me that day, and I heard from friends that it was a sticky day! For me the day was a most glorious one—the high point of my entire life! Here I was, being married to the most wonderful woman in the world. I remember the ceremony itself was short, we were declared man and wife, and I could now kiss my bride!

Dr. Lehman sang in the wedding service—that professor of music and public speaking was a dear and most admired friend of long standing. He must have remembered one of my favorite hymns from seminary days, for he sang "Guide Us, O Thou Great Jehovah." My closet friends from the seminary were there. The Petersons were there. Leon Pacala and Mrs. New (the Chinese woman who was a former delegate to the United Nations by the National Chinese government) were there. My cousin Miron came and Betty Farcas came from Detroit (whose husband received postal cards from my father to be forwarded to me). Some other Rumanian background Baptist folks from Philadelphia were there. All in all, it was not a small wedding.

An unexpected circumstance happened to my friends, Joe and Edith Jenkins from the First Baptist church, Washington, D.C. They arrived in Philadelphia but had some difficulty locating the address of the church, and time was running out. In desperation, they stopped at a private home, knocked on the door, and when the lady came to the door explained to her their plight, and as there was no time to go to a hotel to change, asked if they might change their clothes in her home. She graciously invited them into a room to change and helped speed them on their way to the church. They arrived in time for the services arrayed in their best! Many times we and the Jenkinses remember the incident with delight and remember again the kindness of people shown even to strangers.

The newlyweds left for a trip to the seashore. This honeymoon trip had been long planned, as both enjoyed walking on the sand and dipping into the surf. And now another of my dreams was coming true—to walk as we were, hand in hand as I had seen other couples do, and young parents with children playing in the water. We talked about some day playing on the beach with our own children. Eunice reminisced about her own family—her mother had had five children, she told me. She went on to say this seemed an ideal number of children. I recalled that one of my brothers in Rumania was the father of two and another brother had one child.

Our honeymoon trip was fantastic beyond our wildest dreams. We set out from Cape May, New Jersey, driving and stopping at intervals along the New Jersey shore, until we came to Cape Cod. We continued our leisurely journey along the main shoreline and came to Cape Gaspe Peninsula and the Saint Lawrence shore. We continued our journey to Quebec, Montreal, and Lake George in New York. After a month we returned to Washington, D.C., and our apartment waiting for us.

We attended services at the First Baptist church on the first Sunday after our return to Washington. I was teaching the choir class at that time. Eunice joined the church and the choir in September, 1956, and has since been a member of the choir.

Within an incredibly short time my life settled into an orderly existence: regular hours and working schedules at home and at church. My bride had the faculty of organization on her own initiative. She would often say, "I hope this meets with your approval." It always did.

My wife wanted to continue her profession and wanted to take a job in Washington. With her training as an instructor of nurses and with her experience, she had no difficulty obtaining a position with the District of Columbia Health Department. She enjoyed her work more and more and seemed to derive a great deal of satisfaction in it.

After several months, one evening Eunice told me she believed she was pregnant and wanted to see a doctor as soon as possible. I was wildly excited at the prospect and on top of the world. Dr. Enos Ray assured her that she was pregnant, and we started counting the weeks. Later, she asked me to place my ear near the heartbeat of our child. If the baby is a boy, he must be called George, after me, my father, and my grandfather, but the middle name must be decided. Then I recommended that his middle name be Stewart, Eunice's family name. So it was agreed.

THE CHILDREN

George Stewart

George Stewart arrived June 29, 1957, at Garfield Hospital in the District of Columbia. When I announced the arrival of our son to my class at Sunday School I said our son arrived at Garfinckel's (a department store downtown). Some of the girls looked puzzled, wondering if Eunice had delivered her baby at the department store. But this error was quickly corrected!

It seemed that Eunice had everything in perfect organization prior to the arrival of the baby. It seemed to me that God had certainly endowed her with that extra sense of order and grace. Everything was in place—the crib, the bottles, the clothing and diapers, and even toys were hanging above the crib!

In less than two weeks my wife and baby were ready to go to our church when our baby was dedicated to the Lord by our pastor, Dr. Edward Hughes Pruden. Each Sunday we would take him to the nursery while we were in class. The nurse at that time was Sarah Milburn. (Now, in 1983, she is in her late eighties.)

I could not have asked for any additional good fortune or happiness than I was enjoying with my young family. Cousin Miron came forth with his usual unexpected wit, "It must have taken great courage on Eunice's part to have children at your age!" He is two years my senior.

Eunice had continued working in her job until shortly before our baby was born. After two or three months she decided she would like to take a job, say, over the weekend working as a nurse in one of the hospitals to keep her in touch with her profession and to boost the budget a little.

It was Eunice's idea that we needed to begin thinking of a home of our own, where "the children would have a yard and more space in which to grow." I was reminded again of the loss of my properties to the Communists in Rumania. I had no desire to become attached to property again. But she came back with another view, "Now, you are in an altogether different life situation. You are a husband and a new father."

I could see the sense in what she was saying. We set out to look for a house and finally found one we liked at 6726 Fairwood Road, Landover Estates, Prince Georges County, Maryland. George Stewart was less than five months old when we moved into our new home. Friends from the church and John Hoff helped us move from the apartment in Davis Place to our own home.

I took my young family on a long trek as far as Detroit and then on to Canada and New York and Philadelphia. From there we went to West Virginia "from the mountains to the prairie," and almost from ocean to ocean, showing off my family to the Rumanian Baptist folks scattered throughout America and my friends at CRDS and letting them know just how blessed I was, already a naturalized citizen of the United States of America.

I had heard some of my friends remark that I was a remarkable man. I came back from such saying that the impact of my wife's influence on my life brought forth my courage and perseverance.

I thought back over my life with its crooks and turns. It is said that God moves in mysterious ways, his wonders to perform. The story of Abraham is a fascinating one. He received the inspiration to leave his home in Ur of Chaldea and start out on a varied and exciting journey under God's direction for the promised land, Canaan.

It might have been that such a call, a thought to escape from my country, Rumania, with an ancestry of more than a thousand years, came to me because God was working in my life in his mysterious way. Could it be possible that God was directing my pilgrimage? It is my belief that thinking people must have in mind that faith in something intangible—in God. In this way, can there be any explanation of man's pilgrimage and wandering in this world and finally finding contentment and happiness? I have been called a happy person, seemingly without worry. I account for my happy disposition in the fact that I have the faculty of appreciating my blessings and being thankful for the many wonderful things that happen again and again in my life pilgrimage.

I remarked to my wife one day that George had such beautiful blue eyes and she explained to me that all babies have blue eyes for about six weeks. In time George's eyes turned a very dark blue—like the ocean. He was a healthy, happy, breastfed baby with a bottle supplement, which he called for at about two o'clock in the morning!

I attended night school at the George Washington University Law School five nights a week, going from the office each day and arriving home at about eleven or later. When the weather permitted I took the footpath through the woods, but if it was raining Eunice would meet me at the bus stop. Young George was fast asleep, but on the weekend I was able to enjoy his company to the fullest extent!

After almost 26 years, Dr. Dobbins from our church remembers meeting Eunice, George, and me at the YMCA cafeteria after church one Sunday. George in his high chair looked about and beamed at everyone who spoke to him. He turned about in his high chair and touched the fur hanging over the chair at the next table and called out "dogi, dogi" and the lady turned around, graciously saying, "It's just like dog fur." He was never afraid of strangers at church or going to the store.

Our young son was growing and showing us daily some new word or new aspect of his development. What happy days for the young family! Soon we knew that a second baby was on the way. If a boy, the name would be either Howard John or John Titus. But if a girl, it was decided that the name would be for a good friend I had known at CRDS, Patricia Ann.

Patricia Ann

Patricia Ann arrived on June 20, 1958, just nine days before George Stewart was one year old. I am constantly amazed at Eunice's ingenuity in any situation. The new baby's arrival fit into our home accomodations with ease, and Patricia Ann eventually took over George's playpen. "Daddy! Baby!" George was telling me and pointing his hand toward Patty's crib. What else better could I have expected than to be granted a boy and a girl? Beautiful babies! Once in a while I found Eunice breastfeeding Patty while George was on the floor at her feet playing with some toys or listening to stories Mom was reading from a book with pictures.

By a gift from God and by nature, Eunice knew how to be a perfect mother. I do believe that God has endowed mothers with a gift of knowing how to handle her child. My wife was exceptionally well endowed with such a nature and to that was added her education as a nurse and instructor of nurses.

Patricia Ann had blond hair when born and for many years to come. When she was one year old, talking and walking about freely, we attended a neighborhood contest for children. Patty won first prize as the prettiest child among forty or so children. Mom preserves the silver cup awarded Patty for her beautiful appearance and comportment.

John Titus

The youngest, John, arrived on November 21, 1959, with an

almost white, curly mop of hair. This is an amazing coincidence, because on this date at dawn in 1948 I arrived in Paris, France; the first day I felt free of being hunted by the Communists or by the police of the countries through which I sneaked out to freedom.

All too swiftly the years of their childhood slipped away. We spent every summer at the seashore, mostly at Ocean City. The children enjoyed the water tremendously, surfing on the raft to no end and showing no fear of the water. Building sand castles and taking pictures were enjoyable events for both children and parents.

During the three years that the children were born, I was enrolled in evening classes in the law school at the George Washington University and graduated with a master's degree in comparative law. I was admitted to the bar of Maryland in 1960, memorable dates for me, having been admitted to the Rumanian Bar 30 years earlier.

One summer while at Ocean City, we discovered a post card showing John with a bucket in hand, walking on the sand looking for shells. During the several years that the post card was on the racks of many stores, I purchased many of them and sent them to friends throughout the world.

Eunice took care of our children at all times. When they were about a month old each of them was taken to the First Baptist church for dedication. In this ceremony, Dr. Pruden, the pastor, took the child in his arms as he offered a prayer for the baby and the parents that they would endeavor to bring their baby up in the love and

Parents' pride and blessing, three children—John, Patricia, and George.

285

admonition of the Lord. At this early age they were enrolled in the church school nursery and Mrs. Milburn had complete charge of the babies.

As they advanced in age they attended Sunday school classes and sang with the other children in the choir. When they were eleven or twelve years old, each of them asked to be baptized. They were all baptized in the First Baptist church of Washington, D.C. George and Patty were baptized by Dr. Pruden and John was baptized by Dr. John Howell.

Eunice wanted to introduce the children to good music, or art appreciation as she called it, at an early age. She sang with them at home and they sang at the church, and we all sang together when I was at home. We enjoyed singing together as we drove to visit friends in West Virginia, or when we drove to Skyline Drive in Virginia, or when making the trip to the Rumanian-American Baptist Convention held yearly in Detroit, Michigan. We never missed an opportunity to practice our singing together.

When the children were three or four years old, we taught them to swim at our community swimming pool. Later they wanted to teach me how to dive from the high board. I was reluctant to try, although I had been swimming ever since I knew there was a river. I remember I bruised my nose once in a high jump and I renounced then I would never attempt any such swimming feat again.

When they were four or five years of age, I taught them to ride a bicycle. John was the quickest to learn, and within a half hour he was riding by himself. Patty and George took one or two hours to master the bicycle.

When George graduated from the Bladensburg Junior High School, he received the Superintendent of School Certificate. This indicated he was the top student in all school subjects as well as extracurricular activities at that time. As he graduated from junior high, the integration problem in Prince George's County became paramount. Patty and John were transferred to Kenmore Junior High School, where they graduated amongst the first in their class. This was a newly established school, and I undertook to organize a Parent Teachers Association. I thought the parents and teachers would appreciate the fact that a lawyer with much experience took the interest to charter such an organization.

Because of the integration process in our county, the senior high children were assigned to a school whose principal informed

286

the parents that the school had a low level of educational achievement. It comprised the area where the poorly educated black population lived and despite repeated effort it seemed impossible to raise the level of the educational standards. I was able to have my children transferred to Northwestern High School, provided they were enrolled in the Junior ROTC program. The children agreed to this proposal and were accordingly enrolled. We, the parents, were required to furnish transportation. For six years we drove the children to school, sometimes alternating with neighbors who happened to have a child enrolled in that school.

From the age of seven children went with Eunice for weekly piano lessons. Each day they practiced their music for thirty minutes, which left plenty of time to play with their friends. When John was in the fifth grade, the principal of his school called us to ask whether we were able to buy a violin for John. The music supervising teacher had informed her that John had perfect pitch and when a violin was placed in his hands he was able to perfectly tune it. On another occasion, the principal told us that John had made the highest score possible in the Iowa Test—99 or 100 percent.

At the senior high school, George graduated among the first in his class of six hundred. He received a scholarship from the navy for the ROTC at the Illinois Institute of Technology, which he followed for two years. Then he returned to the East and enrolled in the Rutgers School of Electrical Engineering, from which he graduated. Shortly after graduation, he took a job with the Westinghouse Electric Company, preparing instruction manuals for operating various electrical machines.

Patricia was markedly determined in the pursuit of her musical studies. She enrolled in the Preparatory School of Music at Peabody. Later, she graduated from the Johns Hopkins University, Peabody Institute of Music, with a B.A. in music education with a major in piano. She was on the Dean's list during her college years. She continued her musical education by attending Southern Baptist Seminary, Louisville, Kentucky, graduating with a masters in church music and in Christian education. She is a teacher of music in the elementary schools in Maryland.

John attended the Catholic University College of Liberal Arts and graduated with a B.A. in political science and music performance, with a specialization in violin. His overall average was magna cum laude. He was introduced in the Phi Beta Kappa society as an overall outstanding student. He chose to attend the Georgetown University Law School. During his senior year he was the managing editor of the *Criminal Law Review of America*. Some time before his graduation he accepted an invitation to join the law firm of Reid and Priest in New York City upon completion of his academic classes. Upon graduation, he studied for the New York bar examination, which he took in Albany, New York. Following the exam, he took a five-week trip through Europe by bicycle with his friend, Steve Hunter. Quite a daring adventure and undertaking!

Eunice reiterated time and again her views about our responsibility and caring about the future welfare of our children. She maintained that we would not be able to leave material fortune to each of them, but we should strive to give them the best education possible. Then they would be able to make a sizable contribution to society in their lives on their own initiative and to the best of their individual ability. We have been strengthened and uplifted in our personal life by their individual accomplishments. It has been evi-

All the Crisans, Easter 1967, in front of their church, First Baptist of Washington, D.C.

dent in a real way that they have patterned their living on their faith in a God considered our protector, guide, and assurance for ever ready help.

MY WIFE'S IMPACT ON MY LIFE

I believe that without the helpful influence of my wife, the projection of my own life would have amounted to little notice. I feel that it is chiefly due to her faithful and wise training of our children that they developed to a mature and independent adulthood, enabling each to bring to life individual inborn characteristics and latent talents.

It was Eunice who suggested that we take them to the crib nursery at the church every Sunday and on other occasions. They made wonderful friends for life. Through the years, it was she who was ever mindful of an opportunity to have a family outing; picnic lunches and rest periods along the way were organized in a pleasant manner that made each trip a pleasure to remember.

Her involvement in the church activities, her dedication to her Sunday school work for many years, her continuing choir and musical programs, all contributed to a feeling of pride and of being blessed by her life. When one of the children calls by phone today it is usually to speak to Mom, to ask questions on any number of subjects such as some personal problem, health advice, or just plain etiquette or some middle-of-the-road wisdom.

Friends in our church and friends outside the church have at one time or another remarked, "George, you have raised a fine family of children, and they are a credit to you all because you loved them."

I am quick to reply, "It is to Eunice you may accord the biggest credit to their development in every way, in which I fully supported her at all times."

There is a verse in the book of Ecclesiastes in the Bible that states that a wise wife makes a house a palace for living. I feel it is true that Eunice has indeed made our home beautiful for us. Friends who stop by to see us often make comment on the congenial atmosphere all around and of the pleasant feeling lingering afterward because of it.

XIII

CHURCH AND COMMUNITY WORK

BECOMING A BAPTIST

In Rumania I was baptized at the age of ten days in the Orthodox church, built by my forefathers. At the age of twenty-one I was allowed to be baptized as a Baptist fellow. In Arad, I joined the congregation at the church called "the Hope," at the railroad overpass. I became the attorney of several churches and members of the Baptist faith. Even before my admission to the bar of Arad, I was called to work on the recognition of the Baptists as a denomination. At that time (before 1930 and even after) the Baptists were only tolerated.

The bulk of the Baptists lived along the Crisus Valley. It might have been that some Anabaptist remnant had influenced the people on these slopes of the Transylvanian Alps to seek another way, to try to read the black book, that is, the Bible. They sought to amend their ways, thus to become Repenters.

A seminary was established at the town of Buteny, with the encouragement of the English Baptists and early Southern Baptists of America interested in the Rumanian Baptists. The city of Arad was the center of the Baptists in Rumania. There I had met Dr. Lewis, Dr. Rushbrook, Dr. George Truett, Dr. Mullins, and others. I was delighted to learn that in other countries, there were learned people among the humble and almost illiterate people, as we were considered in Rumania. That gave me much encouragement to stand fast for my faith, when I was called by the bishop and many local priests lost, sold to Beelzebub, heretic, and betrayer of Orthodox Mother Church.

One of the last American missionaries in Rumania was Dr. Roy Starmer of Chattanooga, Tennessee. He was the director of the seminary in Bucharest, established by the Southern Baptist Convention. When the totalitarian regime was imposed on Rumania by Hitler, he had to leave Rumania. At that time almost all the Baptist churches were sealed. They were to be reopened only after the Second World

290

War, not all at once, but here and there, by people who dared to face the consequences.

In my escape, while in Austria, I discovered that a group of refugees had found a place of worship in Salzburg. There I met several Rumanians from the provinces occupied by the Russians, Bessarabia and Bukovina. I attended that meeting place about two Sundays while in Austria.

It might have been that my interest in the Baptist Brotherhood, my wide interest in people regardless of ethnicity or faith, made me look for a Baptist church when I arrived in Paris, November 21, 1948. It was at the Baptist church, 48 Rue de Lille, that I met again Dr. Roy Starmer. He recognized the escapee, George Crisan, took me under his American wing, and made me his assistant in managing the Relief for Refugees in Paris, which had been established by the Baptist World Alliance.

At that church in Paris, in the morning, the French congregation met for services. In the afternoon a small Rumanian-speaking congregation met for services. Again I became involved in the Rumanian Baptist church activities. I organized a Sunday school class among the many Rumanian refugees who had never heard of the word *Baptist*. They were assured that the Rumanians all were orthodox. I spoke to the congregation where there was no pastor and where the older people took turns to speak. I organized a chorus with the help of a Rumanian young lady, Lia Constantinescu (now Sezonov), formerly a singer for the Rumanian Radio and Opera.

Because of this involvement in the church life, I was offered and eventually accepted a scholarship at the Colgate Rochester Divinity School at Rochester, New York.

All these incidents and activities in my life, in Rumania before the war, on the battlefields, in jails, in crossing seven borders—some of them with the peril of death, made me more deeply aware of the Certainty of things unseen—that God does not let even the humblest of his servants perish.

My stay at the Colgate Rochester Divinity School proved to be most enlightening and resulted in the deepening of my faith that my destiny was surely guided by the hand of the Almighty. I felt warm friendship from my professors and the dean and the president. Through their efforts and with the help of Representative Kenneth Keating of the district, a bill was put through Congress making me a permanent resident of the United States of America. Otherwise, I would have remained a foreign student, coming to this country as a stateless person with a French passport for a stateless person, in which case, I would have been returned to France.

In Rochester I became a member of the First Baptist Church of Rochester, New York. Among all the wonderful people I met I made many friends for life. To name a few: Dr. Leon Pacala, who became president of Colgate Rochester Divinity School; Rev. Kenneth Peterson; Rev. Frank Carlson; Eleanor Buzzell, who after about a year in the same class married Robert Pope; Robert Withers, whose father called me to speak to the youth conventions in West Virginia. There were many more along with their wives. I was invited for many Saturday dinners among these kind and caring people.

Several weeks after I moved to Washington, D.C., I received an invitation from Dr. Pruden, pastor of the First Baptist church of Washington, D.C., to address a certain group of people on an evening to tell of my experience in my escape from behind the Iron Curtain.

It was not long before I joined the congregation of the First Baptist church, where I was welcomed into the fellowship. I was soon asked by Wilbur Sparks, a lawyer, to substitute teach the choir class of the Sunday school—about sixty members. I became more and more involved with other groups and committees, including the Board of Deacons.

Parents and children in front of their church, the First Baptist Church of Washington, D.C.

I made scores of friends. A few who stand out specifically were David and Lucille Hunter, Mildred and Quinton Hodges, John and Virginia Rowley, Harold and Helen Kennedy, and John and Barthelia Shouse. Harold and John were very helpful in assisting me in finding a job with the government. I met the late president Harry Truman, who came to the services. I also met the late president Lyndon Johnson. Then I met Jimmy and Rosalynn Carter and their family. Jimmy and Rosalynn were members of the class I used to teach, the couples class now being taught by Fred Gregg—an amazing brother in the faith. Through Fred I was able to send President Carter a letter telling of the Rumanian Baptists under the communistic rule of President Ceausescu, who later came to the White House for a state visit. Eunice and I were guests of honor at that event. President Carter introduced me to President Ceausescu with these words: "Mr. President, this is George Crisan, a good friend of mine."

Eunice joined the choir shortly after our marriage, and she had continued her musical interests there. Her spiritual contribution to our prayer life through the years has been an immeasurable influence in our family life. Our children were always with us attending church from about the age of three or four weeks old until they went away to college or continued in graduate studies. Through the

G.C. reads invocation at the First Baptist Church while President Carter and First Lady Rosalynn Carter stand, March 1978.

unquestionable allegiance from our family members I felt a deep satisfaction in my own life and I had certainly tried to increase in every way I could what talent God so graciously extended to me.

CONTRIBUTING TO RUMANIAN BAPTIST FRIENDS

It was the late Reverend Danila Pascu who had the incredible idea to ask me to come to America and study divinity, although he knew I had been an attorney for eighteen years in Rumania. I did not know the English language, but he vouched to Dr. Dorris Sharpe, the chairman of the board of trustees of Colgate Rochester Divinity School, that "If George is accepted, he will succeed because he keeps his promises!"

I was received as a member of the family by John and Anna Pacala of Indianapolis and their wonderful family; by Stanley Catana of Detroit and Mrs. Catana who gave an affidavit of support for the refugee, George Crisan. Andrisan, the editor of the *Luminatorul-Illuminator*, had asked me to write articles for their publication. I wrote articles almost regularly for more than twenty-five years.

The late Reverend Joseph Ardeleau invited me to preach in his church in Akron, Ohio, during a series of revival meetings. I made many friends among the Rumanian Baptists there.

And on another occasion, Dr. Luke Sezonov and his wife invited me into their home in Chicago, asking me to preach in his church. Luke was an old friend from Rumania and for a short time was the pastor of our church in Arad. He once confided to me, "George, I have been in Rumania visiting with my folks as well as with the brothers and sisters in the faith. It seems their plight is almost hopeless if we write or broadcast through the Voice of America only bad things about the communistic regime. But now, the Baptist Brotherhood is considered on an equal basis with other denominations."

I felt I could be useful by helping people in need, be they of Christian belief or atheistic or communistic. When Pascu and the Reverend Lucaciu visited Rumania and preached in many churches there, I thought that I, too, could attempt to do something in a constructive way by recommending to the United States Congress the extension to Rumania of the Most Favored Nation Tariff Clause on a yearly basis. I have met, and attempted to befriend in every

294

way possible, all the Rumanian ambassadors to the United States of America since diplomatic relations were renewed in 1963.

After I became a member of the bar of the State of Maryland, the presidents of the Rumanian-American Baptist Association of the United States and Canada, year after year, have asked me to be their legal counsel in various matters and resolutions. Then I was elected Editor of the *Illuminator* for many years.

Thus, I have met many people—the old ones who came to America before the First World War and the new ones who came after the Second World War—and through it all I am still known as the Rumanian Baptist lawyer, on whom people may call, from New York to Los Angeles or from Florida to Chicago. I receive calls from Italy, Austria, or France asking for the proper way to get to America as a refugee or how to bring one's family to this country. Such questions about various matters still come my way and probably will continue as long as I am able to handle them or give a legal advice to them in their plight.

I cannot say no. I have kept my natural bent, answering every letter coming to me. It is a source of deep satisfaction that I am able to write to one who is seeking a spark of hope in the dreariness of the life pilgrimage and give a word of encouragement.

Later, the reverends Pascu, Lucaciu, and Lucuta of Windsor, Ontario, Canda, asked me to edit a publication, *The Christian*, which I enthusiastically accepted—and we still publish it. I have written scores of articles for this publication.

Because of my involvement with the Rumanian Baptists in America, I was invited to write for the *American-Rumanian News*, a bilingual periodical of the Rumanian Union and League, a fraternal organization in Cleveland, Ohio, with local organizations in many places in the United States and Canada. Many of my articles were published in the Almanac of the *Rumania-America Newspaper of Cleveland*, which has been issued yearly since the 1930s.

Writing and delivering articles for the Voice of America for almost fifteen years has been another source of satisfaction in my life in America. Through this work, I have met many outstanding people, all working toward a better understanding among the nations of the world, making known in a new way our adopted fatherland, the United States of America, where there is liberty, opportunity, and justice for all.

LOCAL COMMUNITY INVOLVEMENT

All through my life any problem affecting our community or any public controversy caught and held my close attention. I would study the problem myself and try to find a solution to it. This interest in public affairs might have been awakened in me by my grandfather's life. He had been elected mayor of our village more than 20 years by the time I was born. As a miller, my grandfather's days were busily filled with grinding the grain for the people of our village and of neighboring villages.

My father sang in the *strana* as a cantor in the church built by our forefathers in 1760. Father completed his military obligation at an early age. He had an outgoing personality and always had a pleasant chat with everyone who came to the mill. My mother had a friendly greeting for everyone while they were waiting for their flour. She was asking everyone, "Do you care to have a slice of bread while you wait?"

I cannot remember that anyone ever said no.

My grandmom, from the Big Run Valley, often walked me to the mill. She greeted friends and neighbors on every side with, "Good day to you, Joanna," or "How is your husband's cough today?" Then she would turn to me and say, "Basil is sick and it seems recovery is slow in coming. The best thing one can have is good health."

Mother was always saying, "Without health, nothing is worthwhile."

Our literary clubs in school asked me to prepare a paper on a classic or modern subject or write bylaws or minutes. It was a challenge and someone had to do it. I did it and I felt satisfied that I was able to assume that responsibility.

Because of either an inherited aptitude to get along well with people or a desire to find out the truth of things for myself and not by hearsay, I felt there was much logic in the things men do or else absence of it, which is to say lack of wisdom in trying to solve problems.

I was asked to give a short eulogy of my Professor Teodorescu, killed by a Communist-instigated group of workers, at our National Peasant Democratic Club in Arad, which was near my office at that time. I said among other things, "As surely as the sun rises and the earth circles around the sun, so will political movements pass away. And people will finally see the right turn to take."

Well, the president of the college, instead of congratulating me, said he would not have allowed me to speak if he knew I would speak against the communistic bloc or so-called Workers Block party. The local paper, however, carried several sentences of my eulogy.

Later, I learned that those comments stigamatized me as an anti-Communist person. Because of such openness I was the first attorney to be put in jail (in the political jail, as it was called at that time) in September, 1945; then in the secret jail of the People Security Police in November, 1947. While I admired a good speech either by a lawyer, preacher, or a politician, I felt I could do as well, whenever the occasion arose.

While visiting in Rome (1949, Easter) the American Baptist missionary in Rome took me to visit and speak at two Baptist churches in the Rome suburbs. Dr. Moore introduced me to the congregation as "a brother in the faith who escaped from behind the Iron Curtain" and asked me to speak of my flight experience.

I spoke in French and Dr. Moore interpreted for me in Italian. People came to shake hands with me, expressing love, compassion, and thanksgiving for my safe arrival in Western Europe, in the Free World!

At Colgate, Rochester, I was invited by churches, high schools, university student unions, Lions clubs, Rotary clubs, Minute Women societies, et cetera, to relate my story—the escape story. I was only enthused by the reception and the appreciation shown me. After many, many years I have met doctors, lawyers, and other people who remember my telling my story of my experience in flight.

In the divinity school, the dean, the director of research, and many of the professors commended my power of expression. On one occasion Dr. Baker kindly stated that I might have been one of the most illustrious students to have passed through Colgate Rochester Divinity School. It comes to mind that my recognition among my peers came when a professor or a student mentioned that I had given the clearest or most logical answer to the question at hand.

When we moved into our home in Hyattsville, it was a new community and a new development called Landover Estates. Soon afterward, I was approached by some who had lived there about five years to join the Citizens Association. In this organization we have worked hand in hand with the Zoning Commission and other county administrative divisions.

When my firstborn entered school I was asked to be a member of the Parent Teachers Association and to act as treasurer. Later I assumed the presidency of that association. The trees and bushes we planted at that time continue to afford much satisfaction and pleasure as we pass by and see their development and beauty. Some time later I established a parent teacher association in a new school.

The Maryland Assembly passed a resolution that a new constitution be drawn. I put up my candidacy for the constitutional convention. My children and their friends were running up and down the streets handing out pamphlets to publicize my candidacy and my stand on issues. A distinguished friend said, "George, I would not be able to put up my candidacy for an office like that because I would not be able to accept losing."

When I felt and aspired to a certain definite action, it never occurred to me to entertain the thought, *What if I cannot do this or do not succeed?* When I went to Russia to fight a war I did not contemplate the possibility of being killed but rather I prayed within to the Lord that his will be done and to let me die rather than to be left disfigured.

It seems to me that the highest satisfaction I always had was not in the job I held but the real feeling that I was able to be of help to someone either in the courts of law or to the committees and boards in the church, or to many others who asked orally or in writing direction in life in the new environment of America. My clearest advice was and still is that "if you work daytime then go to English school at night; if you go to school in the daytime then go to work during the night." In this way, the new immigrant will learn to apply his or her talents and to multiply them by their best efforts, in freedom with opportunity and justice.

I have never looked for pie in the sky, as the old saying goes. But I have never looked for defects, be they in people, land, homes, or even in attire. Rather I have looked at things that appeal to me and to even take a good example.

While I never aspired to be rich, I once was. Then came the Communists, who took everything and put me in jail. So I was left to live in hiding and barely escaped with my life from the Communists.

Yet in America I became rich far above monetary value in giving instead of getting. The art of giving is what one does. Our close association with our church, our affording the best education possible for our children, having a home organized by my wife with her talent and industry, and the pleasure and educational value of our travels in this country and Canada through Europe, and even behind the Iron Curtain, all make up my riches in life. And I call to mind a most amazing event, being introduced to the Rumanian president Nicolae Ceausescu by President Carter as "a good friend of mine." These riches are beyond my wildest imagination.

While still a young lawyer I helped my brothers with their college expenses as much as I was able. It was a time of deep depression in Europe and America, too, but more so in Rumania. My father had lands, grain, and the mill, but no money to pay taxes. In that period I took the train and went home for a short time on several occasions. I enjoyed walking about barefoot and climbing the hills of childhood with rocks larger than our home. Nothing would grow on those slopes but gypsy cherry trees, which produced sour cherries. But there were sweet strawberries and wild blackberries. I saw again my ancestral home where my parents' forefathers lived their lives. Our family history goes back to the dawn of history of Tisa, which was mentioned in the *Chronical of Csanki* as Thyza, Thiza, or Tyzafalva, in 1436 a well-settled community under the Baron Brancovici (of Siria, 1439) where some ancestors were elevated to the nobility by the Emperors of Austria: Leopold I granted them titles in 1701 and the Holy Roman Emperor Carolus IV granted another one in 1740.

Once when I arrived home my father was not there and my mother said that he was building a new meeting house. When I asked why he was having this done she replied that he carried on his life as he saw fit according to his own plans and ideas. She said he had purchased several strips of land to make a large yard facing the street and the river Crisus and now was in the process of having a new meeting house in stone erected. When I went to the site there were the workers and stone masons at work building the walls. My father was there overseeing everything that was done and directing the workers himself. I asked my father his reason for this new structure while the present building seemed quite adequate. He explained to me his feeling: "Thank you, son, for asking me and for coming to see us. All my life I have given to the Lord as I thought was right. The Lord has given me plenty in my life. I have known people who pinched their pennies and put it all in their belt pocket. I believe nothing good happened to them or their family," he concluded.

I thought about what he had said and I believe I understood the truth he spoke.

XIV

REALITY IS MY CONCLUSION

What is reality? And what is faith and hope? Good questions? Philosophers, theologians, scientists, lawyers, judges, or even people all around ask these same questions. When becoming dissatisfied with things as they are or when an unusual reverse occurs, the question comes to mind—why did this happen to me at this time? Is there a sure answer? Socrates cautioned his disciples, "Know yourself." Paul Tournier, however, said, "It is impossible for one to know his subconscious ego or even his conscious one." The Apostle Paul stated in his letter to the Hebrews that "Faith gives substance to our hopes and makes us certain of realities we do not see." Each of these men show faith in something! The Christians and Jews have faith in Jehovah, the Almighty God, the Creator of the Universe and all things seen and unseen—the creator of man.

The Communists believe that Lenin or Stalin, Marx or Engels speaks the truth or the reality. Of course, they saw reality of things as they stated it.

Khrushchev, and lately Gorbachev and the Chinese, have started to see the reality with their own eyes.

In these conclusions, it is enough to say that everything is in the eye of the beholder; beauty, ugliness, truth, falsehood, good fragrance or unpleasant odors.

Then some of us see the reality of God and His work in the universe and in everything He has created, see His abiding law, inescapable to comprehend.

- Why did I escape the toll of war at Stalingrad?
- Why did I meet the first day in freedom an American missionary in Paris to help me?
- Why was I asked to come to America at the age of forty-two to be a student (after 18 years as an attorney)?
- Why was I asked to work at the Library of Congress?
- Why did I dare to marry at 48 a girl 16 years my junior and raise a family of three children?
- Why has my health remained excellent, mentally and physically, at age 80 as I write these lines in our home in Ocean City, Maryland?

Everyone may look at me in all these happenings with his own eyes, whether physical or mental, and still would not find any final answer.

A cultural counselor at the Rumanian Embassy in Washington once asked me point-blank, "How do you explain how you have accomplished so many things in your life?"

I came back with a quick answer, "God and nature gave me an amazing gift—the ability to forgive. I hold no grudge against anybody, not even against the Communists, who so ill-treated me. The other gift is never to cry over the past."

I think it was a Roman poet who said, "It is futile to cry upon the ruins of Pompeii. The dead will never revive."

He would not say another word on this matter.

In my office I have a little plaque with this inscription: Only one life, t'will soon be past, Only what's done for Christ will last! A client might read the plaque and ask, "Are you a Christian?"

"I am here to help you because God was most loving to me all my life and I can only repay His kindness by helping my fellow man," is my answer. That is the reality I see in things unseen. It is the reality in my inner eye!

INDEX

Gsovski, Dr. Vladimir, 251
Gurahont, village, 145
Gyula, city in Hungary, 9, 10, 29, 30

Halmagel, 54
Halmagean, Mary, 55
Halmagiu, town of, 16, 25, 44, 63, 146
Hans (*John* in English), 198–199
Harding, Byron, 258
Hentiu, Ioan, 91
Herculaneum, 216
Herodotus, 248
Highland Park, Michigan, 190, 223
Hitler, Adolph, 113, 115, 124, 129, 133
Hodges, Quinton and Mildred, 293
Hoff, John and Jean, 271–73, 277
Holland, 251
Hollo Utza (Craven Str.), Budapest, 177
Holy Roman Emperor Carolus IV, 299
Horia, 74
Horia Sima, 118
Hudson, Dr. Winthrop, 238
Hungarians, 23, 143, 155
Hungary, 246
Hunter, David, Lucille, and Steve, 293
Howell, Dr. John, 286
Hutchinson, Edwin, 268

IIT (Illinois Institute of Technology), 287
Idlewild Airport (John F. Kennedy), 223
Iercan, Dr. Nerva, 141
Illuminator, monthly, 295
Ionescu, Prof. George, 62
Iorga, Nicolae, 118
Iowa, 260
Iowa Test, 287
Ireland, 222
Ispravnic, Dr. Sever, 90

Iron Guard, 118, 123, 124, 152
Israel, 235
Iron Curtain, 227–30, 234, 237, 243, 245
Italy, 50, 128
Italian Baptists, 215

Jacob's children, 168
Japan, 241
Jenkins, Joe and Edith, 280
Jaszenko, Kiril, 249, 250
Jenö (*Eugen* in English), 176
Jews, 301
Johns Hopkins University, 287
Jones, Dr. Robert, 252
Jehovah, 214, 280, 301
Julius Caesar, 129, 214
Justinianus, compendium of, 83

Kalnoki, Count Hugo, 248
Karlsruhe, 196, 197
Keating, Kenneth, congressman, 229, 230, 291
Keath, Lawrence, law librarian, 243, 244
Kennedy, Harold and Helen, 255, 293
Kennedy, President, J. F., 259
Khrushchev, 301
King Ferdinand University, Law School, 254
King Carol of Romania, 111
King George Hotel, Paris, 218
King Michael of Romania, 143, 159, 160, 171
Kiser, Rev. Kent, 245
Kishinew, city of, 131
Klein, Dr., 138
Koczvara, V. P., 249
Konigretz, 25
Kurzius, Edwin and Veronica, 255, 256–58

L'Arc de Triomph, Paris, 211, 219
Lake George, New York, 281
Landes, Felix, 61, 67, 122

306